The dynamics of **PLANNED CHANGE**

The dynamics of

Ronald Lippitt
University of Michigan

Jeanne Watson
University of Chicago

Bruce Westley
University of Wisconsin

Harcourt, Brace & World, Inc.

Under the General Editorship of
Willard B. Spalding

PLANNED

CHANGE

a comparative study

of principles and techniques

New York · Chicago · San Francisco · Atlanta

to

Kurt Lewin

and

our colleagues at

The National Training Laboratories

FOREWORD

Change—inevitable and universal—is an element in every human situation, and social scientists and educators are today showing an increasing amount of interest in theories of change and the use of these theories to influence society. The authors of this book fill a longfelt need by undertaking the task of answering some fundamental questions about change. Focusing their attention on the concept of *planned change*, they induce its basic principles from a great variety of the techniques used to effect change throughout a large part of the social scene.

The significance of such a project is self-evident and its value triplefold. As a theoretical analysis, a comparative study, a commentary on research proceedings and professional training, this is a book of high academic consequence. Also important are its widespread practical implications for both professional "change agents" and private citizens who as individuals and as members of groups, organizations, and communities seek to institute change in order to improve some area of personal, group, or social affairs.

A worthy and very serviceable contribution, this book crystallizes our thinking on a challenging and important subject and will prove to be a milestone in the evolution of our knowledge of the phenomenon of change.

Willard B. Spalding

PREFACE

The subject of this book is *planned change*—that is, change which derives from a purposeful decision to effect improvements in a personality system or social system and which is achieved with the help of professional guidance. In the following pages we have undertaken a comparative study of the principles and techniques which furnish the basis of the work of the various types of professional helpers concerned with such change. In addition to the concept of *planned change,* terms such as *change agent, client system, change forces, resistance forces, phases of change,* and *methods of change* are discussed. It is upon the fundamental ideas indicated by these terms that this book is centered.

We are not the originators of any of these ideas. As with the formulation of all new concepts, many influences have stimulated their development. To begin with, the fact that we consider the idea of planned change an important one probably has much to do with our location in Western culture, or, to be more specific, in American culture. Taking initiative to exert control over one's own fate or to influence the fate of others is not a mode of thinking common to all societies.

Then, too, we have been greatly stimulated by the ideas and the example of Kurt Lewin. It was his idea that science and democracy should merge in a widespread sharing of the rational processes of making decisions, taking action, and testing consequences. This means assuming and exploring a wide area of change potential in the individual, the group, and the community. It involves the active use of scientific methods and trained personnel to execute the change goal effectively. Most of all, however, it requires the formulation of a general theory of change, one which can be used to assist in understanding such diverse situations of planned change as are met in psychotherapy, childrearing, industrial management, race relations, and community development.

We are very much aware also of the direction and impetus which has been given to our thinking by the work of the National Training Laboratories. From this enterprise we discovered how much common ground there is for communication and learning when professional workers from such different specializations as clinical practice, group work, community organization, personnel management, industrial relations, public health, education, religion, and international relations gather together for group discussions on mutual interests. From these discussions there emerged an understanding of some of the basic features of the work of the professional change agent, and the ideas about the phases of change which Kurt Lewin suggested in his theorizing were made more concrete by practitioners interested in finding ways to facilitate planned change.

Spurred by the challenge of advancing these ideas, we were moved to make this comparative study of the work of professional change agents. The new vistas that were opened up to us by this comparative approach excited us. At the same time, we were humbled by the complexities of the task we had undertaken and by the many leads we had to leave unexplored. We hope, however, that we have succeeded in our intention of elucidating the principles and problems of planned change in such a way that this book will prove helpful to all, professionals and non-professionals alike.

To the many colleagues who both modified and sharpened our ideas by their thoughtful participation in seminar discussions we want to express our deep appreciation. We hope we can look forward to a similar exchange of ideas with our readers.

Finally, we should like to acknowledge with thanks the financial support of the Russell Sage Foundation and the University of Michigan Faculty Research Fund which made this study possible.

Ronald Lippitt
Institute for Social Research
University of Michigan

Jeanne Watson
Family Study Center
University of Chicago

Bruce Westley
School of Journalism
University of Wisconsin

Contents

OUR ORIENTATION TO
THE PHENOMENA OF PLANNED CHANGE

1

The modern world is, above everything else, a world of rapid change. This is something upon which observers in every field of thought and knowledge are agreed. What does it mean? Many things, of course; but perhaps its primary meaning lies in its effect upon people. It means that people, too, must change, must acquire an unaccustomed facility for change, if they are to live in the modern world. It means that the achievement and maintenance of our mutual well-being is becoming progressively more important and more difficult for us as individuals and as groups. It means that if we are to maintain our health and a creative relationship with the world around us, we must be actively engaged in change efforts directed toward ourselves and toward our material, social, and spiritual environments.

The increased need to modify or invent our patterns of behavior and organization has led naturally to a demand for professional help. This help is now available to assist us in our attempts to meet the problems of personal and social change. Not only is the number of professional helpers increasing very rapidly, but the specialized skills and techniques presented for our consideration offer extraordinary variety. What we attempt to do in this book is to clarify and compare these many different skills and theories, to look for contrasts and similarities among them, and to assist in the development of a general theory of change, a theory which will explicate the process of giving help to people—individuals or groups—who must change in order to improve their level of functioning.

The societal context of change problems

Personal and social aspirations for change seem to emerge from a number of fundamental trends in our current collective life. We might call these trends the forces toward innovation in human society.

First, there is the fact that man is continually seizing new opportunities to use or modify the natural resources of his environment or the technological features of this environment which he has himself created in his previous attempts to solve problems. Dramatic instances of this perennial human effort are put before us every day in the press—weather-control experiments, undersea gardening, the construction of plants for the manufacture of atomic power, traffic-control procedures, jet flight, the chemical control of growth processes, vaccination against disease, and so on. These are efforts to solve problems. They have become so complex in our day that they require an ever more minute specialization of individual skill and knowledge. The result is an intricate division of labor and hence a multifarious interdependence among the units of labor in all of our great variety of problem-solving efforts to use, control, and modify our environment. Out of this fact of interdependence arises the host of problems which have to do with collaboration among workers, the invention of new patterns of working, the needs for new patterns of leadership and co-operation.

A second type of stimulus toward innovation, created by the first, originates in our need to utilize and adjust to the changes that we are constantly creating in our environments. Planners of one kind and another look ahead to adjustments and changes in our way of life. Legislators enact new laws to take account of changed conditions of living and the new resources which have become available; educators organize the specialized units of knowledge which must be transmitted to our young people if they are to engage in these new processes of utilization and adjustment; administrators co-ordinate our adjustmental efforts; and all of us, willy-nilly, grapple with the problems of changing our personal goals, desires, expectations, and patterns of behavior.

From these experiences in exerting our power to shape and refine our environment emerges an image of fluidity. Nothing is static; improvement is always possible, provided, of course, that we can agree on what really constitutes an improvement. Consequently, we are always revising our definition of what is good, of what constitutes good health, good performance, efficiency, effective use of our resources, and so forth. In itself, the idea that we can improve ourselves and our circumstances is a potent push toward innovation.

The essentially competitive process of comparing ourselves with others is another impetus toward innovation. It provides us with a motive for getting ahead through discovering improved, that is to say *changed*, ways of functioning.

The pain and disorganization that arise from finding that our familiar ways of behavior no longer work in a new environment or in one that has been altered are frequently an additional stimulus toward change.

From all these types of innovation forces there derives a multitude of problems which have to do with relating effectively to ourselves and to each other. These become problems which must be worked on at several levels of problem-solving effort.

LEVELS OF PROBLEM-SOLVING EFFORT

Throughout this book we shall focus our discussion upon four types of dynamic systems—the individual personality, the face-to-face group, the organization, and the community. There are, of course, other strata of society at which organized problem-solving efforts and change continually go on, such as the national and international strata. But we have chosen to pay attention to these four types of systems and to a <u>comparison of the ways in which they receive professional help</u>. We have chosen to accept the implicit assumption of the cases which we have analyzed that to some degree systems of each type can be regarded as "closed systems" and that therefore they can be helped without paying attention to systems at the other levels. It is usually recognized that this is only partially true and that in fact there is ordinarily quite a high degree of interdependence between smaller and larger systems, which results in an interdependence in their problem-solving activities.

Another general assumption which we have accepted is that in all of these dynamic systems there is a tendency for the system, in its problem-solving efforts, to arrive at certain patterns of process and structure which are relatively stable and resistant to change. Hence the system is often slow to respond to the external stimuli toward change which are furnished in the movements and pressures of society at large and which we mentioned briefly in the last section. Patterns of response and initiative which have proved successful in solving one problem are likely to be repeated when a new problem arises, even though they are no longer effective. But before we go any further, let us summarize briefly what we mean by the four types of dynamic systems and what we are talking about when we discuss problem-solving processes, their stabilization, and the need for change.

The personality system

If a person has a need to find someone who will fix his shoes or sell him a newspaper, it is quite clear that his need (as one subpart of the personality system) must secure the collaboration of his cognitive and perceptual apparatus (other subparts) if he is to find out where the shoe-repair shop or the newspaper stand is. But suppose the person is in a state of considerable frustration because he has recently been dressed down by his boss. Then his problem is more difficult. He is subject to a conflict between some of his subparts; for instance, his sense of social values may conflict with his need to express hostility, his cognitive structure may deplore the foreseen results of his emotional need to blow off steam. His resolution of these internal, interacting conflicts may be to bury the hostility or to give it vent by castigating his secretary or his wife, or he may go out for a vigorous walk, or he may organize a counterattack against the source of his frustration. Different personality systems have various accustomed ways of solving such problems. Moreover, in addition to these regular patterns of internal behavior, the individual personality system usually creates regular and accustomed patterns of interaction with its environment in order to achieve goals and satisfy needs. In interacting with their social environment, some personality systems, for instance, exhibit patterns of trust, while others exhibit patterns of distrust. Some systems try to create a relationship of submissive dependence; others strive for dominance; still others seek an extreme of independence or minimal contact. As internal or external conditions change, the personality system is confronted with the challenge—and often with the stark necessity—of modifying its customary and stabilized patterns in order to cope more effectively with the new conditions. The desirability of improving one's performance may provide a challenge which incites one to seek help, or the pain of a present maladjustment may create a readiness for change.

The group as a dynamic system

Committees, staffs, families, work groups, clubs, and many other types of small social units make up the large population of social systems which are the focus of attention for students of group dynamics. We can visualize the internal dynamics of these systems much more easily than we can visualize the internal dynamics of individual personality systems. We can watch the interaction between subparts of groups. Everyone is familiar with the sort of conflict which occurs between a chairman and the members of his committee or between the subgroups (cliques, factions, and the like) which compose the system. We know more or less what kinds of division of labor must be instituted within the group if it is to go intelligently about the processes of making decisions and taking action. We are aware, often painfully so, of the interpersonal difficulties that can disrupt the face-to-face groups in which we live. Beyond these problems of internal process and structure, we recognize the fact that most small groups occupy a distinct place in the larger social environment: perhaps they are trying to excel other groups in a competitive context, or perhaps they are trying to bring about a reform in the community at large. As we shall see in Chapter 2 and thereafter, small groups are very often placed in situations where their accustomed patterns of interaction with the larger environment and their characteristic procedures for problem solving have clearly become obsolete; that is to say, they are no longer appropriate to the new circumstances in which the groups find themselves. The result in many cases is the emergence of a desire for change.

The organization as a dynamic system

For our purposes, *organization* means any of the larger social systems which comprise the community. These are the parts of the community which have a more or less clearly defined and specialized function requiring the loyalty and labor of a group of people who are organized in a relatively systematic relationship and whose efforts are co-ordinated by some kind of formal leadership structure. We think of such various systems as business organizations, welfare agencies, educational institutions, government bureaus, religious associations, and political parties. The internal processes of such systems usually involve interactions among officially defined subparts, such as the various departments of a business organization, the professional corps and volunteer units of a welfare agency, the students, teachers, and administrators of a school system. In organizations the relationships among subparts are likely to be formalized, and hence face-to-face interactions are less feasible than in small groups. The result is likely to be a difficulty of communication among the parts of an organization as they attempt to collaborate in a common effort. Externally, that is to say, in relationships involving the organization with its environment, this system may be engaged in such activities as influencing public opinion, competing with other organizations, recruiting new members, or obtaining information about the effectiveness of its work or the marketability of its products. Obviously, in our intensely competitive society many organizations have become very sensitive to the need for internal efficiency and external good will, and they are prepared to consider any change that promises to bring about improvement in internal and external conditions.

The community as a dynamic system

The community, defined politically or ecologically, is made up of a variety of interacting subparts—individual citizens, informal interest groups, organized occupational or political subgroups, economic and social strata, geographical units, political subdivisions, and so forth. The stresses and strains set up by these interacting subparts and the necessity of maintaining community services to all constituent units have resulted in a wide variety of stabilized structural arrangements and problem-solving procedures. Perhaps we tend to view the community in terms of its internal processes more than we do the other three types of systems. These processes are the events we see and hear about as citizens. Of course, there are interactions between a given community and neighboring community systems as well as between the community and larger structures such as state governments. These, however, are very often formalized to such an extent that the community itself, as a single system, can do little to change them.

THE NOTION OF PLANNED CHANGE

As new internal or external situations arising from the innovation forces we have mentioned confront the personality system or the social system, the system itself is challenged to change its structure or its way of functioning in order to cope more effectively with the changed state of affairs. These changes toward the good (that is, effectiveness, adjustment, painlessness) or away from the bad (that is, ineffectiveness, maladjustment, pain) may come about in a number of ways. The system may mobilize its resources to improve and correct its own operation or structure. In other words, it may take matters into its own hands. Or the normal processes of maturation and development may result in the spontaneous evolu-

tion of change from within the system. Or the system may escape
its problem by moving to a new situation where its present methods
and structures are better adapted to the environment. Or changes
in the external environment may actually serve to solve the system's problems instead of creating new ones. A shift in the regional economy, for instance, may produce a better local employ-
ment market and reduce intergroup tensions, thus solving the problems of a local business firm. All of these types of change can be
classified in this analysis of change processes as either spontaneous, developmental changes within the system or fortuitous, un-
planned changes outside the system. These are quite different
things from the type of change which we want to discuss in this
book: the *planned change* that originates in a decision to make a
deliberate effort to improve the system and to obtain the help of
an outside agent in making this improvement. We call this outside
agent a *change agent*.* The decision to make a change may be
made by the system itself, after experiencing pain (malfunctioning) or discovering the possibility of improvement, or by an outside change agent who observes the need for change in a particular
system and takes the initiative in establishing a helping relationship with that system.

We need always to remember that when examined closely all
dynamic systems reveal a continuous process of change—adapta-
tion, adjustment, reorganization. That is what we mean by dynamic, by being alive. We call these processes learning, development, maturation, and growth. But it is equally true, as we can
learn both from experience and from the results of scientific studies, that all these systems exhibit a high degree of stability, con-
stancy, or rigidity, in many aspects of their operation and organization. Often, as external observers, we can note that this stability
is very uncomfortable or even dangerous, not only for the system
in question but for its neighboring systems. In other words, the
natural dynamic processes of change do not occur fast enough to

---

* The term was adopted by the National Training Laboratory staff in
1947 to facilitate discussions among heterogeneous groups of professional
helpers. It is a term which has since proved very useful.

keep pace with the very rapidly changing conditions of our world today.

Since the social organism is often unable to alter these stabilized, but inappropriate, patterns of structure and function itself, outside help—a change agent—is needed. This has led to the development of a great variety of professional helping roles. The study reported in this book was undertaken in an attempt to focus attention on the patterns of collaboration which emerge between the professional helper and the system as they work toward a goal of planned change in the function or structure of the system.

PROFESSIONAL CHANGE AGENTS

When one thinks of the sources of professional help which are accessible to the personality system, a number of specialists come to mind—the psychiatrist, the clinical psychologist, the social worker, the human-relations expert, the parent educator, the marriage counselor, the mental hygienist, and so forth. Some of these professional roles are more fully developed than others and occupy an acknowledged niche in our society. These differences of prestige and sanction, in some cases at least, result in striking inequalities in the kind and amount of professional training available in our society for the assistance of personality systems which are endeavoring to change in order to cope more effectively with internal and external realities.

Other resources are available to group systems. These include group workers, staff consultants, leadership trainers, discussion specialists, conference experts, and the like. Unfortunately, the demand for these helpers exceeds the supply in many cases. The development of professional training curricula in such specializations and the establishment of adequate professional standards have not proceeded fast enough to provide trained workers where they are needed. Nevertheless, a wide variety of professional helping roles has been developed for work with groups as clients.

Similarly, organizational systems faced with problems of social process and social structure can call upon productivity analysts, communications experts, labor-management specialists, labor-relations consultants, and supervisory- and executive-training consultants, among others. As a matter of fact, American industry has sponsored a rapid move toward professionalization in the various fields of industrial development, and we now have an association of industrial consultants and a fairly well-developed graduate curriculum for professional training in these fields. There has been a similar activity in the development of specialists who give consultative help to school systems.

The problems which beset community systems have also attracted attention and stimulated the development of facilities for the training of many different kinds of professional people, including public-administration consultants, community-council organizers, intergroup-relations specialists, community self-survey consultants, and adult educators specializing in the community-development field.

We call all of these helpers, no matter what kind of system they normally work with, change agents. Even when assistance is given by a team of helpers, each contributing a different skill, we shall call the team a change agent.

We shall call the specific system—person or group—that is being helped the *client system.* In earlier discussions of this comparative perspective on different types of professional work, we found that if we used the word "client" alone, professionals working with communities felt left out; they thought the word referred only to individuals. On the other hand, if we used a term such as "social system," those working with individuals felt left out. "Client system," though a trifle unwieldy, is a compromise term denoting systems at any of the four levels.

However, the use of the general term "client system" to refer to a number of different kinds of units may occasionally present semantic difficulties. A group does not consult a change agent in the same way that an individual does, and it does not act in the same way that an individual does. Consequently, it is important to remember that the word "system" always refers to an organization of interrelated parts and that when the system is a multiple-person system these parts may be various types of sub-units—individuals, roles, groups, organizations, communities. Needless to say, sub-parts do not always agree with one another. In much of what follows, however, we shall treat the client system as a single unit. Again, it is a question of simplicity and clarity; it would be tedious to remind ourselves on every page that the client system is not necessarily unitary in every respect and that every action taken and every view held by one part may be disputed by some other part.

When we say, in speaking of a group or organization or community, that "the client system comes to the change agent," or "the client system wants to change," or "the client system holds a distorted view of itself vis-à-vis its environment," we mean that there are some members who act this way, or feel this way, or see things this way. We do not suggest the existence of anything like a group mind or group will.

The same kind of qualification applies, of course, to statements about individuals. Many people undertake their relationship with the change agent only halfheartedly. Like all of us, they are complex creatures; parts of them may want to change, but other parts are quite happy with the status quo. All of us know someone, for instance, who consciously wants to change but unconsciously repeats the same unsatisfactory pattern of behavior over and over again.

The fact that a client system consists of distinct but related parts (or persons) introduces a special difficulty when we wish to talk about the relationship between the change agent and the client system. On one hand, the change agent usually directs his efforts toward the improvement of the entire system; the system, then, is the client. On the other hand, the change agent often is in direct touch with only a part of the system. Thus a change agent who works with a community or an organization must often deal with committees of interested or appointed individuals, not with the entire membership. The same is true in the case of a change agent who is working with a small group or an individual: he may find that although the entire system is physically present parts of it offer him only resistance or mistrust. In short, the change agent often works directly with only a "contracting subpart" of the system, but his objective is to enlarge this contact and in-fluence until he reaches as much of the system as possible. In our shorthand language, we say simply that the change agent works with the client system.

THE OBJECTIVES OF THIS STUDY

We have defined our terms, and we have examined briefly the idea of planned change, the four types of client systems, and the role of the professional change agent. Let us now attempt to for-mulate as briefly as possible the four objectives which we have set for ourselves in the chapters which will compose the rest of this book:

1. To make a comparative study of the ways of defining problems, of the operating principles, and of the methods used by a number of professional change agents who work with the four types of client systems.

2. To explore the possibility of developing a general framework within which the wide variety of helping techniques and profes-sional orientations could be conceptualized.

3. To survey a sampling of the types of research which seem to con-tribute directly to a theory of planned change, and to formulate our notions of research priorities.

4. To derive from our comparative analysis some specific ideas about the training of graduate students, with the hope that students, both as behavioral scientists and as professional change agents, may be made more aware of their precise functions and responsi-bilities in the field of planned change.

It should be clear from the above that what we have in mind is an exploratory study. When we projected our four aims we tried also to clarify some of the things we would not try to do. We de-cided that we would make no ambitious attempt to apply the cur-rent theoretical systems of the behavioral sciences to practical problems. We are interested in appraising the general value of scientific concepts wherever they seem relevant, but this does not mean that we can attempt the ambitious job of linking total systems of conceptualization to areas of applied problems. We also agreed that we could not attempt to be completely interdisciplinary in the creation or use of concepts, nor could we be comprehensive in our discussion of the varieties of professional help techniques. We do, of course, want to look carefully at the work of a reasonable variety of professional helpers, but without aspiring to be inclusive or even completely representative.

In our study of the methods of giving help, we shall not try to present a condensed "how-to-do-it" manual. Instead, we shall try to clarify the precepts which may be derived from a general consideration of ends and means in the change process; we hope that this clarification will assist professional helpers to select or create their own ends and means with more understanding. Hopefully, we shall identify and give form to a number of problems which are related to the techniques of giving help, so that behavioral scientists who are interested in research will find challenging lines of investigation open to them.

We should also call attention to two additional limitations in the scope of our analysis which have been implied in the preceding discussion. First, we have not tried to sample all types of planned change. Instead, we have concentrated primarily upon problems of change which occur in psychological processes, social relations, interpersonal processes, problem-solving procedures, and processes of social alignment or structure. This leaves out a vast swath of change phenomena such as technological change, changing health habits, changing technical skills, changing modes of economic behavior, and the like. Second, we shall look only at those planned operations in which there is a voluntary relationship between an external change agent and a client system. This excludes the many change operations which are carried out by administrators within an organizational system—teachers within the classroom, parents within the family—without any contact with an outside helper. It also omits a fairly large number of relationships in which the change agent's role is primarily a coercive one based upon his power over the system whose problems and change processes are being influenced.

We have not forgotten that all persons, ordinary men and women as well as professionals, very often function as change agents. The duty to give and the opportunity to receive help arise frequently for all of us. In fact, we believe that our analysis of some characteristic instances of professional help is relevant to the roles that all of us play as givers and receivers of help in our daily lives.

OUR CHOICE OF ILLUSTRATIVE CASES

The selection of cases to illustrate our analysis has been determined by our use of several procedures for locating and screening case material.

First, we made a general review of the relevant literature. We found, as we expected to find, that the different kinds of professional help directed toward planned change in each of our four types of systems tended to form into clusters based on techniques and areas of primary concern. We identified these clusters and found that they coincided in most cases with the established fields of specialization: psychotherapy, casework, attitude change, human-relations training, group therapy, staff consultation, organizational surveys, industrial consultation, community organization, intergroup relations, community self-surveys, and so forth.

After this we tried, by talking with colleagues and examining the literature, to discover and identify significant differences of method and point of view within a particular cluster, psychotherapy, for instance, or community organization.

Next, we attempted to find published or unpublished materials or available informants that could provide us with adequate descriptions of the diagnostic procedures and change techniques of actual persons or groups who represented a particular orientation within a cluster. In other words, we tried to pin down the divergences of concept and method between different groups who were trying to achieve the same ends. We made a particular effort to locate case materials which would include some genuine conceptualization of the process of giving help and some reliable descriptions and analyses of the relationships between change agent and client system. Many cases, unfortunately, could not be used because they were confidential or incompletely recorded.

These, then, were our criteria. In using them, we tried not to select any presentations of personality theory, group-dynamics theory, or community theory which did not acknowledge the generic problems and techniques of producing planned change or did not say something about the role of the change agent. There are a few exceptions. In some cases we were unable to locate change agents who could deal abstractly with their diagnostic techniques and their principles and methods of inducing change. This split between those who act and those who conceptualize was particularly and rather painfully conspicuous among change agents working at the level of community systems.

A bibliography of the materials used in our analysis will be found on page 299, and reference numbers used throughout the text are keyed to the bibliography.

THE ORGANIZATION
AND PRESENTATION OF OUR ANALYSIS

The analysis offered in Chapters 2 through 9 is the product of two more or less related processes: (a) our prior theorizing and (b) our attempt to generalize from a comparative study of the case materials. During a period of three years we joined in a number of efforts toward the formulation of a general theory of change. An interdisciplinary seminar on the theory of change, for example, concentrated particularly on a comparative analysis of resistance to change. Also, a staff work group met weekly to discuss the possibility of designing research which would contribute to a theory of change. One of us participated with colleagues at the Tavistock Institute for Human Relations in London in a work group which attempted to explore some of the implications of psychoanalytic theory for an understanding of resistance to change in organizational and community systems. Our first step in preparing the present report was to summarize the notes from these previous discussions and to attempt the formulation of a tentative framework for conceptualizing the role of the change agent and the process of changing. Then, after the selection of our cases for analysis, we undertook a series of discussions about the work of each of the change agents, attempting in our talks to discover where the principles and methods described by the agents helped to clarify and amplify our conceptual framework and where, on the other hand, their descriptions indicated a need for further modifications and additions. This modified framework, very rough and tentative at many points, will be presented in the following sequence.

First, we shall review and compare the ways in which the various change agents approach the diagnostic task of forming and assembling their ideas about the dynamics of a system in need of help. From this follows a comparison of the ways in which they identify the problems of pathology in the given case and evaluate the desirable directions of change. These diagnostic orientations are described in Chapters 2, 3, and 4.

Then we shall attempt what we call an overview of the dimensions of the helping relationship, the helping process, and the role of the change agent in giving help. This overview will occupy Chapter 5.

Next we shall elaborate one of these ideas, the idea that we can look at change in terms of some fairly universal phases in the process of change and can view the work of the change agent in terms of the procedures he uses to give help in each of these different phases. These concepts will be presented in Chapter 6.

We shall then try to summarize and compare the methods of giving help which are used by the various change agents during the different phases of the process of change. These comparisons, which will take into account all the types of client systems, will be presented in Chapters 7, 8, and 9.

In Chapter 10 we shall summarize our ideas about the kind of theorizing and research which should be carried on in the future in order to expedite the development of a theory of change and assist in the evaluation of the various methods of providing help. And finally, in Chapter 11, we shall present our thoughts on improvements which are needed in the graduate training of change agents.

Our hope in writing this report is that it will prove valuable both to our colleagues in the behavioral sciences who are interested in change and to our colleagues in the various fields of professional help who are interested in broadening their view of their roles in social change and who want to clarify and extend their ideas about the methodology of giving help. We have been excited and reassured to find so many interesting points of comparison among the implicit or explicit theories and methods described by the different types of professional workers. These specialists, it seems, have a great deal of help to give to one another—new insights and techniques which can reach usefully across the lines that separate the different professions and disciplines—provided the barriers to communication can be broken down to permit a general exchange of experience. Colleagues who have used earlier drafts of our report have assured us that they have not found it difficult to relate the terms which we have been forced to invent to the terminologies and concepts of their own particular specializations. We hope that this will be true as well for our present readers.

DIAGNOSTIC ORIENTATIONS TOWARD

PROBLEMS OF INTERNAL RELATIONSHIPS

2

In the chapters which follow we should like to share with our readers the experience of looking into the work of many different change agents. We shall discover that, in spite of wide apparent differences in theory and practice, there are enough similarities among the projects described by these agents to allow us to reduce their ideas of how to help with planned change to a limited number of diagnostic orientations.

Our procedure will be quite simple. We shall present selected illustrations of the work done by several change agents who seem to us to proceed upon similar assumptions about what is causing the trouble for their client systems and about how to help the client system move toward a more desirable state of affairs. We will then try to state in general terms the orientation to giving help which we consider to be implicit in the work of this group of change agents. In each case the orientation will be an abstraction derived from the illustrations we shall have cited, but it will not be altogether representative of what any of these particular agents has done, nor will its relevance be limited to this group of agents alone. We can, of course, cite only a few of the examples of each point of view. Our effort will be an attempt to generalize different basic approaches to the task of helping with planned change. We assume that each approach will be used by a number of different change agents and, conversely, that a single change agent may use more than one approach.

We believe that every change agent makes certain assumptions, either consciously or unconsciously. These pertain to (1) the nature of the client system, (2) the process by which the client system got into trouble, (3) the nature of the trouble, (4) the processes which will lead to an amelioration of the trouble, and (5) the ways in which he himself can contribute to bringing about the desired change. These are the assumptions which define his approach to the task of helping with planned change.

The first three of these assumptions will occupy us in Chapters 2 and 3 in our analysis of what we call the "diagnostic orientations" of different change agents; the last two assumptions will be considered in Chapter 5 in our analysis of the functions of the change agent.

We are tentatively proceeding upon the assumption that each diagnostic orientation is equally applicable to units of all sizes, including the individual, the small group, the institution or organization, and the community. In selecting illustrations for the chapters which follow, we have tried to find examples from cases involving as many of the four kinds of client systems as possible. Unfortunately, our success has been only partial. Some of the orientations seem to apply more directly to work with one kind of system than to work with the others. Nevertheless, we feel that an attempt to imagine what a given approach will mean when applied to each of the four kinds of client systems, even though the actual case materials are lacking, may be both stimulating and rewarding. We invite our readers to lend us their imaginative co-operation at the points where our restricted and somewhat arbitrary list of examples breaks off.

Our examination of the case materials has led us to make a major distinction between change agents who concentrate on trying to improve the relationship between the client system and its environment and those who concentrate on helping to bring about change in the system's internal processes. The distinction is a matter of emphasis only. Rarely will a change agent limit himself solely to internal or external considerations. For instance, change agents who are trying to bring about some modification of internal structure or process may use as their ultimate criterion of success a measure of the efficiency with which the system can function in its environment. Correspondingly, change agents who are trying to alter the relationship between a client system and its environment may proceed by first trying to change internal processes. Almost all change agents recognize the importance of both internal and external relationships and are aware of the close interdependence between them. Nevertheless, change efforts tend to focus on one or the other. First priority is given to making a change in either external or internal relationships, and it is assumed that as change occurs in the area of primary interest it will be accompanied by related changes in the other area. Hence we have accepted this distinction as a useful means of arranging the material in this and the following chapter.

INTERNAL DISTRIBUTION OF POWER

The first of the diagnostic orientations which we shall consider derives from the change agent's assumption that the difficulty of the client system arises from a faulty internal distribution of power. Power may be too highly concentrated or too diffuse; it may be exerted in harmful or ineffective ways. The change agent who begins with this assumption will try to help the client system develop a new and more appropriate power structure, either by adding new elements to the existing structure or by revising the relationship between the existing power structure and the system as a whole. Let us turn, therefore, to some examples of change agents whose orientation seems to be toward working with the client system's power structure. We shall consider each type of client system in turn.

Individuals

Among change agents who are working with individual personality systems the ones who seem to be most directly concerned with a redistribution of power and control are the modern ego psychologists. These theorists draw on orthodox psychoanalytic doctrine, but they have moved out of the main line of Freudian development by concentrating on ways to increase ego strength instead of simply on rearranging the boundaries between id, ego, and superego.

Redl and Wineman (13, 14) give us an example of this approach in their report of work with children who are too disturbed to benefit from ordinary psychiatric treatment. The report takes the view that these children have suffered extraordinary traumatic experiences which have made it impossible for them to develop egos capable of sustaining appropriate relationships with others. Redl and Wineman recommend a therapeutic environment which is designed to help the children, first by taking on the responsibility for the work which the ego would normally do (control and direction of behavior) and second by providing opportunities for the development of ego strength. The main objective is to help the child acquire an internal center of strength and organization.

Taft and her co-workers (16), following Rank's emphasis on individual will, have stressed the client's will to change, his determination to achieve more personal control over his own fate. Here a central objective of the helping process is to assist the client in exploring his ambivalences toward the painful work of acquiring and enforcing internal control.

Small groups

Many of the so-called "group dynamics techniques" aim at redistributing power in the group so that it can be guided by the will of its members instead of by tradition or by the ideas of a few persons in positions of central power. (See, for example, Corey, 21.) Thus post-meeting reactions sheets have been found useful for learning how the members of a group evaluate their meetings and for exercising group influence in determining what should be the order of business at the next meeting. Improved procedures for setting an agenda and for recording group progress can be used to make sure that the group spends time on problems which members feel are important. Buzz groups and other techniques of mass participation permit the members of a large group to contribute actively to the formulation of group policies.

Large organizations

The creation of new centers of power in industry is a basic objective in the work of Taylor (50), whose aim was to develop what he called a "third force." Taylor entered industry at a time when a new distribution of power was just occurring, and he became one of the first industrial efficiency experts. He was appalled when he entered a manufacturing establishment as a common laborer to find what he called "soldiering" on the job. Later, as a foreman, he tried driving his men. When this failed, he blamed worker resistance and the unwillingness of management to risk disrupting an uneasy truce. Taylor cast about for a way to bring the benefits of full productivity to both sides, and he decided that the answer could come from a "third force," a group of professional efficiency men whose direct allegiance was to neither management nor workers. Instead, Taylor felt, these professionals would be responsible to their profession and to society as a whole. Isolating them from the work group, he set up a training program for individual workmen, taught them efficient methods, and offered them payments on the basis of increased production. He hoped that his practices would spread throughout industry by contagion. As a matter of fact, his plan did enjoy some success, and a professional class of efficiency experts did eventually come into being. But the independence of this "third force" from management was never clearly established and was, of course, strongly disputed by the labor unions.

A somewhat different approach is described in a report by Coch and French (35) on the methods of retraining the workers in a pajama factory to perform new jobs. When the company adopted a new line of goods requiring changes in production methods, the workers were divided into several groups. One group was merely told about the change and given no chance to plan ways of adapting to it; the workers in this group learned their new tasks slowly and displayed obvious signs of frustration and hostility. A second group, which was given a chance to participate in setting the piece rates for the new items, learned the new tasks more rapidly. A third group, composed of workers who participated fully in all the decisions about how to adapt to the change in production methods, learned even more rapidly and achieved substantially higher production records than had been established in previous work. Thus it appeared that the experience of being coerced impaired the ability of the workers to function effectively, while the experience of being allowed to participate in decisions usually reserved for management increased the workers' effectiveness.

This conclusion was explored further in a study made in the office of a large insurance company (45). The study was based on the concept of axiality, which was defined as the balance between the control which people at a given hierarchical level exercised over their own work and the control which they were called upon to accept from people at a higher hierarchical level. In other words, high axiality means a high degree of control from above. To lower the axiality of workers in the rank and file is to reduce the extent of regulation issuing from above and increase the extent of self-regulation. The change strategy in this case was to lower the axiality of one group of work units and raise it in another, while a third group, in which the axiality was left unchanged, was used as a control with which to evaluate the effects of the changes on the productivity of the other two groups. The hypothesis that lowered axiality would engender increased job satisfaction, greater involvement of workers in their tasks, and stronger motivations was only partially substantiated.

Communities

Change agents who work with community systems seem more inclined than others to conceptualize their work in terms of an internal power conflict. Alinsky (52), like Taylor and Redl and Wineman, speaks frankly of the need for new foci of power. He urges the development of grass-roots groups, or "People's Organizations." A People's Organization, he says, should not be representa-

tive either of the various classes in the community or of the established interest groups; it should be drawn by and large from the
depressed classes. It should mobilize the zeal for betterment which
Alinsky feels may be found abundantly in any depressed people,
and it should utilize the "natural leadership" to be found there.
Through a process of free interaction, the members of the People's
Organization locate their common goals, mobilize their antagonisms toward common enemies, and prepare to fight existing foci
of power (vested interests and the like).

In this case, the role of the change agent lies in helping the
group to locate the common causes of its difficulties, to identify
and bring forward the indigenous leadership, and to use both its
strengths and weaknesses in the mobilization of power. The agent
does not oppose tradition but, on the contrary, uses it in developing and applying organizational forces.

Alinsky contrasts his People's Organization with community
councils and other groups which seek to be both representative
and constituent. The community council, he says, merely provides
a battleground for the various pressure groups in the community,
thus blinding the council to the needs of the community as a whole.
Whatever zeal these pressure groups are able to muster is expended
inwardly in hostilities against each other, rather than outwardly as
an effective force for change.

A second approach to the mobilization of power in a community
is described by Reid (73) in his report on Taos and Taos County,
New Mexico. The area was extremely depressed, fed by pitiably
inadequate agriculture, populated chiefly by a Spanish-language
subculture, and assisted by a large number of agencies at all levels
of government. Each of these agencies had a specified set of goals
and a carefully delimited area of operation, but there was no co-
ordination of effort at the local level. The change agent, therefore, created a county-wide co-ordination-and-action group consisting of representatives both from the communities and from the
various agencies. Informal problem-solving groups were established in each community and connected by channels of communication to the county-wide group. The result was that workers from
the agencies could begin to pay attention to community goals in,

stead of to the limited agency goals, and community leaders could learn to make maximum use of the skills and resources provided by the agencies. The quality of service to the community was greatly improved.

In Montana, Poston (71), Brownell, and associates faced the problem of a declining population and a state-wide community disintegration. Western Montana, the mountainous section of the state, was originally settled during a boom in the mining and lumbering industries. The original development of the country had been largely exploitative, with the usual consequences of depleted resources, a depressed economy, and a high potential for social unrest. A gradual recovery, over long years, was halted by the twentieth-century sequence of war, depression, and another war. New industries did not develop; no stable economy was created; and a selective population decline began. Half the graduates of the state university were leaving the state. In short, the very people who might have provided leadership were instead leaving the area. Moreover, among all the people an essentially frontier scheme of values, based on fiercely guarded individualism and unabashed materialism, persisted and prevented the growth of united action to solve the state's economic problems.

In this predicament, the change agent—in this case a group—believed that its main job was "getting the people to take concerted action to enrich the quality of living in the state, find ways to stabilize the family and small community, and study ways to raise the appreciative and spiritual standard of living." The program proceeded through university extension services, traveling plays and lectures, and a series of local community pageants designed to induce an appreciation of local history among the inhabitants of the stricken areas. In one case the change effort consisted in providing leadership for a successful attempt to establish a much-needed new lumber-products industry.

The program was short-lived. It ran into intransigent opposition from the state's chief mining and industrial syndicate, and the financial, political, and social power of this entrenched interest was enough to destroy the change project.

Thelen (77, 78) and Sarchet (74, 78) report a different type of attempt to cope with community disorganization. They worked in transitional neighborhoods on Chicago's South Side, where wartime population pressures brought Negroes into what had been a more or less settled and homogeneous white neighborhood. Reactions to the new influx ranged over the whole gamut of social hostility, from mere unwillingness to communicate and mild expressions of disunity to outright hysteria. Wartime restrictions contributed to the inability of the city to supply necessary services, and signs of physical deterioration were on every hand. Many of the residents who could flee to other parts of the city did so, and those who remained behind were utterly unable to cope with their new situation.

Thelen and his co-workers tried to meet these problems by the organization of block groups which could mobilize residents to work on immediate local problems. The change program included the training of a local leadership team in each block. The block leaders were connected with each other, with the neighborhood organization, and with a city-wide commission in such a way that they could exert pressure on the city government, but their primary responsibility remained the development of group cultures in the blocks. This was accomplished by bringing together block residents in a series of meetings where a permissive atmosphere was established and where it was possible for individuals to test the rumors, insights, and plans for action which were current in their local areas. Gradually, as there was an increase in communication and a general "sharing of affect" (that is, a mutual sharing of feeling), group cohesiveness developed, and the residents began to acquire a capacity for rational problem-solving behavior. Thus the procedure was twofold: first, to reduce the differences among the ways in which the residents looked at the same set of conditions, thus broadening a sharing of affect, and then to shift from affective to cognitive considerations. As a result, the groups looked more realistically at the sources of strain in their neighborhoods and then tried to develop ways of working on these as objective problems. There was considerable emphasis on the importance of early success in problem solving, and the problems selected were often those which offered a visible and noncontroversial target, such as the lack of an important city service.

Thelen's work is reported here as an example of community disorganization and reorganization. Actually, however, Thelen does not place as much emphasis upon power as he does upon communication. His basic assumption is that communication derives from shared perceptions and culturally validated shared meanings, and that the intermingling of people who lack shared meanings because they came from different cultures must lead to a throttling of communication. At the same time, external change increases the need to communicate. Hence communication in disunited communities is likely to take the form of furtive rumor or expressions of open hostility. A self-reinforcing cycle is set in motion—threat, rumor, factual distortion, and renewed threat. The only way to break this cycle is to clear the channels of communication between the culturally distinct groups so that perceptions can be mutually tested and distortions corrected. Eventually, through the sharing of affect and the successful solving of problems, new shared meanings can be developed to bridge the differences between the culturally disparate elements, and more normal communication can ensue among all the people concerned.

Analysis

In each of the illustrations we have given here the change agent has assumed the existence of a defective power structure within the client system, and as a result he has tried to bring about a new and more appropriate organization of power for problem-solving action. These illustrations, plus a good many others which we do not have the space to include, suggest two approaches which a change agent may use in trying to correct an unbalanced distribution of power. One is to create a new center of power. This new center of power may be conceived as antagonistic to existing centers of power (Alinsky), as separate from but supplementary to existing centers of power (Taylor, Reid), or as emerging from disorganization to provide a rallying point for disaffected subparts of the system (Redl and Wineman, Poston, Thelen). A second approach, alternative and complementary, is to change the functional basis of existing centers of power, allowing a greater flexibility of command so that different parts of the subsystem can more easily make their influence felt (Corey, Coch and French).

In both of these approaches the ultimate objective is to create a broader base for the power structure so that policy and action will more adequately represent the needs of all parts of the system. In certain pathological cases an additional requirement is that the power structure of the system be altered to maximize constructive rather than destructive tendencies.

Our conception of the role of the change agent obliges us to omit a great deal of material about the kind of change which results in active participation in a power struggle. We have committed ourselves to a study of the ways in which a change agent can help a client to help himself, and hence we have arbitrarily excluded any analysis of the ways in which a client may try to help himself solely through the coercive or competitive use of power. This is a job for other authors. However, we do want to point out quite explicitly that many change agents, in the rough and ready circumstances of their jobs, cannot afford to restrict themselves in this way. Every attempt to bring about a change at one level of unit organization raises the possibility that vested interests at other levels, external to the immediate client system (which almost invariably is a subpart of a larger system), may be threatened and may respond with coercive action. Often the change agent must be prepared to deal with an antagonist as well as with a client. In other words, the change agent may from time to time abandon the role of change agent, as we have defined it here, in order to assume the role of protagonist.

In summary, the change agent, acting in his proper role, may be concerned about developing new centers of power or about making old ones more representative of the client system as a whole. His approach is generally to look for new sources of leadership or strength within the client system, to offer the training which will allow this potential power to manifest itself, and to help locate the problems and action strategies by which these new combinations of strength can assume the habits and confidence of authority.

INTERNAL MOBILIZATION OF ENERGY

Another group of change agents is concerned in one way or another, it seems to us, with the channeling and mobilization of energy. There are a number of different reasons why a client may not be able to mobilize energies effectively, and we shall try to illustrate each of them.

Individuals

The assumption of the classical Freudian theorists (7) seems to be that energy is lost in internal conflict between id forces seeking discharge and ego repressions of these forces. The function of therapy is to alter the patient's "instinctive economy," thereby increasing his conscious awareness of the repressed contents of the id and reducing his need for elaborate ego defenses. Id energy which has been dammed up or squandered in unproductive defensive efforts is then released to the control of the conscious ego, and the patient finds himself in possession of greater resources of energy for productive activity.

The therapeutic process depends heavily upon interpretation; the therapist spells out for the patient the nature of his unconscious desires and intentions as they are revealed in free associations, dreams, and transference behavior. As the patient learns to understand the significance of his unconscious behavior, he gains the ability to modify it and make it more consistent with his conscious intent.

Small groups

Allen (17) is a therapist who has shifted his attention from the neurotic individual to the neurotic interpersonal system. Specifically, he is interested in treating children by means of working with the entire parent-child relationship. His assumption is that health consists of uninterrupted personal change in accordance with changing biological and cultural imperatives, with a progressive relinquishment of old interpersonal satisfactions in favor of new ones. When one or both members of a relationship cannot give up the old satisfactions, growth is interrupted and neurosis results.

Therapy requires the treatment of all partners to the relationship, in this case, the child and the parent. The therapist establishes a relationship with each person separately, then proceeds to offer each a series of opportunities to choose between new and past modes of obtaining satisfaction from their relationship. The patient gradually gives up the old satisfactions, frees himself from the neurotic alliance, and becomes ready to resume normal growth. Some case workers concentrating on work with children (Clifton and Hollis, 5) similarly stress this orientation in work with pre-adolescent children and their parents.

Cattell (85) has been particularly explicit in his use of an economy-of-energy model to describe group functioning. For him a group's "synergy" is the total energy it can command. "Maintenance energy" is the part of that energy which is bound up in the group's internal machinery; "effective synergy" is the residue, the energy which is available to the group for use in carrying out its purposes. Thus the more energy the group expends in internal conflict, the less it will have available for carrying on its external business.

The training program inaugurated by Maier (28) for work groups in industrial environments gives attention to both power relationships and communications, but it is pre-eminently an example of the agent's concern for the efficient use of energy. Maier points out that in hierarchical organizations whose chief motivational base is the threat of reprisal the supervisor-employee relationship is unlikely to produce either efficiency or satisfaction. In fact, there is a strong tendency for the system to develop sharp role differentiations with an accompanying tendency toward unilateral authority and accountability. Between hierarchical levels there grow up perceptual discrepancies and defensiveness leading to recriminations and a general sense of threat.

Maier suggests that the solution lies in the introduction of democratic supervisory procedures at all levels of the hierarchy. By this he means that the authority to make decisions at each level should be shifted from the supervisor to the work group. The supervisor should become a democratic leader rather than an official who hands down unilateral decisions. Such an arrangement, Maier says, restores two-way communications, increases the capacity of the work group for meeting and solving problems, and reduces the tendency of persons at all levels to consider new problems as threats to their personal security. This introduction of democratic supervisory procedures is accomplished through special training sessions for supervisors, and Maier describes a number of techniques which can be taught to supervisors to enable them to effect this change in their roles.

Large organizations

Interest in the mobilization of energy is, of course, paramount in industrial concerns, where more energy means higher productivity and greater profits. Industrial consultants have developed a number of ideas about what can be done to organize the available energy in any given system most effectively.

Jaques (36) reports the efforts of a British consulting firm in which several fields of specialization were united to destroy what he called "unwitting collusion" between various staff and employee groups in a foundry. The specialists began by constructing a detailed organizational chart which served as the first step toward a clarification of roles. Then, when they were invited to work with a specific subgroup they would try to locate the underlying and unrecognized forces which interfered with the ability of workers and supervisors to take their assigned roles. The change process was one of "working through," that is, interpreting these concealed forces to the work groups involved. In the process of working through, members of the client system were given plenty of opportunity to discharge their feelings. Naturally, there was resistance to the interpretations made by the change agent, and these resistances of course needed to be interpreted. The objective was to increase the capacity of the group members to tolerate painful insights into negative group phenomena—in other words, to look realistically at themselves, their jobs, and their relationships with other subgroups. This in turn would increase the ability of the whole system to solve its own problems by identifying and working through the irrational elements which from time to time inevitably enter into and distort the operation of a complex organizational system.

Perhaps an example from Jaques' book will help to clarify what is meant by "unwitting collusion." The "Divisional Managers Meeting" asked for help because the members felt that the factory's managing director was moving so rapidly in the field of human relations that technical development was being ignored. The team of consultants discovered that the managing director, on his side, considered the manager group too obtuse to understand his objectives in the field of human relations. The consultants were able to point out that this collusion between the managing director and the manager group in making an issue of the human-relations program actually served to obscure several more basic problems. The managers were blocked by rivalry among them for authority and for the favor of the managing director; the managing director was blocked by his own ambivalent alternation between paternalistic and authoritarian attitudes toward the managers. Thus "the culture of the organization had been fashioned to act as a defensive system against the anxiety of having too explicit responsibility for people" (36, p. 315).

The Scanlon Plan (38, 48) represents another attempt to create more productive energy-releasing relationships between interdependent working groups. It combines a more or less standardized incentive plan with certain other features which are designed to increase the participation of workers in meaningful problem-solving activities that are related to their work. The plan provides for continuing production committees which are to receive suggestions for ways of improving efficiency from line and staff employees at all levels. Daily "feedback" is provided for all workers on the production of their group; that is to say, workers are told what their teams have accomplished each day. Thus the workers can see immediately the effect of any change in production methods upon their efficiency. At the end of each month a bonus is paid to everyone in the organization, based on total production records and worked out jointly by management and the union. This means that individual workers can help one another without loss to themselves; they are encouraged to communicate their special skills to their co-workers. The worker can perceive quite clearly the direct relationship between his own work and the total productivity of the organization as well as the relationship between the productivity of his own group and the amount of the monthly bonus. The effect of the plan is to increase the whole system's productivity by creating a more direct relationship between the individual and the total organization.

The Scanlon Plan agrees substantially with the change model presented by McGregor (92), who suggests that frustration, aggressiveness, and low productivity occur when authority is exercised in such a way as to hamper the satisfaction of the individual worker's needs, whereas increased productivity may be achieved by using authority to facilitate the satisfaction of the individual worker's needs. Scanlon attributes the success of his plan to the fact that workers derive satisfaction from participating in as much as possible of the meaningful activity connected with their jobs, especially in the decisions which have to do with the productivity of the group. In other words, workers enjoy the increased sense of responsibility which comes to them when they are allowed to make the decisions and solve the problems related to their own work.

Communities

The mobilization and channeling of energy has been a factor in the work of a number of community change agents, but it is difficult to find a case in which this is the primary concern. Perhaps Biddle (53) is as good an example as any. He begins with the assumption that communities fail to grow because of apathy and "fragmentation." Apathy originates in past failures, factionalism, loss of communal self-confidence. Fragmentation derives from the tendency to rely on community subgroups (that is, pressure groups) instead of on a community-wide organization, in the belief that one's own group can "gain and hold advantage only at the price of disadvantage" to other groups.

Biddle's solution is the community council. He believes that the council is a device which can restore communication among groups, develop native leadership, and encourage the members of the community to assume a responsibility for solving community problems. The change agent's role in the council sessions is that of a catalyst. His contributions from the floor are aimed at relieving tensions or isolating those in the group who tend to play a negative part. He uses the "method of encouragement" to help the group expand the area within which it is willing to assume responsibilities; he uses the "technique of agreement," which includes permissiveness, catharsis, and the interpretation of one group to another, to help reduce the emotional tensions between groups.

We have noted that objections to the community council have been raised by Alinsky (52), who argues that the council cannot mobilize energy for effective community action because it almost invariably becomes the arena for conflicts between constituent groups. Then the available energy is consumed in internal bickering. He maintains, for instance, that racial dissension and "scapegoating" arise and divert energy from constructive work into futile conflict. It is important, he says, always to keep an external target for the People's Organization to fight against ("a fight in the bank") so that the group can avoid the pitfall of internal dissension.

Total cultures

Only rarely does a change agent find an opportunity to apply his skills to a total culture. One of the few examples is provided by Parsons (95), who was one of a group of social scientists asked by the government to suggest the means of achieving an effective occupation policy in Germany after World War II. His complete analysis and recommendations are far too complex to be described here. But among his important contributions was his recognition of the fact that the Nazis owed their "success" in part to their use of a fundamental dualism in the German ideological structure. On one side, he pointed out, the German national character is predominantly "emotional, idealistic, active, romantic," and on the other, predominantly "orderly, hard-working, hierarchy-preoccupied, methodical, submissive, gregarious, materialistic." The Nazis linked together these components, using the first to create the Hitler myth and the illusion of German invincibility and the second to establish their political goals. The two were combined in a single synthetic ideological motivation. Parsons suggested that "the first task of a program of institutional change is to disrupt this synthesis and create a situation in which the romantic element will again find an apolitical form of expression" (p. 248).

Analysis

The change agent who is concerned with mobilizing or releasing energy usually tries to establish a dramatic contrast between the productive use of energy in rational attempts to solve problems realistically and the nonproductive waste of energy in frustrations and internecine conflicts. We have noted a number of ways in which energy is wasted—in the persistence of internal conflict within the system (Freud, Alinsky), in the displacement of energy into irrelevant activities (Freud, Jaques, Alinsky), and in the investment of energy in modes of behavior which produce only negative or destructive effects either in the client system or in neighboring systems (Allen, Maier, Parsons). In all of these cases the first job of the change agent is to interrupt or prevent the wasteful use of energy. Then he must work with the client system to establish new and more productive patterns of energy use.

In addition, we found that several of the change agents whose work we discussed were concerned not with correcting pathological wastefulness but with bringing an even better economy of energy use into systems which were already relatively healthy (Cattell, Scanlon, Maier, McGregor, Biddle). These agents assume that ways can be found to relate the subparts of a system more effectively to the whole and that when this has been done the energy and ideas originating in the subparts will become more fully available to the whole client system.

INTERNAL COMMUNICATION

Virtually all of the change agents whose work we are reviewing here gave at least some attention to the importance of good communication between the subparts of a client system. But let us summarize now some of the cases in which the change agent seemed to feel that an actual breakdown in communication was the primary cause of difficulty.

Individuals

Carl Rogers is well known for theories of personality and therapy which emphasize the self-percept and the individual's ability or inability to organize his experience into a meaningful whole based upon the self-percept. Experience which bears no discernible relation to the self-structure is likely to be ignored; experience which seems to be inconsistent with the individual's view of himself is likely to be distorted or denied. "Psychological maladjustment exists when the organism denies to awareness significant sensory and visceral experiences, which consequently are not symbolized and organized into the gestalt of the self-structure" (15, p. 510).

Therapy, for Rogers, is basically "the experiencing of inadequacies in old ways of perceiving, the experiencing of new and more accurate and adequate perceptions and the recognition of significant relationships between perceptions" (p. 222). The therapist's job is to provide a setting in which the client finds a maximum opportunity to experience these changes in the perception of himself. The therapist does not question, does not evaluate, but only accepts and affirms; he introduces no content; he gives the client acceptance, understanding, and support. The client enters therapy with a rigid and limited self-percept, highly vulnerable to the contradictory realities which may be thrust upon it by the environment. In the course of therapy the client moves first to a state in which the self-percept breaks down and becomes disorganized, and then to a reorganization of the self-percept, permitting it to incorporate previously contradictory elements. This comes about because the therapist accepts the aspects of the patient's self which have been previously denied or distorted, so that eventually the patient learns that he, too, can accept these aspects of his personality. Aptekar (80) describes a somewhat similar casework orientation which he calls "dynamic passivity."

Frieda Fromm-Reichmann (8) is a therapist who is interested primarily in the modes of communication between the patient and other individuals. Strongly influenced by Sullivan, she defines psychiatry as the study of interpersonal communication and mental disease as the disturbance of interpersonal relations. Disturbance originates, for example, in the relationship between a child and the adults who are close to him when the adults communicate to the child things about himself which he cannot accept or things which are false. Later the disturbance may be perpetuated when the child, as he grows older, attributes to other adults the same unacceptable appraisals of himself which he encountered in his earlier childhood environment. Therapy in this case proceeds mainly through the observation and investigation of the doctor-patient relationship. The therapist offers interpretations which will show how the patient's behavior in this relationship is influenced by dissociated (repressed) residues from past relationships.

A study by Gordon Lippitt (11) in a nontherapeutic setting shows that communications from other people about oneself can become an important force for change when they are depersonalized and made explicit. The individuals in a training group were asked to evaluate one another on various aspects of participation in group discussions and to indicate how they wished their colleagues would change. Through diagnostic interviews with members of the research staff, some of the members of the group were told how the others wished them to change; the rest had no such interviews. This "feedback" of information had a measurable effect. Those who were interviewed responded very positively to the receipt of the guiding information and began to change in the desired direction more rapidly than those who did not receive the information.

Small groups

Mutual or multiple ignorance has been found by change agents in many groups, organizations, and communities. Lau (25), who conducted a study among members of college fraternities, found that a preponderance of fraternity boys tended to believe that their fellow fraternity members were more "conservative" than they were themselves. When they were shown the results of a survey which revealed the real attitudes of the members of their own and other fraternity houses, the resulting discussions served as a stimulus toward change. That is to say, the distribution of correct information about the willingness of members to admit Negroes, Orientals, or Jews often led members to re-examine their opinion of what the official house membership practices should be.

Gomberg (see Taft, 31), in reporting a process of family casework in which the change agent met regularly with the husband and wife in separate sessions, describe the negative relationship of noncommunication that had developed between the husband and wife. The casework process was believed to be instrumental in opening up blocked channels of communication within the family group.

Large organizations

An interesting discussion of communication problems in a large organization occurs in the report by Jaques (36) on the work of the interdisciplinary team from Tavistock Institute at a British foundry. Part of this report has already been presented; more can be added here.

Jaques and his associates do not make the usual assumption that a restoration of communication will invariably produce a positive effect upon the efficiency of the system. In an industrial environment certain kinds of communication are necessary and others are not. The communication network must provide the links among the three interdependent systems which are identifiable in any factory: the social structure, the culture, and the personality. Within this network constructive barriers must be erected to prevent communication from flowing too freely ("adaptive segregation"). On the other hand, misplaced barriers can cause damage; barriers erected as a defense against recognizing and dealing with the stresses which develop between subparts fall into the category of "maladaptive segmentation." The creative use of selective barriers is the means by which communication among subgroups can be regulated in a proper and reasonable flow. Effective communication follows from a "known and comprehensive communications structure, a code governing relations between roles, and a quality of relationship between persons such that adaptive segregation may be mutually agreed upon and rigid segmentation is unnecessary."

Communication is defined as the sum total of information about feelings, attitudes, and wishes, transmitted directly and indirectly, consciously and unconsciously. Whenever social equilibrium is upset communication occurs. It is the means, therefore, by which a system takes corrective action in the presence of difficulty; obviously, communication is essential if the source of the difficulty is to be diagnosed. In a hierarchical structure, communication must proceed both ways, up and down. Upward communication can be effective only when the bottom and middle are free from any sense of intimidation and when the top accepts and even seeks communication from below.

Examples of attempts to improve communications among different segments of an organization are given by Bradford and Lippitt (34, 39, 40) in their reports on supervisory-training programs in government and hospital settings and by Jenkins and Lippitt (24) in their study of interpersonal perceptions of parents, students, and teachers. In the hospital study a "work problems" group was established at each of three different hierarchical levels, and the groups met regularly to consider work problems and their causes. It soon became apparent that most problems involved workers at all levels, but that each problem was perceived and interpreted differently by workers at the different levels. The change agents were given permission to tell the workers in each group how the workers in the other groups were reacting to specific problems. This led to further discussions and to attempts at diagnostic role playing—that is, putting oneself in the role of those at a different level of the structure—to clarify the ways in which the problems appeared to workers at all three levels. Eventually, direct communication was established between the different hierarchical groups. As a result, the staff acquired a greater capacity to solve problems in the best interests of the total organization.

In the Jenkins and Lippitt study, parents, teachers, and students were asked to tell what they liked and disliked about each other. That is, parents were asked to report on teachers and students, teachers were asked to report on parents and students, and students expressed themselves about parents and teachers. Striking differences in perception were revealed. The findings of the survey were discussed first in each group alone, then in meetings among the groups. These discussions led to a greater mutual understanding of one another's needs and problems and hence to a greater ability to meet these needs and problems.

Mann (42, 43, 44) used a similar survey-plus-feedback technique in working with the accounting departments of a large public utility. Survey data had been collected which included (1) information about the perceptions of workers and supervisors of themselves and one another and (2) departmental comparisons of these employee attitudes. The data were presented in a booklet which was given to supervisors and division heads. A tentative program was worked out in which discussions of the results of the survey were to be carried out among supervisors, between department heads and employees, and among employees. The program was not carried out with equal completeness in all divisions or in all departments of a single division, since the responsibility for planning the kind and amount of "feedback" to employees was left for decision by individual supervisors in consultation with the change agent. A comparison of workers' attitudes and behavior before and after the study showed a significant change among the workers who had been given the results of the survey and especially in those groups where the results had been discussed by the supervisors and employees together.

Communities

Community change agents have confronted various kinds of communication problems. We have already mentioned Thelen's work (76) in stimulating communication among culturally distinct and socially antagonistic groups. In much the same way, Biddle (53) has tried to create opportunities for communication between representatives of competing forces in the community.

Lindemann and his associates (51,* 64) report on the work of an interdisciplinary team which undertook the job of introducing preventive psychiatry in a particular community. Instead of locating and treating every case of mental disease, the group emphasized the treatment of unhealthy interaction situations. A fairly comprehensive referral system was established, so that interpersonal situations which seemed dangerous (as between teacher and student, parent and child, teacher and parents, and so forth) could be located and treated quickly. Treatment usually involved a number of approaches. An unhealthy parent-child relationship, for instance, might be remedied through the use of controlling group atmospheres in the child's classroom, teacher-parent conferences designed to further an understanding of aggressive behavior in children, and perhaps an approach to the child through his group activities. In the case of serious mental disorders, of course, psychiatric treatment was given.

Hence we see that communication is important at two points: first, in finding and identifying the place where treatment is needed; and second, in conveying information to the persons involved about what they could do to improve the situation.

The multiple-ignorance model is found in a number of community studies, especially those with a distinctly cognitive orientation. In the study of "Baytown" by Festinger and Kelley (62), for instance, the mutual hostility of residents in a wartime housing project was attributed to multiple ignorance. The study was conducted in a New England city where the old residents regarded their town as a "one-class" community. They resented the presence of newcomers who seemed to them to belong to a lower class. On the other hand, the residents of the housing project felt themselves rejected by the town and for this reason assigned a lower-class status to each other. In the housing project, there was little communication and much hostility. The truth was, however, that there was no real difference in social values between the residents of the housing project and those of the town. Thus ignorance caused the

---

* It will be noted that reference number 51 refers in the bibliography to an article by David F. Aberle. Although Aberle wrote the article in question, Erich Lindemann was director of the project described in the Aberle report.

trouble in the first place and lack of communication perpetuated it.

When the change agent, in this case a group, entered the scene, it seemed wise to attempt to increase the contacts among the residents of the housing project in order to dispel their false impressions about each other, while also trying to prevent any increase in contact between the project residents and the town. The hypothesis was that as the project residents came to know each other better they would create a more positive image of themselves and that this image would in turn reach into the town. The experiment was cut short, however, by resistance which developed against the change agent within the housing project.

The community self-survey is another form of the communication model which is used by community change agents. As an example, consider the report by Selltiz and Wormser (75) on a community self-survey in a small northern city which was beset by problems of discrimination. The survey was made by a group of community members, and the change agent functioned primarily as a technical consultant. The survey brought into vivid prominence the facts on the extent and magnitude of discrimination in the community. Those who participated in making the survey came to feel responsible for the outcome of the study and for making the findings known to the entire community. More and more, they came to feel responsible for correcting the injustices they had seen; they wanted to reaffirm the American doctrine of equality. Once the violations of this doctrine became inescapably visible to everyone, community members felt obliged to take action against the discrimination in their midst, and the moral position of those who openly defended discrimination became clearly untenable.

In Puerto Rico the Commonwealth government established a community action program which operated at the local level but was conceived as extending throughout the country. It is described by Cannell, Wale, and Withey (58).

Puerto Rico's problems were intense and concentrated—a growing population, very rapid urbanization, increasing social and economic dislocation throughout the country. Individual citizens were inclined to submit passively to these changes and wait for a wealthy landowner or powerful government to set things right again. On the other hand, the government's program, known as the Community Education Program, aimed to stimulate self-help at the community level.

The program called for the selection of individual citizens from each community to receive training in leadership, the administration of this training, and then a continuing relationship with the local leaders after they had returned to their communities. Within the community the program emphasized the identification of local problems, the discussion of these problems in order to stimulate concern about them, and finally the development of a plan of action for solving the problems. Widespread community participation was made one of the program's major points in the hope that this would both disseminate a realistic appraisal of the nature of local problems and lead to a vigorously pursued campaign to solve them.

The program emphasized communication in two ways. First, it was important to establish communication among members of the community. Many individuals were themselves concerned about local problems, but they felt that others were not. This was a form of multiple ignorance, and obviously it had to be corrected. Second, mass media were used extensively in teaching citizens the methods of solving the problems of their communities. Integrated campaigns using movies, booklets, and posters were designed to inform, persuade, and stimulate. Except for the radio, rural Puerto Rico had previously been exposed to very little mass communication, and hence this campaign was particularly effective.

Analysis

We have combined here two kinds of examples—change agents who try to correct defective patterns of communication within a client system and change agents who use communication as a means of exerting pressure on the client system to change. In the latter cases we may infer that the change agents assume their client's ordinary communication patterns are inadequate, though not necessarily pathologically defective.

Pathologically defective communication arises when maladaptive barriers are erected between the subparts of the client system. If the client is an individual, we speak of repression, dissociation, and the denial of significant aspects of experience (Freud, Fromm-Reichmann, Rogers). If the client system is a group or organization or institution, we speak of barriers between hierarchical levels and between different functional subparts (Taft, Jaques, Bradford and Lippitt, Jenkins and Lippitt, Mann). In a community there may be barriers between different cultural groups (Thelen), between different interest groups (Biddle), and between groups with different residential or historical backgrounds (Festinger and Kelley). Once they are established these barriers seem to be not only self-perpetuating but self-aggravating. Defensive responses, distorted perceptions, and mutual antagonisms come to characterize the relationships between subparts. The role of the change agent, therefore, is to serve as a neutral but friendly intermediary between the various subparts, first transmitting information from one part to another and eventually preparing the various subparts for direct intercommunication. Once this is genuinely established, the subparts can work together on their mutual problems.

The change agent who assumes that his client's trouble is ignorance rather than a pathological defect is not concerned with the removal of barriers so much as with stimulating an increased flow of information. This information may be designed to heighten self-awareness by providing data on the feelings and beliefs of all the people in the system (Lau, Selltiz and Wormser, Cannell, Wale, and Withey) or by providing information about the behavioral practices of people throughout the system (Selltiz and Wormser). On the other hand, the information may derive from the relationship between the client system and its environment; it may constitute a transmittal of the desires or expectations of other systems in respect to change in the client system (Gordon Lippitt). The change agent may produce external information which apprises the client system of the possible types and methods of change (Lindemann, Cannell, Wale, and Withey). It should be noticed that in the latter cases the pressure for change originates outside the client system, although the change itself occurs within the system and not primarily between the system and its environment. Almost all cases in which the change agent believes that his client system's chief problem is ignorance fall into this last category.

In this chapter we have looked at the work of a number of change agents who have tried to facilitate change within a client system. In our analysis of what it is that these agents want to change, we suggested three different diagnostic orientations. The agent may concentrate on changing the distribution of power within the client system, on altering its characteristic ways of mobilizing energy, or on correcting its patterns of communication. In addition, we noticed that within each of these major orientations there is a difference between change agents who want to destroy old patterns of behavior in order to make way for new ones, on the one hand, and change agents who simply want to add something new, on the other. This distinction is roughly one between agents who are concerned with curing a pathological condition and agents whose interest is in bringing about an improvement in a relatively normal condition.

These three diagnostic orientations are by no means mutually exclusive. In fact, most change agents probably pay attention to two or even three of the dimensions we have discussed here. But for conceptual purposes it seems helpful to treat them separately. Having done this, perhaps we can think more clearly about the assumptions which are implied in each of these orientations, specifically the assumptions about the kinds of situations which lead client systems to ask for help and the ways in which this help may best be given.

DIAGNOSTIC ORIENTATIONS TOWARD
PROBLEMS OF EXTERNAL RELATIONSHIPS

3

Some change agents are primarily concerned not with changing the relationships between parts of a client system but with changing the relationship between the client system and its environment. This is a diagnostic orientation which appears most frequently among change agents who work with individuals, but it may also be used by change agents working with other kinds of systems. In addition, of course, there are many cases in which a change agent who is working directly with the subparts of a client system tries to change the relationship between a subpart and its environment. Hence the question of whether a change agent is working with "internal" or "external" relationships depends to a certain extent upon an arbitrary definition of what constitutes the client system: is the unit with which the change agent is directly concerned defined as a system, or as a subpart of a significant larger system? The answer will vary from case to case. Moreover, one must remember that the difference between an orientation toward internal relationships and an orientation toward external relationships is a matter of relative emphasis. Change agents are seldom concerned exclusively with one or the other. They always pay at least some attention to both. A healthy client system is one whose internal and external relationships are both good.

CORRESPONDENCE BETWEEN
INTERNAL AND EXTERNAL REALITY

One way to think about the difficulties which may arise between a system and its environment is to consider the discrepancy between the environment as it actually exists and as it is perceived by the system or by the members of the system. Some of the conceptual notions which have been used to describe this discrepancy include projection, autism, and inappropriate frame of reference. In the first case, the client system introduces a constant bias into its perceptions of reality, using idiosyncratic instead of objective standards of interpretation. In the second case, the client isolates itself from surrounding systems, refusing to communicate with them and thereby restricting or destroying its chance of receiving accurate impressions of them. In the third case, the client system is unable to understand the messages which come to it from the environment because in interpreting them it uses a frame of reference which differs significantly from the frame of reference of the sender. Let us consider some examples.

Individuals

Bettelheim (1) and Redl and Wineman (13, 14) appear to be concerned primarily with projection in their efforts to treat extremely disturbed children through the use of special therapeutic environments. The child who enters Bettelheim's Orthogenic School or Redl's Pioneer House usually assumes that every other person in the world is hostile to him; this is his bias. The job of the adults on the counseling staff is to prove to him that his assumption is wrong and that adults are really not at all what he imagines them to be.

The techniques for doing this are many and varied, but through them all runs the thread of the need for a consistently positive response to the child. The adult must try to meet the child's physical and emotional needs as well as the situation permits, and he must try to avoid being provoked into hostility or enmity. Occasionally interpretation is used to make explicit the discrepancy between what the child expects, or projects, and what actually occurs. Most of the time, however, the child is simply confronted with a real world of loving adults and left to learn for himself that the hostility which he anticipates will not arise. When he begins to learn this and to relinquish his inappropriate expectations about other people, he is ready to start on the road toward socialization.

A similar case, involving the environmental treatment of disturbed adults, is reported by Curle and Trist (6). Transitional communities were established in England to facilitate the return of British prisoners of war to normal living. Many of the returned prisoners suffered from a sense of alienation; they were separated from their friends and loved ones by "a gulf of experience impossible to share." The roles, responsibilities, and relationships which they had left when they entered military service no longer seemed valid, and consequently the prisoners were unable to resume their civilian status. The transitional community adopted anchoring points from the POW culture—maternal medical care, for example, and a strong group democracy—and used these as a context for interpreting the contemporary life from which the POWs were estranged. Gradually a bridge was built from one culture to another, and the POWs regained and even expanded their capacities for participation in contemporary life. In other words, a correspondence had been set up between the internalized culture of the POWs—that is, their wartime frame of reference—and the culture of the people with whom they would have to live as civilians.

The effect of differences in internalized culture is seen even more clearly in studies of foreign visitors. Watson and Lippitt (33), for instance, report that Germans who visited America as guests of the United States Government after the war perceived American culture in ways which were consistent with the German frame of reference. Where Germans and Americans shared the same values, as they did in respect to the desirability of raising children to be responsible and independent, the Germans were eager to explore and learn from American practices. On the other hand, where German and American values differed, as they did in respect to the division of responsibility between the sexes, the visitors disliked the American pattern and were unwilling to learn from it. These discrepancies between German and American frames of reference were not much influenced by the visit to America. However, they did serve to define and limit the points at which communication between Germans and Americans—that is, between the client system and the change agent—could occur.

Perhaps the clearest example of a change agent's attempt to decrease autism is to be found in the work of the National Training Laboratory in Group Development (3). In the training groups of the summer laboratory individuals have a chance to learn both about group development and about themselves. Discussion groups of approximately fifteen people meet for several hours each day. Part of each meeting is devoted to a discussion of the things the members have seen and felt in their own group. Such discussions inevitably include reactions to individual members of the group, and hence these individuals often discover things about themselves which they had not known before. When this kind of candid "feedback" is encouraged, individual "social blindness" is greatly reduced.

Small groups

Some of the cases we have already mentioned could serve as well to illustrate the situation of the small group whose members share a distorted or inappropriate view of reality. For instance, the frame of reference of the foreign visitors is to some degree anchored in face-to-face group relationships, and so is that of the returned British POWs.

From another context we may remind ourselves of the case studies cited in the discussion of communication, notably the cases in which the client system was a large organization or institution. We saw that Bradford and Lippitt (34) and Jenkins and Lippitt (24), were working to correct the perceptual discrepancies which had arisen between different subparts of an organization. If we were to say that one of these subparts was a client system, we

would have an example of a small group with a distorted view of
its environment. In these cases the change procedure was to improve and increase the communication between the different subparts, first through the change agent working as an intermediary,
then through direct face-to-face contact. The Gomberg report (31)
on family casework (see p. 41) is another illustration of this intermediary role.

A report by Hogrefe (23) supplies another kind of example of
a small group which is out of touch with its environment. He dis-
cusses the efforts of a neighborhood agency to make contact with
a teen-age Manhattanville gang. The gang possessed an elaborate
group culture of its own as well as effective means for keeping at
a distance any groups or persons who might threaten the integrity
or identity of the gang. Field workers from the agency eventually
made contact with the gang by simulating their norms of behavior.
Specifically, the workers tried to make suggestions which would
serve what Hogrefe considers the relevant needs of young people
in a gang situation: status, unity, freedom, and adventure. The
workers' immediate objective was to win personal acceptance,
though without disguising their agency connections. The ultimate
objective, of course, would be to use this personal acceptance as a
means of broadening the favorable contacts between the gang and
society at large.

Large-scale organizations and communities

The further one ascends in the scale of unit size, the fewer examples one finds of work with systems which are diagnosed as being out of touch with their environment. As a matter of fact, we
did not find any cases in which organizations or communities
asked for help with this kind of problem, a point which raises
some interesting theoretical speculations. Is it, for instance, because the larger unit creates its own environment? Or because the
relationship between a large unit and its environment is so se-
curely established that change is impossible? Or perhaps because a
large number of people, all related in one unit, cannot share the
same delusions for very long at a time? Or is it because when
alienation does occur on a large scale it is solved by some form

of power struggle, not by the more rational means of consultation with a change agent?

Analysis

The cases which we have presented here as examples of a lack of correspondence between internal and external reality illustrate the various forms of discrepancy which we mentioned at the beginning: projection, autism, and noncongruent frames of reference. It would be possible to consider all of these problems as examples of disturbances in communication, and this indeed is one of their consequences. But they take on a special interest from the fact that the very nature of reality, as perceived by the client system, makes it difficult for communication to occur. The change agent must alter the way in which the client system experiences reality before effective communication can begin. Generally speaking, the means by which a client system is helped toward a new experience of reality is the creation of a special reality which will simplify and emphasize the cues needed for objective perception. Such a special environment may be created to help the client learn new ways of relating to other systems around him. It may, for instance, be a therapeutic environment designed to correct an emotional disorder (Bettelheim, Redl and Wineman); a transitional environment designed to facilitate a shift from one culture to another (Curle and Trist); or a laboratory environment designed to encourage unusually free interpersonal communication and to stimulate the practice of new relationship skills (National Training Laboratories). If special environments cannot be created, then the change agent may try to enter into the environment of the client system (Hogrefe) or transplant the client system out of its own environment and into the environment of the change agent (Watson and Lippitt). In all these cases the change plan is similar. The object is to bring the client system into an active relationship with the change agent or his representatives, to provide opportunities for the client to discover and reject the inappropriate ways in which he has been relating to others, and to help the client learn and practice new ways of relating to others.

GOALS AND VALUES FOR ACTION

We have not made any attempt to introduce into this book examples from the vast literature which deals with the conditions and techniques for changing attitudes. Partly, this is because most reports of attempts to change attitudes describe efforts of persuasion or indoctrination; these are not collaborative and do not involve a helping relationship between a change agent and a client system. Furthermore, most reports of attempts to change attitudes do not meet the criterion of being interested in changes of overt behavior as well as cognitive orientations.

However, some attempts to bring about change in the goals and values which guide the behavior of the client system do seem to fall within the range of our definition of change activities. Specifically, these are projects in which the change agent tries to (1) provide new information which (2) leads the client system to engage in new behavior which, in turn, (3) leads the client system to adopt new values or attitudes.

Individuals

One relevant example comes from Brim's (4) experimental attempt to increase the permissiveness of mothers whose children had become feeding problems. When a mother went to her doctor for help with her child, the doctor suggested that she try behaving in a more permissive way, gave her reasons to support the recommended change, and warned her that this technique might not produce immediate results. He also gave her resource material on other possible ways of behaving. This standardized "training session" was repeated with a large number of mothers from similar socioeconomic and ethnic backgrounds. Follow-up research resulted in a classification of the mothers into three groups: those who did not try to change, those who tried but gave up, and those who changed and persisted in their change. These differences in behavior were related to such things as the prestige of the change agent (the doctor) in the eyes of the mother, the mother's emotional needs with respect to the child, and the degree of support or nonsupport which the mother's plan of changed behavior received from neighbors, from popular literature, and especially from her husband.

Small groups

The work done by Lewin and his associates (26) indicates that the technique of "group decision" is an effective instrument for goal change and behavioral change. During World War II, when meat was scarce and expensive, change agents held meetings with groups of housewives to discuss the possibility of their using sweet-breads, kidneys, hearts, and similar meats. The housewives were given information about the food value of these unpopular meats together with suggestions for cooking them. In some groups this information was dispensed and nothing more was done. In others, where the group-discussion technique was applied, the housewives were encouraged to talk about their reactions to the change agent's suggestions, and eventually they were asked to indicate by a show of hands how many actually planned to try these meats in their family menus. The results showed that women from the groups which had held public discussions were much more likely to accept the change agent's recommendations than were women from the groups which had received precisely the same information but had not been given an opportunity to discuss it or to arrive at a public decision.

Organizations

The very interesting and well-reported project of Sorenson and Dimock (49) on institutional change emphasizes the importance of a change in values (that is, organizational policy and philoso-phy) as a basic concern of the change agent who is beginning a process of change in the functioning of an organization. Such a change in values must be followed, they report, by a major program of staff training in the means of actualizing the new values.

Communities

In the context of community work, Clark (59) has provided an outstanding survey of cases of attitudinal and behavioral change in intergroup relations. His results argue strongly for the thesis that if the *situation* is changed, behavioral and then attitudinal changes will follow. He finds that the most successful instances of desegregation occurred in communities and institutions where the people in power simply introduced an abrupt and irreversible change, where the sanctions for the change were firm, painful, and without exception, and where the new policy was clear and unequivocal. In these conditions it was possible to obtain behavioral change without initial attitudinal change; very often, however, the change was evaluated affirmatively after the fact.

Another approach to changing attitudes is represented by change agents who believe that greater contact among persons will reduce their hostilities. Festinger and Kelley (62), for example, tried to reduce the mutual antagonisms among the residents of a housing project by increasing the amount of contact among the residents. Many other workers in the field of intergroup relations have concentrated on finding ways to increase interaction among different groups. The implied assumption is that hostility between groups is irrational and arises from distorted perceptions, that free interaction will dispel the distortion by showing each group what the members of the other group are really like, and that this change in understanding will eventually produce a change in feelings.

Analysis

In all of the cases reported here the change agent makes a direct attempt to change behavior and hopes that changes in values and attitudes will follow. In some cases (Brim, Lewin) he simply asks the client system to give the new behavior a trial in order to see if it isn't more satisfactory than the old. In other cases the client's situation is changed so that it is either forced into new behavior (Clark) or led into it naturally (Festinger and Kelley). There seems to be an implied assumption that it is more legitimate for the change agent to suggest a change in behavior than a change in attitudes, but that once new behavior patterns are developed the client system will work out new attitudes for itself.

Note also that in every case there is a strong emphasis on the importance of social support for the new modes of behavior. It is assumed that people will change much more readily when their change wins general approval than when it does not.

SKILLS AND STRATEGIES FOR ACTION

A third way to help a client system improve its external relationships is to help it develop new skills which can be used in problem solving or improving human relations. This approach implies that every client system encounters an unceasing series of challenges and opportunities and that difficulties in the relationship between the system and its environment arise when the system lacks the skills which would lead to effective action in meeting these challenges and opportunities.

Individuals

Blocksma, Fox, and Lippitt (2) have attempted to carry this approach into the elementary-school classroom. Sociometric measures were used to identify an experimental population of more than two hundred rejected children. Three different techniques were compared for their effectiveness in raising the status of these children among their peers: change agents provided special training to improve the skill of rejected children in social sensitivity and interpersonal relationships; they provided special training to give the high-status children skill in supporting and encouraging the low-status children; and they also supplied training to give teachers skill in developing group standards within the classroom which would be helpful to the low-status members. These techniques were compared for effectiveness both in changing the behavior of the rejected children and in changing their sociometric position within the group.

At the National Training Laboratory in Group Development (3) skill training is given to individuals and to the training group as such. Individuals are taught the skills of group management and leadership, and in addition they are helped through consultation to meet the specific change problems which await them at home. At the level of the *small group*, each training group is helped to increase its ability to recognize and solve its own problems of group process and leadership so that by the end of the training session it is more ready to turn from internal to external problems.

Large organizations

An example of the way in which change agents trained at the National Training Laboratory use their skills to effect changes in their own organizations after they have returned to their homes is reported by Nylen and his associates in a study of the Seattle public-school system (46). The school system had recently undergone a period of rapid expansion, and the usual results—excessive specialization at each level and formalization of communication between levels—were apparent. Several members of the school system who had received special change-agent training formed a nucleus of people interested in working on these problems by introducing throughout the system better group techniques for problem solving. This nuclear group was gradually enlarged as other members of the system were invited to join it or became involved in the processes of its work. Ultimately, it became the Puget Sound Group Development Laboratory, serving not only Seattle but the surrounding region.

The activities of this enlarged group have expanded to include a number of goals. These are (1) to change attitudes toward the study of group development, not only through experience in groups but also through a successful television program; (2) to engage the support of the school administration, chiefly by communicating regularly with a sympathetic superintendent and Superintendent's Conference; (3) to use existing resources, including excellent school facilities and the traditional rewards in the educational system, for self-improvement activities; (4) to attract key people from the school system by inviting them to join the nuclear group and by extending responsibility to them; and (5) to conduct frequent institutes for training in human relations. The result of these activities has been to spark a diffusion throughout the entire school system of a set of skills and attitudes which members of the system can profitably employ in meeting new problems wherever they arise.

There are some very interesting parallels to the Seattle case just mentioned in the report of Sorenson and Dimock (49) on the extensive program of in-service training which is required to support major policy changes in a large organization.

Maier's description of a program for training in human relations in industry (28) has already been cited as an example of an effort to rechannel energies within the client system. But it could be listed here also, since it was an attempt to expand problem-solving skills at all levels within the system.

Communities

Many change agents who work with communities devote large parts of their programs to training in the skills and techniques of problem solving. By way of example, we shall mention only McClusky (66, 67, 79 *). He and his associates at the University of Michigan are engaged in a community-development program which offers help on request to voluntary problem-solving groups in Michigan communities. The help consists of training in the skills of identifying, discussing, and solving community problems, with emphasis on democratic procedures. Various techniques are used, including special lectures by members of the community-development staff, extension courses, area conferences in which key people from several neighboring communities are brought together, and continuing consultations with community councils which request them.

Analysis

The illustrations which we have given here are all characterized by the transfer of skills from the change agent to the client system and, in the case of multiperson systems, by the diffusion of these skills as widely as possible throughout the system. If the emphasis is upon problem solving (Blocksma, National Training Laboratories, McClusky), the system is considered as an actor, acting upon

---

* Reference number 79 in the bibliography refers to a report by Alvin Zander on one project in the community-development program which was carried out under his direction.

problems located in the environment and in some sense external to the system. If the emphasis is upon human relations (Maier, Nylen, *et al.*), then the need for interaction among people who are trying to solve problems is stressed just as much as the external problems themselves. Thus the system becomes both the actor and the thing to be acted upon. In both cases the ultimate objective is to improve the skill repertoire of the system so that it can deal with problems presented either by changes within the system or by changes in the environment.

Change agents who offer training in human relations and problem solving often assume that there exists a series of steps or activities which are required for successful response to a new challenge. Thus there are skills which are associated, first, with sensitivity or the perception of significant changes inside or outside the system; second, with the interpretation and evaluation of these perceived changes; third, with knowing when and how to gather additional information; fourth, with planning action steps; fifth, with the execution of the action plan; and sixth, with maintaining opportunities for a continuous feedback of information relevant to the success or failure of the plan.

There is one aspect of problem solving which is sometimes singled out for special attention and which is of particular interest to students of change. This is the characteristic of flexibility or, as it has sometimes been called, changeability. Some change agents consider this the key to the entire problem-solving process. They believe that if a system can be made sufficiently flexible first to recognize the changes indicated by the incoming information about itself or its environment and then to create new and effective patterns of response to meet these changes, the system will be successful.

It is the role of the change agent who offers help in the areas of human relations or problem solving to act as both a resource and a catalyst. He gives training in techniques, and he tries to stimulate the client system's interest in using these techniques. However, he does not allow a dependency relationship to spring up between himself and the client system, and he does not attempt to impose his own goals for change. From the beginning he tries to create situations in which the client system can learn by doing; he tries to encourage in the system a creative and successful independence.

In this chapter we have looked at illustrations of the work of selected change agents who emphasize the change process as improvement in the relationship of the client system to its environment. We have seen that these change agents may proceed from three different orientations, not mutually exclusive but distinct enough to be separated in this analysis. One orientation is that which looks for discrepancies between the real and the perceived environment and attempts to adjust them by correcting the client system's unrealistic perceptions. A second orientation assumes that the values and behavioral goals of the client system are at variance with its own best interests and that the client can be led to adopt more appropriate goals and values by undertaking new modes of behavior and new experiences. A third orientation emphasizes the skills and strategies which the client system may use to solve the problems which are presented either by the external environment or by the patterns of human interaction within the system.

Each of these orientations emphasizes the indispensable autonomy of the client system as a participant in the change process. Essentially, this means that the change agent may not identify himself with the environmental forces which confront the client system. Instead he makes himself helpful to the client system in whatever ways he can, but leaves the responsibility for understanding and dealing with the environment squarely up to the client. Hence, when change occurs the client can justify it in terms of his own experience and cannot shift the responsibility for it to the change agent.

SOME GENERALIZATIONS

In the last two chapters we have examined the work of a number of different change agents in an attempt to understand and classify what we have called their "diagnostic orientations." One reason for doing this, of course, is an academic interest in comprehending precisely what it is that change agents are trying to change. But beyond this is our conviction that the diagnostic orientation of the change agent constitutes an important part of the help which he has to offer.

Why is this so? Because, in the first place, the diagnostic orientation of the change agent is in many ways a self-fulfilling prediction. If he looks for difficulties in communication, for instance, he will find them; and if his help is directed toward improving communication patterns, success will demonstrate to the client system that a solution of communication problems necessarily results in a more satisfactory state of affairs. The same thing is true for each of the other sets of assumptions about the sources of difficulty and the desirable ways of giving help. The orientation of the change agent is a primary factor in determining the "facts" which the client system will discover to be true about its own situation.

If this is the case, then it is important for the change agent to be explicit, at least to himself, about what diagnostic assumptions he is making. Furthermore, he needs to understand clearly and realistically the usefulness of his own assumptions; that is to say, he needs to know what kinds of clients and what kinds of difficulties correspond well enough to his assumptions to make the assumptions valid, thus enabling him to offer effective help. We were dismayed by the large number of cases we encountered in which the change agent was not explicit in stating what he wanted to change and how he expected his help to function in the change process. In such cases, of course, we were reduced to inferring the agent's diagnostic orientation from a careful study of his procedures. On the other hand, we should point out that a good many agents have been very explicit in describing what they were trying to do, not only to their readers but in some cases also to their clients.

Change agents differ greatly in the extent to which they try to share their diagnostic orientations with the client system. Often the client system holds well-established, not to say hidebound, views of itself; these views are hard to change, yet they must be changed if any lasting improvement is to occur. Thus much of the change process may consist of interaction between the change agent and the client system, directed toward a questioning of the client's self-image and an acceptance of some of the diagnostic insights offered by the change agent.

It is worth noting some of the reasons for ignorance and distortion in the self-image of an individual and in the ideas which the members of a group, organization, or community share about the system to which they belong. If the system is currently in pain or trouble, this in itself may generate defensive obstacles to accurate self-diagnosis. The pain may be so great that attention is riveted upon symptoms; the client's only clear thought is that the symptoms must be removed. At the same time, both individuals and groups may be afflicted by a motivated inability to see their own responsibility for their pain: it is hard to admit one's own shortcomings, whether they be simple disabilities or complex expressions of hostility and destructiveness. Moreover, the factors which permitted the system to get into trouble in the first place are still working to sustain the trouble and block alternative courses of action.

In the case of a system which suffers no special pain or difficulty, but which does aspire to move from its present healthy state into one which is even better, the stumbling blocks are more likely to arise from ignorance than from defensiveness. It is difficult for the system to visualize the unknown state in which things will be better and to ascertain the unfamiliar path which leads to it.

The knowledge and experience of the change agent enable him to view the situation of the client system in a way which is neither defensive nor ignorant. He is more objective and more informed than the client system. His informed objectivity may be said to depend upon three axioms, which can be summarized as follows.

First, the change agent who is approached by a system in difficulty may assume that he understands the *general cause-and-effect sequence* which led to the difficulty. For example, a personality theorist may assume that certain kinds of childhood experience account for difficulty in adulthood. Or a sociologist may explain the decline of a rural community in terms of too rapid industrialization and mass production. In such cases, the change agent works with the client system in trying to discover the specific variation of the general cause-and-effect sequence which occurred in the case in question and in trying to evolve recommendations for change which will be suited to the capacities and conditions of the client. Thus the change activity is partly didactic or pedagogic, giving the client a theoretical familiarity with the cause-and-effect model. It is also partly a matter of application: the change agent seeks points at which the general model is relevant to an understanding and changing of the client's particular situation.

A second axiom specifies the use of certain *diagnostic procedures*. These are expected to provide information which the change agent can use, either alone or in consultation with the client system, to analyze the change needs of the system. The diagnostic procedure focuses attention on selected aspects of the client's situation. Information will be collected about some things but not about others. Once collected the information will be interpreted in terms of the same frame of reference which governed the collection of the information. And of course thinking about what kind of change is desirable will also be carried on within this same framework.

The third axiom concerns the *subject matter of the change*. The change agent, for instance, may be convinced that an appropriate area for change lies in the practice of human relations, or in the techniques for problem solving, or in the methods of inter-agency co-operation. Beginning with this premise, he then works jointly with the client system in an examination of current practices in the selected area, emphasizing existing difficulties and points of possible improvement. This diagnosis leads to the development of plans for changing the practices in question. Again, the collection of information is selective, and the plans for change are restricted accordingly.

Now we see that these axioms which give a change agent independence and objectivity in his work with a client system also serve to restrict and guide his attention. He is sensitive not to all difficulties and all needs for change but only to those with which he becomes familiar. Similarly, he is not prepared to engage in all the ways of giving help; he can give only the help which he has been trained to give and which he thinks is appropriate in the particular circumstances. In addition, change agents are just as selective in their views of how they should relate to the client system and what they should do to facilitate change as they are in their diagnostic evaluations of the client system's difficulties. These axioms and assumptions which are related to helping with change define what we call the change-agent function and will be discussed at greater length in Chapter 5. At present, let it suffice to say that the change agent's ideas about how to help with change are intimately bound up with his diagnosis of why the client system got into difficulty in the first place and what kind of help it needs. The two sets of ideas should be considered in relation to one another in any analysis of the work of a given change agent.

MOTIVATION OF THE CLIENT SYSTEM

4

In the two preceding chapters we have used case materials to summarize our observations about approaches to the job of planned change and to clarify some of the different kinds of diagnostic thinking which a change agent may apply to a client system. In this chapter and the two that follow we shall draw on this same material to formulate a more abstract analysis of the processes of planned change.

We shall begin this analysis with a consideration of the motivation of the client system. What makes an individual or a group or any other social system decide that change is desirable? Is the decision to change or not to change ever unequivocal? What are the various arguments that can be advanced for and against beginning a change project or continuing one that has already begun?

These are the questions which interest us, but we shall not try to answer them in specific terms. Specific answers can be given only in a study of a particular client system in a particular situation. Rather, we shall try to develop a general classification of the forces which may increase or decrease the readiness of a client system to change. We shall call these *change forces* and *resistance forces*.

A change force has its origin in any aspect of the situation which increases the willingness of the client system to make a proposed change. A resistance force has its origin in any aspect of the situation which reduces the willingness of the system to make a change. Either kind of force may be rational or irrational, recognized or unrecognized, general or specific. It may originate in the client system, in the environment, or with the change agent. It may be a driving force pushing the system into action or a restraining force which blocks action. In short, the definitions of change force and resistance force are both highly general. They specify whether the direction of the force is toward or away from the change goal, but that is all. The notion of a resistance force as it is used here, for example, includes the psychoanalytic concept of a motivated defense in neurosis, but it also includes the rational objections to change which might arise from an objective assessment of reality.

Change forces and resistance forces are both operating in almost every situation. In a group or community, for example, people will disagree about whether or not to try doing things in a new way. Some people will want a change, others will want to maintain the status quo. Many people will have conflicting desires. They would like to see the benefits change might bring, but they are afraid to give up the security and satisfaction which they currently enjoy. In the case of a disturbed individual the ambivalence may be extremely intense. He wants relief from his painful symptoms, but he finds it almost impossible to give up the defenses which generate these symptoms.

Whether the conflict between change forces and resistance forces takes the form of individual ambivalence, argument between individuals, or formal conflict between subgroups, its resolution is an important part of the change process. If a careful evaluation of change and resistance forces indicates extensive opposition to the change project when it is first proposed, the change agent may not want to proceed further. He may decide to give up the idea of trying to introduce significant change, or he may at least postpone doing anything until conditions are more favorable.

Once a change project has been undertaken, however, the object of both change agent and client system is to swing the balance of forces as much as possible in favor of change. This may mean strengthening the change forces, weakening the resistance forces, or both. Maintaining a favorable balance of forces is a continuous job for the change agent and client system, beginning with the initial decision to undertake a change project or helping relationship and continuing until the project has been completed.

Every specific situation creates its own constellation of change and resistance forces which must be understood in its own terms. However, from our review of case materials, it seems possible to set up a classification of possible change forces and resistance forces which will serve as a general framework to guide the assessment of any particular situation.

INITIAL FORCES TOWARD CHANGE

At the beginning of the change process the change forces are likely to be rather general in character. They may consist of unfavorable judgments of the existing situation or favorable judgments of a potential future situation. Four different types of motivation may be distinguished.

The client system may feel dissatisfaction or pain associated with the present situation. Then the change force is a desire for relief. Thus the sick individual wants to be cured of his symptoms and the unproductive group or organization wants to find a way to do things more efficiently.

Sometimes the dissatisfaction arises from a perceived discrepancy between what is and what might be. For example, community members may not feel any real dissatisfaction with their local government, but when they see the improvements which have been introduced in other communities they may begin to want some of the same things for themselves. Or again, the discrepancy may be an internal one, as when a system is confronted with the fact that it does not practice what it preaches. For example, officials of a school system may want to be democratic, yet may be unable to free themselves from autocratic practices. If this discrepancy were brought into focus together with suggestions about what to do, they might very well respond with a desire for change.

Sometimes external pressures will be brought to bear upon the client system to make it change its behavior. One example of such environmental "requiredness" is the expectation of society that an individual will change his behavior as he grows older, as he develops from an infant into an adult. More striking, perhaps, is the demand that a foreign visitor conform to the norms of the host culture. In industry there may be competitive pressures which make it necessary for each firm to take advantage of every new technological and psychological advance. Sometimes the simple fact of hiring a new personnel man or a consultant in human relations will set up an opportunity which members of the system feel obliged to utilize, thus establishing a special kind of environmental "requiredness."

Finally, there is the possibility that some internal requiredness will set up pressures toward change. This assumption is made most often in the case of individuals, where it is easy to talk about "natural drives" toward health or growth. In industry the parallel would be an assumed general force toward higher productivity, and in small groups one might talk about a preference for rational and efficient problem solving. These needs are assumed to be steady forces operating within the system. When they are not satisfied, they become pressures toward change. This kind of assumption implies that one need only remove the block which has prevented their satisfaction and that then the system will proceed automatically to create a more satisfactory state of affairs.

EMERGENT FORCES TOWARD CHANGE

As the change enterprise proceeds, there is a gradual shift in the constellation of change forces. The completion of early steps in the sequence sets up additional forces to stay with the project until the final change objective has been achieved. These additional change forces are of several kinds.

First there is the need to complete a task which has been begun. For example, if a community undertakes a self-survey, the people involved feel some obligation to act upon the results which it produces. Similarly, people or organizations who sponsor a workshop will look for ways to show that it has some positive effect. Kurt Lewin (87) has discussed this point, noting that up to a certain critical point an individual or group may show strong resistance to starting on a sequence of activities. Once this point has been passed and the system has acquired some investment in the process, there is a dramatic reversal. Forces which were once opposed to the change come to its support. Old change forces persist. Energies are directed toward completing the change process and obtaining the final reward.

Change agents have noted two requirements which must be met in order that this reversal occur and produce a maximum effect. The first is that the client system must feel that it, rather than the change agent, has taken the responsibility for the first steps. Then the new change forces which arise after the critical point is passed result from the client system's own action and are binding upon it.

The second requirement is that the client system not be allowed to complete the change process too rapidly. There may be a tendency for the client system to look for and be satisfied with half-way measures or partial solutions. Or the client system may try to act before it is really able to do so. A community, for example, may try to elect the officials to carry through a new enterprise before people have any understanding of what that enterprise will involve or of what qualities of leadership are needed. If inadequate or premature solutions are permitted, they may discharge the existing energies toward change and leave the client system without motivation to go further. Thus the change agent may have to take responsibility for forestalling premature solutions and for helping the client system to maintain for a long period of time its tolerance for uncertainty, exploration, and change.

A different kind of emergent change force arises in the relationship between the client system and the change agent. As they work together they develop expectations regarding the results of their work. The client system learns that the change agent expects certain things of it, and these expectations constitute a force for change. The influence of the desires and expectations of the change agent will increase in accordance with the esteem and liking for him felt by the client system. In addition to the voluntary influence processes generated by the relationship, there may be occasional coercion. Thus if the change process reaches a stage where some next step is clearly indicated but the client system is unable to bring itself to the point of taking action, the change agent may insist. He may give the small shove which is necessary to get the client system over the hump.

Sometimes the change process will produce qualitative changes in parts of the client system which then permit or require further adaptive change throughout the rest of the system. This kind of emergent change force is stressed particularly by individual therapists. For example, one frequent therapeutic aim is to increase an individual's insight about himself. The assumption is that this increase in insight will create pressure within the person for changes in values and behavior. Similarly, the therapist who thinks in terms of distribution of energy may say that the object of therapy is to release energy which has been tied up in fruitless internal conflicts and free it for new and more constructive use by the client system. Or it may be said that as therapy proceeds there is an increase in ego strength for the individual, so that he becomes increasingly able to handle the psychological problems which have been giving him difficulty.

There are parallel emergent change forces in multiperson client systems. A group which acquires an insight into the various forces influencing its behavior is probably better able to handle these forces. A system of conflicting subparts will benefit if the conflict can be reduced. Perhaps the most commonly mentioned qualitative change is an increase in capacity for effective problem-solving behavior. It is generally assumed that a system can make progress by working on small and immediate problems first, thus gradually developing a capacity for dealing with the larger problems. Once this capacity exists, the system is able to face its larger problems, and the pressure to solve them, or to change, is clearly present.

INTERDEPENDENCE AS A SOURCE OF
CHANGE AND RESISTANCE FORCES

The existence of interdependence among the subparts of a system and between the system and its environment has so many implications for change that it warrants separate discussion. We have noted in general terms that interdependence can generate an emergent force toward change if change in one part of a system sets up forces on other parts to match the change or utilize the new resources. By the same token, interdependence can serve as a source of resistance. Readiness for change in one part of a system may be negated by the unwillingness or inability of other interdependent parts to change. A change sequence which would be strong enough to modify a subpart if it existed in isolation may have no effect on the system as a whole, and consequently it may fail to have any effect on any part of the system.

Essentially, the problem that is involved here is the definition of an appropriate unit for change. If the subpart is too small to cope with a given problem, it will be unable to change because of resistance originating outside the subpart, coming either from the larger systems in which it is embedded or from parallel systems to which it is related. If the unit is too large and includes semi-autonomous subsystems which are not directly involved in the change process, it may be unable to change because of resistance originating within the system. On the other hand, if the size of the unit selected as a client system is appropriate for a particular change objective and if several subparts of this system all become committed to achieving the same objective, the motivation and energy available to the system for working on change will be intensified by the interdependence and interaction among the subparts.

It may be helpful to describe some of the mechanisms by which the condition of interdependence becomes converted into a source of force. Each of the following mechanisms may operate to produce either change forces or resistance forces.

Expectations

In systems consisting of more than one individual, the expectations held by one person or group about the behavior of other persons or groups serve as an important determinant of behavior. People do what others expect them to do. This tends to be true even when people know how to behave differently, in ways which would be more satisfactory but which would run contrary to expectations.

As an example of how behavioral expectations can prevent change from occurring, consider the hypothetical case of a human-relations training program in industry. Suppose that foremen are taken off their jobs and given training in new ways of behaving toward their men. Then they are returned to their original positions. The men, meantime, have received no training and have retained their old behavior patterns and their old expectations about how the foremen will behave. Under these conditions, we should expect most foremen to resume their old patterns of supervision almost immediately. Some might try the new techniques, but when these were interpreted by the men in the light of old and inappropriate expectations, they would not have the desired results. Then these foremen, too, would return to the old patterns of supervision. In short, it is quite likely that the workers would be so sure about what to expect from their foremen that they would be unable to perceive, understand, or accept any significant changes in supervisory behavior.

Another example of the same situation can be used to illustrate the mobilization of expectations as a force for change. Suppose that instead of removing the foremen from the job situation for special training, the training program is designed to reach foremen and workers simultaneously. After some preparatory sessions with foremen and workers separately, each foreman meets with his own work group to decide how supervisory matters should be handled in the future. Then the foreman and his workers are all committed to the new plan. Each person expects others to live up to it and knows that he, in turn, will be expected to do the same. Each person encounters daily evidence of the changed expectations of others. Under these conditions it is likely that both foreman and workers will be able to initiate and maintain the new and more satisfactory behavior patterns.

Simultaneous satisfaction of different needs

Many behavior patterns characteristic of a given system will have multiple meanings for that system. A single act serves several different purposes at the same time. In this analysis, we may consider that each purpose, or need, is anchored in a different subpart of the system. Each subpart has its own impulses to act, but the unitary nature of the system makes separate and independent action by the subparts impossible. Therefore some compromise is developed so that the system can act in a way that is generally satisfactory to all of its subparts but not exclusively or fully satisfactory to any of them.

At the level of the individual, there are many examples of what are sometimes called substitute gratifications. The individual who enjoys oral stimulation may take up cigarette smoking. This gives only partial satisfaction of his oral needs, but it also gives partial satisfaction to his need to be socialized and rational. If he were exclusively oral, he might concentrate on eating, kissing, thumb-sucking; and if he were exclusively rational, he might avoid cigarettes because of their cost and their possible danger as a source of cancer. Being both oral and rational, he makes cigarette smoking one of his regular pleasures.

In work situations we find many instances where formal job definitions have been modified to permit the simultaneous satisfaction of work requirements and the personal needs of workers. Thus, for example, one teacher working with his students in a variety of extracurricular activities may develop very close and co-operative relations with them. Another teacher may be aloof and formal, restricting his contact with students to lectures and occasional office hours. Both conform to the minimum work requirement that they meet their classes, but beyond this each defines the job of teaching in ways which suit his own personal needs. In industrial settings, too, job definitions reflect both the need to get work done and the need to keep workers moderately well satisfied while they are doing the work.

Parsons describes a case of multiple determination of behavior in his analysis of how to influence Germany to change from a totalitarian to a democratic state. His analysis pays particular attention to the interlocking of the motivational structure of individuals with the institutional structure of society. In Hitler's Germany, for example, both structures included strong hierarchical-authoritarian elements. The result of such coincidence of personal motivation and institutional requiredness is that "in institutional behavior 'self-interested' elements of motivation and 'disinterested' moral sentiments of duty tend to motivate to the same concrete goals" (95, p. 240).

A similar dovetailing occurs at the level of values. Here, as we have seen, Parsons points to a "romantic" tradition and a "methodical" tradition as peculiarly characteristic of German culture. The Nazis succeeded in uniting the two in support of their political goals. Any new political solution, then, would be obliged not only to disrupt the synthesis of the two value traditions but also to find new channels of expression for each. Otherwise, the tendency would be for the system to return to the political organization which so nicely gave simultaneous expression to both of these traditional themes.

Let us consider now how the multiple determination of behavior which is likely to occur in any system of interdependent parts can contribute to the promotion or obstruction of change. The occurrence of resistance to change is easy to understand. If a change is proposed which would meet some of the needs satisfied by the existing arrangements and ignore others, then the subparts whose needs are ignored would oppose the change and insist on preservation of the status quo. On the other hand, forces toward change would be generated if the proposed change seemed likely to give satisfaction to subparts not previously satisfied, or if it led to new coalitions within the system.

Once again we turn to Parsons for an example. He points out that in Nazi Germany there was a conflict between the value placed on individual achievement and the status system which subordinated individual achievement to hierarchical position. He planned to use this point of strain in the system as the opening wedge in his program of change, with the ultimate objective of forming a new coalition between individual personality structure and institutional structure. His proposal was that change efforts be directed toward the economic-occupational system, with the object of stressing functional achievement roles and de-emphasizing status, hierachy, authoritarianism, and formalism. The new coalition between personality structure and institutional structure would center upon the value of individual achievement but would include also the de-emphasis of hierarchical values. The new patterns of behavior would derive support both by satisfying multiple needs and by relieving previous strain and tension.

Vulnerability to threat

To the extent that one system or subsystem is dependent on another, it wants to see the other maintain both its good health and its good will. One member of a partnership will be threatened by any indication that another member is not able to do what is required of him or, alternatively, that he is exploiting the partnership for selfish purposes. The vulnerability to threat, of course, depends on the extent to which the partners are committed to one another or, to put it differently, the degree to which the observing partner has the freedom and ability to dissolve the relationship.

Let us consider first the way in which this aspect of interdependence may create forces toward change. If the failure of any subpart of a system can cause failure for the system as a whole, then anything which threatens a part threatens the whole. No part of the system can be allowed to suffer too much difficulty. Thus pain originating in one part of a system may become sufficiently important to the total system to make it willing to undertake the necessary corrective action, even if this is costly or difficult. As examples, consider the businessman who spends long hours commuting so that his wife may live in a neighborhood she likes, or the industrial organization which offers employee benefits over and beyond those demanded by the union, or the individual who enters psychotherapy because it is the only way he knows of to get rid of his severe headaches.

Resistance occurs when a proposed change seems to promise benefits to one part of the client system at the expense of other parts. This suspicion of one part by another may or may not be justified by the facts. Often it is enough for one person or group to know that a related person or group is trying to accomplish changes. The immediate conclusion is that this other person or group must be trying to gain some special advantage. The defensive reaction, of course, is to oppose the change automatically without even considering its actual advantages or disadvantages. This readiness to feel threatened can occur both among competing subparts which share more or less equal benefits under the existing arrangements and among subparts which benefit quite differently from the existing arrangements. Community workers would call it a problem of vested interests. Change agents working with large organizations have recognized the importance of "multiple entry," a procedure which ensures that the change proposal is associated not exclusively with one part of the system but with all parts. Whatever the terminology, the point is that interdependence among the parts of a system is often associated with a fear that the improvement of one part can be gained only at the expense of another, and there is thus a tendency to feel threatened by any proposal for change except, perhaps, one's own.

Resistance based on threat is particularly a problem because of the psychological concomitants of a state of threat. These include a constricted field of attention and a need to find some way of controlling whatever it is that threatens. The former makes it difficult for the threatened subsystem to envisage or believe in new and improved ways of operation. The need for control makes it imperative that existing sanctions be applied to punish the deviant or recalcitrant part and restore familiar patterns of control. Change, therefore, is the very thing which is most intolerable to a system or subsystem experiencing a high degree of threat.

On the other hand, it must be remembered that it is not pleasant to feel threatened and that pain can become a force toward change. The system experiencing threat will try first and most urgently to return to old and secure patterns of behavior. If this course of action is blocked off, however, it may be willing to try something new. In a state of crisis any change may be viewed as an improvement.

RESISTANCE FORCES

Let us turn now from our discussion of the change and resistance forces specifically associated with interdependence to a more general discussion of resistance forces. In discussing change forces we made a distinction between those which are likely to be present at the beginning of the change process and those which emerge only after the change project is under way.

With resistance forces this distinction seems to be somewhat less helpful. Many types of resistance may emerge either at the beginning of the change process or after it is under way, or both at the beginning and later on. While there are some types of resistance which are more likely to occur early in the process and others which are more likely to occur later, these are so few in comparison with the number which may occur at either time that we shall not group them into separate sections.

It is important to note that resistance forces, like change forces, may increase in intensity for a while after the change project begins. Thus it may seem for a time as if no progress is being made toward a resolution of the conflict between change forces and resistance forces. Rather, the conflict is intensified as forces in both directions are strengthened. Eventually, however, the deadlock may be broken either by "working through" and weakening a resistance force or by some success or crisis which strengthens a change force.

One form of resistance which is most likely to occur at the beginning of the change process is a general opposition to any kind of change. Often this grows out of a combination of fear and ignorance. The client system may fear that it will be unable to change successfully or that, once accomplished, the change will require things of people which they are unable to deliver. Only the status quo seems safe; anything else seems to carry a threat of failure.

Sometimes these feelings of inadequacy are quite justified. The client system may in fact lack the skill, experience, or capacity for action which would be necessary to carry through a change. This actual inability would result in opposition to all proposals for change and would lead to failure if change were undertaken.

A special case of this type of resistance is the system already mobilized for defense against an internal or external threat. If the threat is real and not imagined and if the change agent can offer no protection against it, then it would be dangerous for the client system to relax its defenses. It could not afford to consider a change which would even temporarily weaken its defense structure.

Sometimes resistance is organized not against change in general but against a particular proposed change objective. It may be judged as undesirable, irrelevant, or altogether impossible. In the first case the client system would oppose any effort to achieve the change, and in the second case such an effort would be seen as a waste of time. Sometimes the change objective appears to be of doubtful value, and the question is whether or not it is safe to experiment. Then attention is centered as much on the possibilities of turning back as on the merit of the proposed destination. Under these conditions a change proposal is more acceptable if it can be tried on a tentative basis, with the final decision postponed until after the trial period.

Perhaps the most familiar notion of resistance is that of clinging to existing satisfactions. This includes the situation in which subparts with vested interests know that they benefit from the status quo and want to keep it that way, as well as the situation in which the client system as a whole is reluctant to give up familiar types of satisfaction. The familiar satisfactions may be ways of getting reward, ways of avoiding pain or anxiety, ways of thinking about itself, or even ways of thinking about the external world. Any one of these may be threatened by the proposed change. We might also include among familiar satisfactions the modeling of present behavior on past traditions, for the conviction that things are being done now as they have always been done can be a source of great pleasure and security.

Resistance is sometimes centered in the relationship between the client system and the change agent. This kind of resistance may mean different things, depending on whether it appears early or late in the change process. At the beginning of the change process the change agent and his form of help are unfamiliar to the client system. The client system, therefore, may be suspicious and doubtful of the value of the help which the change agent has to give. Also, because the change agent is a stranger, he may seem at first to be more alien or unfriendly than he really is. These difficulties are often reduced by further acquaintance. On the other hand, we must recognize that not all change agents are equally acceptable to a given client system and that if initial feelings of mistrust and incompatibility persist they may be adequate reason for ending a relationship.

Dissatisfaction with the change agent which occurs later in the change project may reflect either genuine disappointment with what he has to offer or an unconscious attempt to avoid responsibility for the change process and thus to escape the necessity of making a change. The first kind of resistance may constitute a rational reason for ending the change relationship; the second kind needs interpretation so that the real reasons behind it become clear to the client system.

Emergent resistance forces may be created when factors in the situation which were unnoticed or unimportant at the beginning of the change process turn out to be major obstacles to change. For instance, the client system may be related to systems in its environment which are opposed to change. This opposition may be discounted at the beginning of the change process, but it may turn out to be a serious obstacle. Or the cost of the change project in terms of time, money, or energy may turn out to be more than the client system can handle.

A special case of this problem of growing resistance to the cost of the change project occurs when the initial diagnostic phase of the project consumes so much time and energy that nothing is left for the work of changing. Thus, for example, a community may spend much energy on a self-survey and, when the results are in, may find that there is no longer any interest in acting on the results of the survey. There may be other cases, too, where the initial phases of the project are so exhausting that the client system becomes unwilling to continue further.

The impending end of the relationship with the change agent may set up either change or resistance forces. With the imminent loss of help and support from the change agent, the client system may decide either that it must hurry up and get something done or that, since there is no time to finish anything anyway, it would be better not to start anything.

It is of interest that many resistance forces can be converted into change forces. Resistance forces come into being originally in response to certain needs of the client system. If the client is saying, in effect, that the status quo must be maintained because it is the best way to meet these needs, the change agent may be able to show that the same needs would be met even more satisfactorily in a changed set of conditions. Then the very energy which the client system once used to maintain the status quo may shift direction and become an impetus toward change.

Some change agents, and in particular those who are psychoanalytically oriented, welcome the appearance of resistance because it gives information about the important motivations and difficulties of the client system. If the client system can learn to interpret this information correctly, it will have made an important gain in self-understanding. Thus therapy is sometimes said to consist of working through a series of resistances.

INTERFERENCE

We have defined resistance as any force directed away from the change objective. Sometimes, however, the change process may run into difficulty not because of opposing forces but because of competing forces. Thus, for example, a proposal to build a new city hall might be defeated not because of opposition to such a building, but because it seemed that a new school building was even more urgent. The considerations affecting a decision about the desirability of a city hall might be quite independent of those affecting a decision about the desirability of a school building. Each project could be said to involve its own change and resistance forces. The projects would not be related to each other except at the point of requesting funds. At that point a choice would be necessary. Defeat of the city-hall proposal might be motivated primarily by convictions about the need for a school building, that is, by "extraneous" considerations. Forces of this kind, which hamper progress toward the change objective without being directly concerned with it, may be called *interference*. Interference is most likely to be a problem in cases where the client system has inadequate time, money, or energy. It must try to do first things first. Or interference may be a problem when there are too many competing proposals. The client system need not necessarily feel limited in time or energy to realize that it cannot accept every proposal that comes along and that it must make some choices.

In addition to interference which arises because a client system must choose between competing goals or because it must conserve energy, there is interference which arises because of the sheer difficulty of a proposed change project. The difficulty may take the form of a lack of ideas or of too many ideas. The client system may lack the necessary information, skill, or understanding and therefore be unable to execute the change project. This is a problem particularly if the help of a change agent is unavailable or difficult to obtain. Or the client system may be attracted by the change objective but in conflict about how to achieve it. Discussion and argument about what steps to take in order to reach the objective may consume so much time and energy that the entire project is discarded as unworkable.

A last type of interference is that which originates in the environment or in the relation of the system to its environment. A client system may be willing and able to undertake a change project and still be prevented from doing so by an intractable environment. Intractability might take the form of the absence of necessary resources and particularly of change agents, of rigorous demands or restraints which leave the client system little energy for its own use, or of such severe opposition to change that the risks involved for the client system would outweigh the potential benefits.

It is not always possible for the change agent or even the client system to distinguish between interference and resistance. For example, if a client system says that it is impossible to undertake a change project at present because of lack of time, it is extremely difficult to know whether the client system actually does not have the time or whether this is an excuse which covers motivated resistance. It may take considerable exploration to find out whether or not the excuse is valid. However, it is quite important to distinguish between resistance and interference. Resistance forces originate in the reactions of the client system to the change agent or change objective. They are likely to continue indefinitely as active determinants of the change-relevant behavior of the client system. They may or may not be potential sources of new change forces. Interference, however, is not directly linked to the change project and may disappear from the situation. Such forces can never be converted into change forces, but their disappearance may facilitate the achievement of change.

In this chapter we have described a number of change forces which might motivate a client system to make a change, resistance forces which might motivate it not to make a change, and interferences which might obstruct a change without being directly related to it.

Among the change forces which might be present at the beginning of a change project we noted dissatisfaction and pain, perceived discrepancy between the state of affairs as it is and as it might be, and a demand, arising either from the environment or from within the system, that it change in order to keep up with varying sets of requirements. Forces which might emerge during the change process include the need to complete a task which has been begun, the need to meet the expectations and demands of the change agent, and the need for change to be established throughout the system after one part of the system is significantly changed.

A discussion of interdependence which exists both among the subparts of a system and between the system and its environment indicated that interdependence can generate both change forces and resistance forces. The mechanisms by which interdependence becomes a force for or against change include expectations, the simultaneous satisfactions of many needs in one pattern of behavior, and the vulnerability to threat which exists when the well-being of one system or subsystem depends upon the good health or good will of another.

Resistance forces which might arise early in the change project include a general opposition to change, actual inability to change, opposition to a proposed change objective, and a desire to preserve existing satisfactions. Resistance may also arise from the relationship between the client system and the change agent. Most of these forms of resistance can occur early or late in the change process. In addition, there are some resistance forces which can arise after the project is underway. These include a re-evaluation of costs and difficulties which seemed possible to handle at the beginning but which the client system later finds it cannot handle, a loss of energy and motivation through excessive prolongation of the diagnostic phase of the project, and a premature cessation of change activities because of the impending end of the relationship with the change agent.

Interference was described as a type of force which is not specifically opposed to the change objective, but which nevertheless diverts the energies of the client system away from the change objective. Interference may arise when other projects compete with the change project for the time, energy, and money of the client system; when there is a shortage of time, energy, or money; when there is a lack of information or conflicting information about how to execute the change project; or when the environment is simply intractable.

All of the forces described in this chapter are assumed to be representations of motives, capacities, and situational factors which influence the behavior of the client system. The formal descriptions presented here, which we have abstracted from case materials, are offered not as a substitute for the analysis of specific forces operating in specific situations but rather as an aid to such analysis.

VARIOUS ASPECTS OF
THE CHANGE AGENT'S ROLE

In this chapter we shall summarize the various aspects of the change agent's job as they seem to appear explicitly or implicitly in the descriptions which have been given to us by professional helpers. We must do this in order to prepare ourselves for an examination of the actual procedures which change agents use in carrying out their functions.

Two of the functions have already been discussed; they can be mentioned here briefly as part of this summary.

A DIAGNOSTIC CLARIFICATION

OF THE PROBLEM

In Chapters 2 and 3 we reviewed the approaches which change agents use in answering for themselves the two questions: What is the trouble? What is causing the trouble? We shall see later that change agents differ a good deal in the degree to which they make this diagnostic function an initial and formal part of the helping process. Some reject a formal diagnosis separated from the other processes of giving help; some emphasize the need to share the diagnostic responsibility with the client system; and still others use diagnosis simply as a private guide for their own role in the change process. But whatever they think about the formal place of diagnosis in their operational scheme, nearly all change agents reveal in their reports a recognition of their responsibility to think diagnostically about the nature of the client system's problem.

ASSESSMENT OF THE CLIENT SYSTEM'S
MOTIVATION AND CAPACITY TO CHANGE

In Chapter 4 we concentrated on another part of the change agent's job. The biggest share of the work in any change effort must be done by the client system. Consequently, the degree and quality of change which the client achieves will depend very largely upon how much energy and ability it itself can bring to the working relationship. The change agent must assess the client's readiness to enter into a helping relationship, and he must determine whether or not the client possesses sufficient motivation and capacity to hold up its end of the partnership. This involves, as we have seen, an appraisal of the change and resistance forces which are present in the client system at the beginning of the change process as well as others which may be revealed as the process advances. Being continuously sensitive to the constellation of change forces and resistance forces is one of the most creative parts of the change agent's job.

ASSESSMENT OF THE CHANGE AGENT'S
MOTIVATIONS AND RESOURCES

Perhaps the first question to be asked in any examination of the process of giving help is whether or not the change agent actually possesses the motivations and resources which are required for his job. If he does not, no amount of clinical sensitivity or theoretical acumen will be sufficient.

Consider first the question of motivation. Presumably the change agent is motivated by a desire to help other people. But why does he want to help them? Is he genuinely interested in their welfare? Or—and this is sometimes the case—does he enjoy giving help solely because it inspires feelings of power, assurance, or self-righteousness in him? Usually, of course, motivation is complex and involves both altruism and self-interest. This is not bad in itself. The danger comes at the point where the change agent is so busy creating a situation which will satisfy his own needs that he is unable to respond to the needs of the client system. When this happens his "help" may actually be a hindrance and, whatever it is, it is likely to be rejected.

Even apart from the conflict of needs which may arise between them, the change agent may find that his motivation is challenged by the client system. Altruism in our culture is suspect. The person who says that he is more interested in helping others than in helping himself invites skepticism, and often he may find that he cannot explain himself in terms which are acceptable to his listeners. The rewards which he wants for himself, for instance, may sound so exceedingly strange to other people that they simply do not believe him.

In more than one American community a team of change agents has tried to offer its services without first giving an adequate explanation of its motives. Suddenly people in the community found their own explanation: the newcomers must be representatives of some kind of outside vested interest, or perhaps they have a new "racket" to promote. If the agents can't explain what they want, in other words, it must be because their objectives are suspect. At once the community is on guard, the change agents are thrown out, and any incipient sentiments for change which may have existed before are throttled.

A cognate illustration can be drawn from a different field. An anthropologist told us about his difficulties in winning acceptance from an American Indian tribe. He tried to explain to the Indians that he was interested in research among different cultures and particularly in the history of their particular tribe, but it all sounded dubious to them. Finally he hit on an explanation which they could accept: he had been ordered to do this by his boss. This was something they could understand, and from then on they lost their suspicion and let him go about freely collecting "meaningless" information for his boss. In this case the important thing was not an accurate explanation but one that would be acceptable. The anthropologist's activities had to "make sense" before his clients would co-operate with him.

Sometimes the change agent himself will experience uneasiness about the justification for what he is trying to do. The causes of his uneasiness may be rational or irrational, and the uneasiness itself may assume any one of a number of forms. The change agent whose clients refuse his help may wonder, for instance, if he really has much to offer them. Or he may wonder about his own emotional involvement in his client's problems: perhaps he cares too much or too little, or perhaps he is merely attributing to the client certain problems which are really his own. Some change agents may become disturbed because they think the client system is not being treated fairly. If the change agent, for example, is trying to collect research data as well as give help to his client, he may feel that the requirements of the research project constitute an unwarranted demand on the time and energy of the client system. Again, perhaps the change process is moving more slowly than the agent anticipated, so that the cost to the client system in time, money, and emotional strain is unexpectedly high.

Uneasiness of any kind is easily transmitted from the change agent to the client system, and if it is unresolved it remains to plague them both. Clearly, then, it seems important for the change agent to feel right about what he is doing, just as it is important for the client system to be convinced that it is receiving friendly and competent help.

This line of analysis seems to indicate that an important function of the change agent is an honest self-examination. He needs to think through for himself the reasons why he wants to help others. Included in this question is the matter of what rewards he wants for himself—money, prestige, professional advancement, research data, emotional support from the client system, or simply satisfaction in seeing an important job done well. These rewards must be examined in terms of what the client system needs and what it is able to give. If it seems that the needs of the change agent can be met without interfering with his ability to help the client system, then the work at hand can proceed.

Often the uneasiness of a change agent may arise from his unconscious tensions and anxieties. Unresolved personal problems may inhibit his ability to respond to others in an appropriate and helpful way. The individual-oriented agent, therefore, may stress personal therapy as an important aspect of professional training in order to help minimize the distortions that arise from unconscious modes of response. Personal therapy cannot, of course, eliminate the need for self-examination—in fact, it will probably impress upon the individual the need for continuous self-examination—but it will give him a clearer understanding of his own needs as a functioning personality.

By no means, however, can all of the emotional stress experienced by change agents be attributed to unconscious personal difficulties. The task itself—trying to help other people—often creates special strains. Interpersonal relationships between client and agent become unexpectedly difficult. The client's tensions seem to increase when they should decrease. Unanticipated difficulties arise. The change agent often is hard pressed to keep a grip on his sense of direction and time perspective. He is bewildered and not sure what should be done next. We find illuminating comments on these problems by Fromm-Reichmann (8), Rogers (15), Biddle (53), and Mann (43).

Some large change projects have met this problem by creating a special place for a consultant within the change-agent team. In a counseling center, for example, the counselors may meet each week with a psychiatrist to discuss their work—that is, to raise troublesome questions which they cannot answer by themselves. The questions may concern a client, the agent himself, or the relationship between them. Whatever the problem, a discussion with a competent adviser can help to reduce anxiety and restore self-confidence. The same effect can be achieved in a workshop or in any other setting where a group of individual agents is working with different client systems. The opportunity to raise and discuss disturbing questions with fellow change agents or with an expert consultant can provide both reassurance and direct help, and the resulting gain in the change agent's security and self-confidence can give both stability and a sharper focus to the change process.

Of course the personal problems and anxieties of change agents are of various kinds. Perhaps the only clear generalization which can be made is that the change agent's problems of motivation cannot be safely ignored. No change agent can afford to take himself for granted. His objectives must be clear to himself and to others. The emotional reactions which he experiences as a result of his participation in the change process become a part of that process itself, and thus it is his responsibility to be aware of these emotional reactions, to minimize their irrational elements, and to keep the rational elements in proper perspective. He can be sure that many of his feelings about the change project will be communicated to the client system. Both members—agent and client—will function more effectively if these feelings are channeled into confidence and realistic optimism than if they are dissipated in anxiety, uncertainty, and self-doubt.

This brings us to the matter of professional responsibility. A change agent normally possesses specific and limited skills which enable him to offer his particular kind of help. One of the first questions he must consider in deciding whether or not to work with a given client system is the relevance of his specialized kind of help to the problem at hand. If he decides that he can offer effective help, then he incurs a further responsibility for defining what may reasonably be expected from the change project. Gradually he and the client system must work out a realistic view of the job to be done and the roles of the various participants. In this way the objectives can be made specific and limited; success becomes approachable through a fairly well-defined sequence of procedures. Then the change agent and client system both have definite jobs to do, and both are protected from exaggerated or visionary expectations of impossible achievements.

A second aspect of the change agent's professional responsibility is the "charge" he makes for his services. The word is enclosed in quotation marks because often the charge is far from being any kind of a fee. Some teams of community workers ask nothing more than a chance to show what they can do. Their immediate expenses are usually met by some outside group or higher government agency, and their ultimate reward is a general improvement in living standards. Similarly, agents may organize special training programs in industrial or educational institutions with no charge but a request for co-operation. In the majority of cases, however, the change agent must obtain some financial support from the client system for his services.

Then, too, in more and more kinds of change projects, the agent may want to gather research data which will contribute to a general understanding of the change process. Other demands may be implicit in the agent's definition of the client system's obligations. For instance, a patient undergoing psychotherapy must be willing to commit himself to visit the therapist for a given number of hours each week. A community self-improvement program, to give another example, must have the support and co-operation of a number of community agencies. Whatever the demands on the client system may be, whether they involve time, money, research opportunities, or emotional commitment, it is important that they be fully considered early in the change process. Change agent and client system each must feel that the balance of costs and rewards will be fair and that it will be sufficiently favorable to each to make the change project worthwhile.

Beyond the problem of professional responsibility is the problem of professional ethics. Frequently the change agent will meet this problem in the form of a challenge to his ethical position as a manipulator of personal and social destinies. What right, people will ask, has any man to remake another? Change agents in every profession have answered this challenge by pointing out the safeguards which protect the integrity and autonomoy of the client system. These safeguards are of different kinds. Some professional groups have clearly defined codes of ethical conduct. Some change agents stress the voluntary nature of the change relationship and the ability of the client system to withdraw from the relationship if it is not satisfactory. Others are more concerned about the decision-making process in which the change agent and the client system are engaged. They want to be sure that decisions are made in the best interests of the client system. Thus the change agent may restrict his help to providing effective means and let the client system decide about goals. Or he may work with the client system to clarify and expand the definition of goal possibilities and then leave to the client system the final choice of which goals to pursue. Even in cases where the change agent feels obliged to begin by insisting upon acceptance of his ideas, he usually expects a later improvement in the decision-making ability of the client system, which will bring about an increase in its autonomy and independence of action.

A second kind of ethical problem involves the choice of clients to whom help will be given. Usually there is a minimum commitment to give help only to those systems in which positive improvement seems a possibility and to withhold help in cases where it seems likely to yield negligible or harmful results. It may, however, be necessary to choose among requests for help even when they come from desirable clients. Here there are many possible criteria for selection. Clients may be selected on the basis of the extent of their need for help or the extent to which it seems probable that they may actually benefit from it. They may be chosen to meet the needs of the change agent, as when preference is given to persons or groups who are congenial or from whom the change agent has something to learn. Another possible criterion is the potential distribution of benefits to society at large: client systems may be chosen because they are particularly prominent or influential, so that improvements achieved in them will be emulated by other systems.

This brings us back again to our starting point. The Judaeo-Christian democratic ethic provides various general prescriptions which can guide the activities of an agent. Professional groups, too, have developed codes of ethics. Within such a framework, however, the agent must refer to his own needs, his personal preferences, and his sense of right and wrong. It is at this point that self-insight and a clear sense of direction become important to the change agent.

SELECTING APPROPRIATE CHANGE OBJECTIVES

Usually the change agent must provide some initiative in the decisions about "what are we aiming at," "how shall we go about it," and "what shall we do first." The client may know in general terms what he wants, but the agent's unique skill and experience are needed to give these wants shape and plausibility. We have already examined the various ways in which change agents approach a definition of the change objective. In terms of the diagnostic orientations discussed in Chapters 2 and 3, the change objective may be a different internal balance of power, a new pattern of communication, a release of additional energy, a re-evaluation of goals, an adjustment between external and internal reality, or the development of more effective problem-solving procedures. In other words, the goal is always some change in the structure or functioning of the client system. As we shall see later, there are significant differences in the extent to which change agents emphasize "methodological" and "end state" goals.

Briefly, professional helpers who emphasize methodological objectives describe their goal as the achievement of a certain process (or method) of "working through" the problem with the client system. These agents believe that if the working-through process (that is, a self-survey, nondirective discussions, and so forth) can be developed, then the client system will proceed more or less on its own toward a desirable change goal. Other agents, on the contrary, emphasize the importance of forming a clear image of the final change goal (that is, fewer levels of hierarchy, the organization of a community council, less repression, and so forth). In other words, some agents feel that the process of change itself, if it is properly conducted, will determine the goal and lead the client to it, while other agents believe that the change process must be organized from the beginning in terms of a distinctly outlined objective.

Another point of difference among agents is the degree to which they develop change goals in collaboration with the client system, share their goals with the system, or use the goals primarily as a private source of guidance. In this respect, of course, much depends upon the kind of system with which one is working and the nature of the change problem.

In their formulations of change objectives, most change agents reveal an implicit assumption that movement toward the final change goal is a sequential process which requires a number of subgoals. Therefore, the starting point in the helping process must be chosen in the light of certain strategic conceptions of the most effective sequence of steps to be taken toward the final change goal. This starting point we shall call the leverage point of the agent's help-giving program.

The strategies of choosing a leverage point, as they have been described by various change agents, reveal two different ideas about the sequence of change.

One line of thought emphasizes the persons or subgroups with whom the agent ought to work directly if he is to make reasonable headway in his change program. According to this view, the client system is composed of interdependent subparts, that is, groups or persons. In respect to the change process, some of these units occupy a more salient position than others, and of course some are more readily accessible than others. With whom should one talk first? Who will do the most work in the beginning? Who should be drawn into the change process by the time it is finished? These are typical questions which the change agent must answer. He needs all the information he can obtain about the interest and availability of different people; he needs to know which people or groups can influence others. He uses this information to decide which specified group or person within the client system will be his best ally in taking the first step. That is to say, he uses this group or person as a leverage point for the beginning of a process of change which may eventually spread throughout the whole system.

A second line of thought emphasizes not the persons or parts of the client system where a beginning should be made but the beginning point of a sequence of changes in the client system's structural or functional components which will lead eventually to the final change goal. In a formal organization, for example, the change goal may be a new pattern of communications. The steps for achieving this goal may include, first, a meeting in which people from different parts of the organization discuss with each other their current discontents and expectations; then a period of heightened interaction during which people in different groups revise their ideas about each other; and finally a revised stabilization of the patterns of interaction and communication among groups. Such a sequence uses as the starting point or leverage point the original perceptions which the people in each group share. These perceptions are changed first, with the expectation that this change will lead to a change in communication patterns.

In other words, the leverage point may be either a strategically located unit in the client system's structure of influence or a particular aspect of the client system's dynamic existence.

Change agents who work with individual clients may talk about moving from one level of internal process to another or from one problem area to another, and this is much the same thing as we have already observed. They are talking in terms of leverage points and sequential processes. Consider, for instance, the case of an individual whose contact with reality is impaired. The change goal might be to increase his awareness of things previously repressed, thus giving him a keener insight into himself and the nature of the world around him. If the therapeutic technique is to interpret or reflect his free associations about current activities, emotions, and fantasies, then the leverage point is his own initial insights into current behavior. The assumption is that if the patient can be helped to ask the pertinent questions about his current behavior, then he will be led into a train of analysis which will take him eventually to a rediscovery of the relevant repressed material.

Again, this same case might be approached by establishing at the outset the final goal of a closer correspondence between external and internal reality. This might mean that the leverage point would actually be outside the system. The first step in the change process might be to make external reality comprehensible to the patient, that is, to create a special environment in which all symbols were direct and simple. In this case, the change sequence would progress from this simplified external reality to the patient's correct internal understanding of it and thence to a revision of the client's perceptual mechanisms as applied to all external realities.

From all this it can be seen that two considerations govern the choice of leverage point. The first is *accessibility:* the leverage point must be open to the influence of the change agent and his allies, at least enough to allow the change process to begin. The second consideration is a matter of *linkage:* there must be at least a possible line of change progress from the leverage point to the change objective. The ideal linkage is one which permits a direct, rapid, and easy spread of change from the leverage point to the change objective.

Let us look first at the notion of accessibility. We can see right away that the accessibility of any potential leverage point depends upon its position in the client system and its susceptibility to change.

Position is obviously important because, first of all, the leverage point must be accessible from outside the system; it must be within reach of the influence of the change agent. Therefore, at the level of individual systems we might expect behavioral skills to be more accessible to outside influence than are attitudes, and attitudes to be more accessible than repressed material. Similarly, current experience is more accessible than past experience. In short, certain components of any system, whether an individual, group, or community, are easier for the outsider to get to than are others.

The susceptibility of a leverage point refers to its openness to change, and here we are concerned with various forms of rigidity and flexibility. In one way or another the leverage point should be receptive and responsive to new influences or ideas. Sometimes the degree of susceptibility of a leverage point depends upon the nature of the persons or functions of which it is comprised, sometimes upon the way in which it is related to other parts of the system. Past failures may have spoiled certain subgroups or functions for later change activity and thus reduced their usefulness as leverage points. For example, if a given community feels that it has been "surveyed to death," a new self-survey is not likely to be a good leverage point for a program of community development. People would resist the survey at the very start, and the program would never really begin. Similarly, if an individual is very much interested in improving his speed of reading, his most susceptible leverage point might be the initial activity of practicing to read quickly. In most communities only a small subgroup is genuinely alarmed about the rise of delinquency, and this group, having the highest susceptibility to change, provides the change agent with his best leverage point in launching a program of community endeavor to reduce delinquency. Complications may arise when the criteria of position and susceptibility do not coincide: the person or subpart which occupies an accessible position may not be susceptible to change. For example, the persons in an organization who are highly sensitive to problems of communication and are thus susceptible to change efforts in this area may be scattered throughout the lower levels of the organizational structure and may be virtually inaccessible in terms of their position and distribution. On the other hand, the top management corps, which may be thoroughly accessible in terms of position, may lack susceptibility to change in matters of communication and hence be a difficult leverage point.

This brings us to the second main criterion for the selection of leverage points, the concept of linkage. What linkage means, in effect, is the kind of connection between the leverage point and other parts or functions of the system. Other things being equal, the best leverage point is the one which triggers off a distribution of change to other parts of the system or which introduces a therapeutic chain of processes leading to the final change goal. Many factors may affect the linkage that extends from any given person or subgroup to the rest of the system, for instance, questions of power, respect, prominence, and so forth. Combinations of these factors may give any potential leverage point effective or ineffective linkage.

We shall return later to some of the techniques used by change agents to select leverage points. However, it seems clear from what we have said so far that the agent's diagnostic interpretations in his determination of a starting point, a sequence of steps, and an ultimate change goal are exceedingly important aspects of his job.

CHOOSING THE APPROPRIATE HELPING ROLE

Another aspect of the change agent's strategic considerations is the selection of the role he himself will take in making his contribution to the change process. Shall he mediate or counsel? Shall he demonstrate or encourage? Shall he identify himself with external reality or with the distorted projections of the client system? The cases of change which we have reviewed seem to reveal five types of helping role. Some change agents in describing their work said that they assumed more than one role during a particular change job, and others said that they always specialized in a single type of role with all client systems. Undoubtedly our classification of helping roles is incomplete and will need modifications as it is tested further.

Mediating and stimulating new connections within the client system

One way in which a change agent can help a client system is to make possible new connections among its subparts and to reorganize old connections. In any established system the pattern of internal relationships is well stabilized. Usually it is also accepted without question by the members of the organization: no alternative pattern of relationships occurs to them as possible or even desirable. Hence the position of the change agent as an outsider gives him a unique view of these relationships which is often quite different from that of insiders. This is his advantage; it is his external perspective which allows the change agent to help.

There are various techniques for opening up new connections within a system. Psychiatrists who are engaged in individual therapy or group work rely heavily upon interpretation. Essentially this means that the change agent places himself in a position to receive and evaluate information about the significance of the client's unconscious behavior; then he transmits this information to the client in an attempt to stimulate a conscious awareness of what has previously been unconscious. In individual therapy it is assumed that this interpretation is made to an "observing ego," that is, to a "part" of the individual personality which is listening and trying to understand what the therapist says. In work with groups or organizations the change agent may offer his interpretations in special meetings of all the persons concerned or in reports to select groups of official representatives. In either case persons within the client system try to understand and come to terms with new information, a process which gradually fashions for them a new picture of themselves as a social unit. The change process begins with the development of this new insight, and it often continues until the insight has been substantiated by altered values, activities, and attitudes.

A similar result is achieved by the change agent who collects information from the separated parts of a system and reports it back to the representatives of the whole. In this category we can include both the nondirective therapist who reflects what a patient says without offering an interpretation and the survey-research team which collects information from individual members of a community or organization and then reports or "feeds back" its findings. These change agents, in effect, hold up a mirror in which the client system sees itself more clearly than it did before, but they do not try to add any coloring to the mirror. They avoid any interpretation of material elicited from the unconscious and thus differ sharply from the psychoanalysts. Nevertheless, the primary function seems much the same. It is, in each case, to help the client attain a more extensive and accurate self-awareness.

A third means of achieving this result is proposed by the exponents of the self-survey. In effect, they teach the client system how to make a mirror, and then they let the system itself hold up the mirror and make its own self-examination. At this point, however, a shift occurs in the function of the change agent. In the previous examples the change agent was able to help because he himself was in touch with different parts of the system, parts which were not in touch with each other. He acted as an intermediary. But in the case of the self-survey, the change agent's ability to help derives from his general knowledge of procedures, not from his specific knowledge of the client system. This leads us into the second type of role which the change agent can assume.

Presenting expert knowledge on procedures

A frequent role of many change agents is that of functioning as an expert in matters of procedure. In this role the change agent does not attempt to influence the client system directly, that is, to influence its goals. Instead he offers services in organizing more effective procedures—better means to achieve existing goals. The term "procedure" is used here to mean anything from a single new technique to a major reorganization of processes within the client system. The change agent's role is to bring his previous experience with other systems to bear upon the problems of internal function and organization which are beyond the knowledge and experience of the client.

We have already mentioned one type of procedural help. The change agent may make it possible for the client system to find out more about itself. The techniques for this vary, but they include self-surveys, work conferences, and a variety of self-evaluational devices for small groups.

Another kind of help goes beyond self-examination to assistance in solving the problems which self-examination uncovers. Thus consultants are available to communities which wish to undertake programs of self-improvement, to industrial firms which want to raise production standards, and to individuals who want help in vocational planning or marital adjustment.

Change agents who specialize in human relations emphasize the relationships between persons and between groups. They suggest ways to improve these relationships whether they are dealing with individuals, groups, or whole social units. Their help may consist of skill training, sensitivity training, or recommendations for revised administrative practices. It may be directed either toward internal relationships or toward relationships between the client and the environment. Essentially, however, help of this kind consists of introducing a new perspective on problems of human relations and then assisting the client to adjust his behavior to this new point of view.

Obviously the most drastic procedural recommendation is one which essays a major reorganization within the client system. Any of the types of help we have mentioned may reach this point at the end of a step-by-step process of change. Sometimes, however, the change process begins with a proposal for reorganization or at least for attempting something which is quite without precedent in the client system. Examples of such far-reaching programs are Scanlon's approach to the revision of production methods in industry, Thelen's work in creating local block units in mixed Negro-white neighborhoods, and Wale's effort to promote community problem-solving programs in rural Puerto Rico. The change agent in such projects is much more than a neutral procedural resource. He is an active partisan, trying to explain, popularize, and eventually introduce procedures which are strange and perhaps even repugnant to the client. The agent's role resembles that of a doctor with a sick patient. If an operation is required to save a man's life, the doctor does not wait for approval from the patient but accepts the authorization of a close relative. In the case of a sick community or organization, the relative does not exist. The change agent must make decisions on his own authority, but at the same time he must maintain a constant effort to win the approval and participation of the client as the change program proceeds.

Very often the change agent whose chief stock in trade is his expert knowledge of procedure will find that he must engage in a rather active program of "selling" his wares and himself. He cannot simply hang out his shingle and wait for business to come to him. Instead he must go out among potential clients and stir things up. He may call meetings, organize workshops, or circulate reports on the success of his methods in cases he has handled previously. He may talk with people in order to challenge their satisfaction with the status quo and encourage their hope that better conditions are possible. However he goes about it, his object is to create enough awareness of existing problems to induce his potential clients to seek his assistance.

Once he has established a relationship with a client system, the change agent may still be required to do a certain amount of prodding. A simple decision to begin some process of change does not necessarily signify a determination to carry it through to completion. As his new procedures become familiar and established, however, the change agent will probably be able to withdraw more and more and allow the client system to handle its own affairs. When his knowledge and point of view have become thoroughly familiar to the client system, he no longer has any special function to perform and his relationship to the client is terminated.

Providing strength from within

Sometimes a change agent will try to change the state of affairs in a community or organization by joining it as an autonomous subpart to help provide internal strength. The use of this role is seen most clearly among agents who advocate the use of forceful influence efforts by one part of a client system against another. In this category, for example, we should include the union organizer who joins with his workers to increase their strength vis-à-vis management and the community worker who tries to mobilize the residents of a city block in their fight for better living conditions. In such cases one group of people is judged to be oppressed by another, and the apparent solution is to augment the power of the oppressed group to fight back.

In other situations there may be a conflict between ideas or norms rather than between people. Then the change agent uses whatever power he possesses to strengthen one view relative to the other. In this category we should include not only efforts to change attitudes and values by persuasion but also the use of sanctioned authority to enforce changes in behavior. An outstanding example was the decision by the United States Supreme Court which outlawed segregation in the southern schools. The court did not actually belong to any of the school systems affected by the decision. Yet it possessed authority over them, and in a certain sense it can be said to have "entered" each system when it introduced the new element of compulsion.

The purpose of entering a client system is not always to strengthen one side in a conflict. Sometimes the change agent may enter a system in order to provide it with special nontransferable resources. An example is the TVA, which entered the Tennessee Valley (99) with a specific function to perform. A second example is the community mental-health team which enters a community in order to provide special health facilities. Neither the TVA nor the mental-health team has any intention of training substitutes and then withdrawing. Each considers itself a permanent addition to the community. The change goal requires the establishment of new relationships with other elements in the system, the indoctrination of community members to popularize the new resource, and finally the provision of a new kind of service.

In addition, there are a number of cases in which the change agent may enter a system to provide a service for a temporary or indeterminable period of time. These cases include the community services provided by housing projects as well as such special community projects as those undertaken by Biddle (53) or the Quaker work camps. To classify the function of these change agents one must turn to the rationale which supports the specific project. If the intention is simply to fill a need which is felt to exist, then the function of the change agent is to provide a specialized resource. In many cases, however, the projects themselves are a means toward some other end. For example, Festinger and Kelley (62) report a community-service project which was designed to promote interaction among the residents of a housing project. The real end sought by the program was not the specific service provided by the new group but rather a reduction of the negative and stereotyped attitudes which governed the residents' views of each other and themselves. Here the role of the change agent was to create a special environment in which the residents of the project could most easily undergo a new and strange process of learning. This leads us to the next type of role.

Creating special environments

There is another group of change agents whose special role—although in practice one cannot always readily differentiate it from other functions—seems to be the creation of environments or situations which are conducive to learning, that is to say, environments or situations in which the client system will find it easy to learn something new or strange. Perhaps the most obvious representatives of this classification are the psychiatrists who have established special institutions for intensive programs in environmental therapy. They assume, among other things, that the concentrated use of environment will provide the patient with a variety of opportunities to learn—to learn about himself, about other people, and about the world in which he lives. The patient's improvement comes about not from any single aspect of treatment but from the cumulation of different kinds of learning.

The social worker who attempts to bring young people off the streets and into a settlement house is operating on the basis of a similar assumption. Presumably one of the reasons for wanting young people to spend their time in a settlement house is the hope that this contact will provide them with an opportunity to learn good things about the people on the staff and, through them, about society at large.

Change agents in a variety of other situations try to create special environments to facilitate learning. Efforts to change the attitudes of one group toward another, for instance, often involve the creation of a situation in which the people from the different groups can enjoy doing things together. It is a technique which has proved effective in meeting problems of race relations, and we have already pointed out how it was used by Festinger and Kelley to attempt to heighten morale and self-esteem in a new housing project. The point is that whenever the change agent wants people to like each other, he may find he can achieve his end better by creating an environment in which friendly personal relationships are a natural by-product than by attempting to influence the clients directly to behave and feel differently toward each other.

For a long time trainers and educators have been creating special environments for learning. The traditional ivory tower may have been far from the world of reality, but it nevertheless did what it was supposed to do: it facilitated an intimate acquaintance with the world of ideas. The importance of an academic environment in establishing a context for learning is illustrated in a trivial way by the standard recommendation in study guides that the student choose one place in which to study and a different place for recreation. This means not that the environment itself produces learning or a change in the student but only that the environment and the stimulus to change—in this case, books—are all of a piece and should not be separated.

Theories of progressive education have embodied the same idea, the distinction being that progressive teachers are interested in different and broadened educational content and hence in a different environment for learning. They move the school and the classroom into the community, thus providing the student with many new opportunities to learn about the world around him.

One extension of this concept has been the development of the "cultural island" (3). The theory holds that in order to train adults in new patterns of interpersonal behavior it is desirable to remove them from their standard environments and place them in special environments where they are free to innovate, practice, and test new behaviors. Home environments reinforce old patterns and make change difficult. Movement to a special "cultural island," however, where all forces are directed toward change, makes it possible for individuals to try something new.

A rather different use of environments is demonstrated by change agents who want to produce a change in group norms. The environment which they try to create is one in which the group is free to examine and question its own assumptions after these assumptions have been challenged by the presentation of new precepts and points of view. Directing attention to these challenges is only a small part of the change agent's job; the creation of an atmosphere in which the group is free to examine itself is usually much more important.

In short, the role of the change agent who creates special environments for learning takes many forms. Sometimes the agent himself may be an important part of the new environment, as is true in the case of special training or therapeutic institutions. In other cases the change agent may prefer to keep himself apart, thus allowing the client to learn from direct interaction with the environment. Sometimes the environment is a direct impetus toward change, constituting in itself a change force; in other cases it may be merely a necessary background which must be present to promote the effectiveness of other change forces. In all cases, however, the change agent must assume responsibility for designing an environment which will maximize the possibilities of change.

Giving support during the process of change

So far each role of the change agent which we have discussed has involved the introduction of something new into the life of the client system: new connections between subparts, new procedures, new resources for use by the system, new environments. In each case the new element has been something designed to stimulate change by altering the balance of forces at work in the client system. But in addition to organizing new forces which challenge the status quo and impel the client system toward change, the change agent usually gives active help in the process of change itself. He helps the client system to meet the challenge which he himself may have originated. We shall consider the various means of direct help as different aspects of a single role.

One way of helping is to encourage and support the client system's belief that change is actually possible. This is a process which begins as soon as the relationship with the change agent is established. Often the very fact that someone has made himself available for help with problems of change makes it more relevant for the client system to think about change. Problems which had formerly been pushed aside now become important; they are brought forward for study and action. Specifically, the person who enters therapy can begin to raise questions about himself which in the past he has tried to ignore. The community which establishes a tentative relationship with a consultant can begin to look for problems which will require the consultant's services. Whereas emphasis had been placed on maintaining a good appearance, now it shifts to the importance of making good use of the help which is available for correcting past errors and weaknesses. The contribution of the change agent to this beginning process of self-examination is his assurance that it is really all right—that is, not dangerous—for the client system to look at its own weaknesses.

Later, as new ideas and new patterns of behavior begin to emerge, the change agent can offer a different kind of support. Now it becomes important for the client system to test these new ideas and new patterns of behavior. Encouragement from the change agent may make it easier for the client system to try something new. His encouragement may consist simply of praise and approval, or it may include preparation of specific procedures to assist in these critical trials. Sometimes it is possible for the change agent to enter directly into the operating theater, so to speak, and give immediate support. Thus, for example, one project dealing with deviant children (2) has included arrangements for an adult to stand by while the child tests a new way of behaving with his classmates. This allows an opportunity to give immediate praise and advice when the child has passed through a difficult new experience.

Sometimes the client system may be so disturbed by doubt about the advisability of continuing the change process that a different kind of help is needed. The client's hesitation may indicate a high level of ambivalence which requires a reassessment of the original decision to work with the change agent. In this case the change agent can help by making sure that both the negative and positive aspects of the client's feelings receive equally careful attention.

In other circumstances the client's hesitation may arise from his uneasiness about departing from the established ways of doing things or from his reluctance to question legitimate authority. Here the change agent may be able to serve as a competing source of authority. Thus, for example, if the workers in one industrial plant hesitate to change their system of production, they may be reassured if the change agent tells them that the same changes have been made successfully in other companies. The change agent presumably possesses authoritative knowledge of the alternatives to conventional practice, and he can vouch for the acceptability and effectiveness of the new methods.

Many change agents accept a general responsibility for what we call *rational reality testing.* In other words, they try to see that the client system maintains a reasonable, objective, and realistic view of the processes of change. There are at least two aspects of this responsibility. First, the change agent tries to encourage a reasonable perspective of the change process itself. This means that he tries to counteract both the hope of a sudden, one-step solution and the despairing conviction that nothing will ever change. It means giving help in the establishment of short-range goals which can serve as steps toward the ultimate objective. Finally, it means helping to sustain the client's motivation toward change through a long period of uncertainty and equivocal progress. The client system may sometimes lose sight of the goal, but the change agent must keep it firmly in mind.

Second, another kind of reality testing concerns the appropriateness of the change plans which have been adopted by the client system. If the change agent encourages the client system to adopt new ideas and new patterns of behavior, he usually also offers some implicit assurance that the client's changed methods and beliefs will not create new difficulties. He may provide this protection either by vetoing the client's proposals when they are irrational or impossible or by helping to establish reasonable procedures for reaching decisions. The latter would include techniques for gathering relevant information in advance, for evaluating each new test before moving on to the next step, and for avoiding stereotyped judgments of good and bad.

Toward the end of the change process the change agent may find that he is required to give a different kind of help. Often the client system will feel that some gains have been made but that more are needed. The client system may be doubtful about its ability to sustain the level of achievement already reached, its ability to progress further, or both. The change agent can help to allay these doubts by inculcating feelings of security and self-confidence. Sometimes an intermittent relationship between client system and change agent can be maintained for an indefinite period after the change process itself is completed. A university consultation service, for example, may withdraw from a particular community when one project is finished, but it will remain on call if new needs for help arise in the future. Sometimes the client system can be put in touch with other systems which are moving in the same direction and with whom future co-operation may be possible; numbers provide strength. Thus people who are returning from a workshop may want to know about other alumni who have had the same kind of training and who are now interested in similar activities. In other cases the client system may expect to be self-sufficient and may be concerned only with its own level of competence. Various things can be done at this point to help increase the client's confidence and readiness for independent action. In general, the point to be emphasized is that the client system should be able to continue progress on its own; the end of a particular relationship or project terminates one phase of the change process but does not necessarily end all endeavor toward change.

ESTABLISHMENT AND MAINTENANCE OF
THE RELATIONSHIP WITH THE CLIENT SYSTEM

All of the change agent's diagnostic and helping activities are conducted in the context of the particular relationship which he has developed with the client system. We shall call this relationship the *change relationship*. It encompasses the joint plans, shared experiences, and mutual expectations which over a period of time the change agent and client system have developed together. At any given time this relationship defines the appropriate and inappropriate behavior for each member and provides the background in terms of which particular acts are to be interpreted. In a very real sense it governs the kind and amount of help which the change agent can give as well as the kind and amount of change which the client system can effect.

Strong convictions about what constitutes an appropriate helping relationship are held by many professional change agents.

Their convictions do not always agree; in fact, they often provoke doctrinaire disputes between one school and another. Naturally, different ideas about the change relationship ensue from experiences with different kinds of client systems and from the various specialized ways of giving help. Change agents who work with individuals rely upon a change relationship different from that of those who work with communities or organizations. Similarly, change agents whose work engages them in long periods of intensive collaboration define the relationship differently from those who offer only occasional consultation. Despite these differences, however, certain aspects of the change relationship are of common concern to many different kinds of professional agents, and these concerns are briefly summarized here.

The need for adequate sanction

Most change agents assume that a change relationship can be satisfactory only if it is based upon the voluntary co-operation of all participants. If this positive attitude of willingness does not exist in the client system, the change agent will either try to develop it or refuse his help altogether.

Change agents do not always agree on what it is that the client system must accept. Some believe that the client system should agree to the desirability of making at least some change, either a specified change or one that is only partly understood beforehand. Others are content if the client system is merely willing to enter into a relationship with the change agent on a trial basis; if they then discover work to be done or a change to be made they can proceed from that point in whatever manner seems best. In either case it is important not to try to trick the client. The change agent who offers as bait a quick and easy solution or an attractive service is likely to find himself with clients who accept the bait but don't want anything else. If he wants clients who are motivated strongly enough to undertake a significant job of self-evaluation and self-improvement, then he must let them know that this is what he expects. He must tell them precisely what kind of a job awaits them. Obviously, one cannot expect clients to do such hard work without being prepared for it.

Once he knows the kind of commitment he wants, the change agent still must select the persons from whom the commitment is to be obtained. For agents who deal with individuals this is no problem. A relationship is established directly with each person who asks for help, although occasionally the agent may resort to referral procedures in the treatment of unwilling clients. Even in the latter case, however, the agent will usually try to win the confidence of the client before the program of treatment is begun.

The change agent who works with social systems faces a more complicated decision. Who should be included in the change relationship? Here we can distinguish between change agents who approach a system in terms of its officially organized leadership or subgroup structure and those who begin work with any available nucleus of people.

The first group, those who are concerned with structure and organization, may in turn adopt either of two approaches. First is the approach which has been called "multiple entry," a term originally coined by Merton (94) and later expanded by Mann and others. In this method of approach, the agent assumes that there are two or more significant segments in the client system and that each segment demands an independent opportunity to accept or reject the change agent's offer of help. In an industrial firm, for example, this would mean that union and management should each agree to a joint working relationship with the change agent before anything else is done. The change agent would not work with either segment alone, nor would he do anything in conjunction with one segment without the knowledge and approval of both. He would plan to keep all segments equally well related to the single change project. The second method of approach advocated by agents who choose to work through structure and organization is the concentration upon a single focus of leadership within the system, as, for example, a community council or an association president. The agent who follows this method will approach only the official leaders within his client system, and he will plan to work with the system only through established channels of power and authority. In this case the responsibility for satisfying the different needs of the different subparts rests primarily with the officials of the system, not with the change agent.

An entirely different approach is used by change agents who are willing to work with any group of interested people, wherever they may be encountered in the structure of the client system. The assumption of these agents seems to be that the important point is to get the project under way with any available leverage point. Once this is done, the work will spread, it is hoped, to other parts of the system. This is an approach used most often in work with communities, where it is impossible to approach all the people at once. Any approach, in fact, would reach only a small part of the system, and hence the change agent often decides to work with that part of the system which is already most interested or most accessible. He may select a group of civic leaders or any group of previously inactive "ordinary" citizens.

Sometimes it is not enough to win sanction from the client system. There may be other persons or groups, external to the system, whose approval is also needed. Thus a child cannot enter therapy without the approval of his parents. A local agency or union may be unable to introduce major changes without approval from the national headquarters. A community cannot ignore the external economic and political factors which govern its way of life. Inadequate attention to these external sources of power is one of the most frequently reported causes of failure among change agents.

Failure to secure sanction from external authorities may be the result of either accident or design. An example of oversight is contained in the report of a change agent who neglected to inform either the project manager or the existing Tenant Council when he organized a new community-service program in a housing project. It is a good deal more serious, of course, when the external authorities willfully withhold their approval. Such a situation is described by Poston (71). The University of Montana, he reports, was interested at one point in a state-wide program of community development. Support was obtained from community leaders throughout the state, but in spite of repeated efforts, no inducement could win the co-operation of "the Company," the monolithic organization which dominated much of the industrial and financial activity in the state. The economic and political power of the Company was so great that eventually its opposition led to the total defeat of the program. Still another situation is created by the change agent who decides to defy the existing power structure. He hopes to win by force rather than by persuasion. One of his principal hazards is an underestimation of the power or skill of his opponent. Here we find an example in Bowens' (54) efforts to create an active tenants' organization and his defeat by a landlord who granted just enough minor but well-chosen concessions to disorganize the opposition.

All these examples serve to remind us that the change agent's efforts to help will often take him into a complex system of relationships between persons and groups. He may need co-operation from several sources, both inside and outside the client system. None of these can be taken for granted. Each must be approached separately, and each must be given an opportunity to raise questions and to arrive at an independent decision concerning the wisdom of co-operating in the proposed relationship. Otherwise, questions which are left unanswered may become a source of serious resistance later in the program of change.

Clarifying expectations about the change relationship

When he has completed the preliminaries the change agent usually finds that he must suggest a pattern of co-operation which will be satisfactory to both the client system and himself. Some of the points which may be incorporated in this primary definition of roles are discussed in the following paragraphs.

First, the change agent must decide what parts of the client system will be directly involved in the change relationship. The relevant considerations here have already been analyzed in our discussion of leverage points. The change agent who is working with a multiperson system will select as allies those persons or groups who are accessible and who demonstrate spread potential, that is, he will choose to work with persons whom he can influence and who in turn can influence others. He may decide to work with everyone in the client system or with only those in one part of the system, or he may decide to establish relationships of varying intensity with different parts of the system.

Each part of the system which is in contact with the change agent will be told, at least in general, what it may expect from that contact. How frequently will meetings with the change agent occur? What procedures will be followed in the meetings? Who will be responsible for conducting the meetings? In general, what responsibilities will be assumed by the change agent, and what responsibilities will be assigned to the client? Precisely what work will they be trying to do and how will it be done?

In addition to these expectations about the work itself, there will be expectations about the emotional content of the change relationship. Will the feeling or tone of the meetings be pleasant or unpleasant? Will the change relationship and the change process be fairly superficial experiences for the persons who participate in them, or will they stimulate strong emotional interest and involvement? Will the change agent take a dominant role and encourage a relationship of dependency in the client system, or will he put the emphasis on self-help? Will he want to know about matters which are private, habitual, and perhaps rooted in the unconscious, or will he be content with the subjects of public record and conscious awareness?

The client's expectations for the relationship of day-to-day interaction with the change agent are usually formed in the context of long-range expectations about the change project. How long will the relationship with the change agent continue? Will the relationship continue on an even course throughout the entire project, or will it move through different phases? In some cases, for example, the change agent may establish an expectation for an early period during which the client system will be heavily dependent, a later period of tentative experimentation, and a final period during which the client system will be relatively autonomous and will call upon the change agent for only occasional assistance.

Change agents will differ, of course, in their beliefs concerning what expectations should be created in the client system as well as in their methods for eliciting expectation. Some will communicate expectations by explicit agreements, others by implicit examples and demonstrations. In all cases, however, the early period of the change relationship will be partially devoted to preparing the way for what is to come later.

Regulating the intensity and quality of the helping relationship

Therapists, both those who work with individuals and those who work with groups, pay a great deal of attention to this question. Most other change agents, however, give very little data on their theories or methods of controlling the emotional content of the change relationship.

Some change agents who work with individuals emphasize the responsibility of the agent in controlling and using the emotional intensities which are generated in the helping relationship itself. The objective is to maintain the relationship as an effective medium for learning. These therapists believe that when difficulties arise in the relationship between agent and client they constitute a valuable opportunity for learning. If the client can "work through" these difficulties and discover new ways of relating to the change agent, he will have made important gains in his general ability to relate to others. Thus it is important that the change relationship offer freedom to act out and explore new realities. This point is stressed by many therapists, including those who work with cultural-island training projects, with children, and with low-status groups in hierarchical organizations.

Some change agents, especially some therapists, object to the emphasis which is often placed on the need for maintaining an objective outside role. It is more important, they believe, to obtain from the client a kind of affective acceptance or trust which will allow him to act freely and experimentally. Such an affective acceptance can best be brought about, they feel, by emphasizing not the aloofness of the change agent or his status as an objective scientist but the mutuality of the helping engagement. To a certain extent this attitude has invaded other areas of helping where some workers now advocate change-agent teams which are composed both of some workers who are oriented sympathetically toward the personal involvements of the client system and other workers who are oriented as experts solely toward the change task itself.

Change agents who work with organizations and communities often feel that they must insist on preventing the development of dependency in the client system. This is not simply because these agents lack training in psychodynamics. When the change process is brief or diffused among many different persons, as it usually is in projects of community development, a relationship of excessive dependency would be an intolerable burden for the change agent and would prolong the change process beyond its normal termination point, thus forcing the agent to continue in his helping capacity after he no longer has any useful function to perform. Moreover, in work with communities the change effort is not a resolution of personal emotional disturbances but a project involving training and social action. The appropriate intensity of the helping relationship is therefore different from that in cases of individual therapy. We shall continue to watch for clues to this difficult question of emotional intensity in the change relationship as we go through the case material in Chapters 7, 8, and 9.

RECOGNIZING AND GUIDING
THE PHASES OF CHANGE

All of the change agents whose work we have investigated recognize that change progresses through certain phases of movement or development, but none of them has identified these phases very clearly. We shall summarize briefly here, and then expand later, our own attempt to classify the phases of planned change. These seem to us to represent the ideas about the development of the helping relationship which are used at least implicitly by many change agents.

The phases of planned change

The seven phases of planned change which we have identified will be discussed at some length in the next chapter, and so we shall merely list them here.

Phase 1: The client system discovers the need for help, sometimes with stimulation by the change agent.

Phase 2: The helping relationship is established and defined.

Phase 3: The change problem is identified and clarified.

Phase 4: Alternative possibilities for change are examined; change goals or intentions are established.

Phase 5: Change efforts in the "reality situation" are attempted.

Phase 6: Change is generalized and stabilized.

Phase 7: The helping relationship ends or a different type of continuing relationship is defined.

The emotional themes of the helping relationship

The affective relationship between the change agent and the client system varies, of course, as the change process progresses. However, we have not been able to draw up a classification like the one above to discriminate among the various phases or levels of this relationship. Most change agents who have written about their work do not describe very clearly this dimension of their experience with the helping process.

Even though we have restricted our consideration solely to cases of *voluntary* helping relationships, we have found a variety of clues which indicate that the emotional content of the relationship varies widely, not only from case to case but from time to time within a single case. At one point, for instance, the relationship may be characterized primarily by feelings of hostility and distrust, at another by feelings of admiration and even affection, and at yet another by a businesslike interest in getting the work done. In fact, there are many possible motifs and each of them may appear many times or not at all in the course of a given relationship. This is true, one might say, of any relationship, whatever its purpose and composition. But in a change relationship there are, in addition, special problems which derive from the fact that one party is receiving help from another on matters of emotional importance. The client system, for instance, may hope very profoundly that the change agent will be able to help and, motivated by this hope, may exaggerate the assistance which the agent is actually able to render. This exaggeration immediately fosters another one, equally dangerous: if the change agent has so much power to help, he must have an equal power to hurt. Thus one exaggeration leads to another, and the agent is feared and hated even while he is wanted and, in some cases, loved. On the other hand, the client's immense desire for help may lead him to disparage the actual power of any particular helper: no one, the client feels, could do as much as he needs, and therefore anyone who claims to be able to do so must be a fraud.

Obviously, irrational responses of this type require special attention. If he does not recognize them and allows them to go unchecked, the agent will find that they interfere seriously with his efforts to give help effectively. They must therefore be taken into account. Often they may serve as important stimuli to learning. Naturally the extent of these irrational responses and the degree of attention they require vary greatly from case to case, but in one way or another the change agent must be able to solve the multifaceted problems which are created when the client system projects its own unrealistic desires into the change relationship.

Emotional reactions may enter the change relationship in still another way. The client system may be preoccupied with an emotional problem which is not specifically relevant to the change relationship but which nevertheless encroaches upon it. Thus an individual in therapy may react to the therapist in ways that are dictated by his own needs. When he is struggling with the general problem of dependency, for instance, he may make unusual demands on the therapist for guidance and support; when he is trying to "work through" his own hostility, he may be unusually critical of the therapist and everything he says. Similarly, a group which is seeking a way to cope with an autocratic leader may refuse to be influenced by anybody, even the change agent, whereas a group which has suddenly been deprived of leadership may want to be told exactly what to do, even in matters which have previously been in the province of routine. In these cases the change agent may want to help the client system understand and overcome the immediate emotional problem, or he may prefer to work around it. Either way, he must know what the problem is. His own contribution to the change relationship is most effective when he recognizes and properly evaluates the current motivation of the client system.

These emotional themes in the change relationship point our attention to the various ways in which the relationship itself may shift as it proceeds. In Chapters 7, 8, and 9, we shall explore this aspect of the problem of help as fully as our limited data will permit.

CHOOSING APPROPRIATE SPECIFIC TECHNIQUES AND MODES OF BEHAVIOR

The change agent is faced with an incessant demand for concrete decisions. What shall he do and what shall he say at this particular moment? Using whatever criteria he has available, he must choose from his repertoire of helping skills the precise means to deal with each progressive moment of decision. Some change agents depend very much on the behavior of the client system; they regulate their own contribution to the helping process in accordance with the progressive responses of the client. For other agents it is a matter of taking the next step in a prepared sequence of procedures. Unfortunately, most of the reports which have been given us by change agents do not contain satisfactory descriptions of these moment-to-moment requirements of their jobs, nor do they contain explanations of the criteria which the agents use in reaching decisions on immediate problems of procedure or behavior. These are problems of decision which we have done our best to infer from the case materials, and we shall present our findings in greater detail in Chapters 7, 8, and 9.

CONTRIBUTING TO PROFESSIONAL DEVELOPMENT
BY RESEARCH AND CONCEPTUALIZATION

Finally, the professional change agent has the job of stimulating his own growth and that of the helping professions by constantly attempting to develop and test new insights about the helping process and the role of the helper. Often this contribution can be made by making research activity a component part of the change project or by organizing one's observations of the helping relationship and then reflecting and reporting on the meaning and general significance of these observations. In Chapters 10 and 11 we shall look at some of the priorities for research in the profession as well as at some of the needs for broadening the training of change agents so that they can make contributions to the theory of planned change more effectively.

In this chapter we have reviewed what seem to us, on the basis of our comparative analysis, to be the main dimensions of the change agent's job of giving help. These are the things which all change agents must do in order to fulfill the whole range of their responsibilities, whatever their particular fields of specialization may be. Fuller discussions of these different functions appear in other chapters. Here we can perhaps recapitulate by simply listing the different functions as we have reviewed them in this chapter.

The change agent's role includes the following activities: (1) diagnosing the nature of the client system's problem; (2) assessing the client system's motivations and capacities to change; (3) appraising the agent's own motivations and resources; (4) selecting appropriate change objectives; (5) choosing an appropriate type of helping role; (6) establishing and maintaining the helping relationship; (7) recognizing and guiding the phases of the change process; (8) choosing the specific techniques and modes of behavior which will be appropriate to each progressive encounter in the change relationship; and (9) contributing to the development of the basic skills and theories of the profession.

THE PHASES OF PLANNED CHANGE

6

Kurt Lewin, in his pioneering analysis of the process of change in individual and group performances, suggested three phases. He wrote:

> A change toward a higher level of group performance is frequently short-lived; after a "shot in the arm," group life soon returns to the previous level. This indicates that it does not suffice to define the objective of planned change in group performance as the reaching of a different level. Permanency of the new level, or permanency for a desired period, should be included in the objective. A successful change includes, therefore, three aspects: *unfreezing* (if necessary) the present level, *moving* to the new level, and *freezing* group life on the new level. [87, p. 34]

Our study of the work done by various change agents seems to suggest that this conception of three phases can be somewhat expanded.

The literature of change suggests that most change agents are oriented toward two objectives when it comes to selecting the methods of giving help. First, they try to choose techniques which will help the client system to solve its problems and thereby achieve a desirable change. The second objective, corollary to the first, is to choose techniques which will develop and maintain an appropriate relationship between the change agent and the client system so that the client will willingly acknowledge and use the resources offered by the agent. The change agent's influence must be acceptable to the client system if the helping process is to develop. Both of these objectives are constantly shaping the change agent's course of action. In fact, concern about the relationship between the agent and the client occupies such a prominent place in the literature of change that we have felt obliged to give it an explicit locus in our formulation of the phases of planned change. Consequently, we have expanded Lewin's three phases and propose below a list of five general phases of change process.

1. Development of a need for change ("unfreezing").
2. Establishment of a change relationship.
3. Working toward change ("moving").
4. Generalization and stabilization of change ("freezing").
5. Achieving a terminal relationship.

We shall see later in this chapter that the third phase can in turn be divided into three separate subphases, each embodying important characteristics of its own. This, therefore, makes a total of seven phases in all.

We do not suggest that all planned change necessarily progresses in an orderly sequential way through each of these stages of change. Indeed, one can usually see more than one phase going on at the same time. Most change processes probably proceed by a kind of cyclic motion, starting over and over again as one set of problems is solved and a new set is encountered; hence the different phases become mixed up and the final objective may be achieved by a process which seems rather muddled to the observer who is looking for a clear-cut developmental sequence. Nevertheless, we have found it helpful to review descriptions of change—in persons, groups, organizations, and communities—in terms of this sequence of phases. And we have found it very helpful to use these phases in separating and classifying the specific helping techniques.

In this chapter we shall describe briefly the characteristics of the seven phases as they have emerged from our comparative assessment of the case materials. Then, in Chapters 7, 8, and 9, we shall describe the specific helping techniques which are pertinent to each phase.

PHASE 1. THE DEVELOPMENT OF
A NEED FOR CHANGE

In Chapters 2 and 3 we identified some of the types of problems which create stress or disruption within a system or between a system and its environment. Before a process of planned change can begin, these difficulties usually must be translated into actual "problem awareness," that is, into a desire to change and a desire to seek help from outside the system. The various subparts of systems at the group level usually evidence different degrees of awareness of the system's difficulties, and consequently the total system lacks concerted sensitivity to the problems which may demand change effort and help. Even the subparts of a personality system are usually divided or ambivalent about the need for help. As we have seen, there are frequently vested interests in the system which are motivated to reject or prevent an awareness of serious problems. And there may be communication blockages which inhibit the spread of awareness. In the case of young children studies (90) have indicated that there are significant developmental age differences in their ability to recognize personal and interpersonal problems.

Moreover, problem awareness is not automatically translated into a desire for change. First there must be at least some confidence in the possibility of a more desirable state of affairs. Any system is likely to face a number of resistances within itself when it comes to setting a level of aspiration for change. Perhaps, for example, a group or organization has already attempted several times to solve its difficulties and has met only with failure. This may lead to a defeatist belief that the system is completely incapable of dealing with its problems, even though there is a high level of problem awareness within the system.

Finally, of course, problem awareness and a desire for change lead to an explicit desire for help from outside the system. But before this can happen, the system, or at least some influential sub-part of it, must believe that external help is relevant and available. Such a belief is by no means to be taken for granted. Frequently there is an awareness of problems and a genuine desire to do something about them, but these are accompanied by resistance to the idea of help from outside. A parent, for instance, may feel that an appeal for outside help is an admission of his failure as a parent; a company president may believe that he himself must be responsible for solving his company's problems and that he should not thrust this responsibility upon an outside agent; a teacher may feel that he is jeopardizing his chance for promotion if he seeks help from his supervisor or from some other external source.

In some cases the system may be quite ready to take advantage of outside help but may not know where to find it. Parents, for instance, may not know where to turn. Their only previous experience with professional helpers may have been with their family doctor, with their church leader, or perhaps with a social-welfare agency, and none of these sources may appear to offer relevant help.

Among different cultures and subcultures there may be a good deal of variation in sensitivity to different types of problems as well as in readiness to accept certain types of problems as "legitimate" ones to be aware of or to admit to others. There are also great differences in the accessibility, influence, and acceptability of various types of change agents. All of these factors bear heavily upon the question of how the first phase of the change process is triggered off.

This first or "unfreezing" phase in the change process usually occurs in one of three different ways in the cases which we have reviewed.

First, a change agent discovers or hypothesizes a certain difficulty in a potential client system and offers his help directly or takes steps to stimulate an awareness of the difficulty in the system. Again we cite two examples from our case materials. The staff of a community mental-health clinic invites the parents of all children who are experiencing difficulty in school to attend discussion groups sponsored by the staff. A management consultant requests an appointment with a company president to tell him about the executive-development program which is available to his firm if it is needed.

Second, a third party, connected with both the change agent and the potential client system, becomes aware of the system's difficulty and brings the two together. For example, a mother who is disturbed by the fact that her ten-year-old child refuses to eat takes him to see a child therapist. Or a philanthropic foundation which is interested in the welfare and development of a particular community invites an adult-education team from a nearby university to offer a series of institutes on community development in order to stimulate the interest of community leaders.

Third, the potential client system becomes aware of its own difficulty and itself seeks help from an outside source. This is the most common way for the change process to begin. No doubt nearly everyone can give illustrations. One example from our case materials concerns an individual whose anxieties become intolerable and who consequently makes an appointment with a psychotherapist; another concerns a group of citizens who, becoming worried about the way in which their neighborhood is going downhill in terms of real-estate values and community services, set out to seek the advice of a community consultant.

In the next chapter we shall review some of the techniques which are used by change agents in guiding this first phase of the change process.

PHASE 2. THE ESTABLISHMENT OF
A CHANGE RELATIONSHIP

The development of a working relationship with the change agent raises a good many new problems for the client system. There is, for instance, the problem of communicating the need for help in such a way that the potential change agent can understand and accept it and agree to the relevance of his type of help. Or, in cases where the potential change agent has himself taken the initiative to stimulate a need for help, the client system must try to assess the validity of the change agent's diagnoses and the expedience of his recommendations.

One of the most crucial features of this second phase is the way in which the client system first begins to think about the potential change agent. First impressions can do a good deal to determine the future of any human relationship. Polansky and Kounin (96) have studied the development of first impressions in helping situations. Their work shows how very actively the client system forms its early conceptions of the change agent, particularly in respect to estimates of his ability to give help, his inferred motives, and his attributed friendliness or unfriendliness. When a change agent offers to help in solving a problem which involves labor-management relations, he may be sure that the president of the company and the president of the union are both very much concerned to discover and evaluate his personal attitudes toward labor and management. The mother whose child needs the attention of a psychotherapist may be very much disturbed by the prospect of exposing her own inadequacies by communicating with a particular change agent. The individual who needs to enter psychotherapy may use his first appointment in trying to decide whether or not a particular agent is competent to work on his problems.

Often the client system seems to be seeking assurance that the potential change agent is different enough from the client system to be a real expert and yet enough like it to be thoroughly understandable and approachable. What the client system really wants is two change agents in one. It wants an agent who will identify himself with the client system's problems and sympathize with the system's needs and values, but who will at the same time be neutral enough to take a genuinely objective and different view of the system's predicament.

Another pitfall which the client system must negotiate in this second phase is the arrival at an understanding about the kind and degree of effort which must be put forth in the collaboration with the potential change agent. The client must not only understand the arrangement but he must at least tentatively agree to it. Frequently, wishful thinking deludes the client system; the change process is thought to be easier and speedier than it actually can be. When this happens the relationship between client system and change agent is likely to get off on the wrong foot. When the agent tries to clarify his time perspective and his view of the client's responsibilities later in the change process, the relationship may be severely disrupted.

If the client system is a group, an organization, or a community, this second phase of the change process is likely to raise important organizational or procedural questions within the client system. Usually one subpart is more ready to change than others. Hence this subpart must attempt to engage the sympathy of the other subparts toward the projected plan of establishing a working relationship with an outside source of help. A good many problems may be encountered. Who is to pay the change agent's fee? Who is to deal with him? Who is to accept responsibility for the change project if it is a failure? These and many other questions must be settled before the subparts can agree to admit the change agent and work with him. Even in the case of change in an individual, the various segments of the personality must be brought into some kind of basic agreement on the wisdom of establishing a relationship with the change agent.

Very often the client system, the change agent, or both ask for a trial period, and nothing could be more understandable. There are so many contingencies, so many imponderables, at the beginning of the change relationship that neither party can be sure the relationship will progress satisfactorily. Recently a survey was conducted among a small sample of change agents who were at work on various group and organizational projects. They agreed that this second phase of the change process, the phase during which the parties must arrive intelligently at a decision to work together, is one of the really crucial steps in the whole change process, perhaps the most important of all. The success or failure of almost any change project depends heavily upon the quality and the workability of the relationship between the change agent and the client system, and many aspects of this relationship are established very early in the helping relationship.

PHASES 3, 4 AND 5.

WORKING TOWARD CHANGE

We have already pointed out that in our analysis the third phase, the process of changing, divides naturally into three subphases, each of which seems important enough to be identified as a major stage of the change process. Lewin referred generally to this part of the change process as "moving," proceeding from one level of function or performance to another. We think that this part of the change program can be viewed most fruitfully as being composed of the following three phases.

1. The clarification or diagnosis of the client system's problem. (Phase 3)
2. The examination of alternative routes and goals; establishing goals and intentions of action. (Phase 4)
3. The transformation of intentions into actual change efforts. (Phase 5)

Let us look briefly at some of the aspects of these three processes.

Phase 3. The clarification or diagnosis of the client system's problem

One important task which must be undertaken by the client system is to collaborate with the change agent in diagnosing the nature of the client system's difficulties. This is likely to raise a number of problems. First of all, the change agent needs information. How shall it be obtained? It may be only a matter of making the client system available for observation and testing, as when a team of interviewers is invited to ask questions of a company's personnel or when an individual submits to a Rorschach test. On the other hand, this business of providing information may involve the client in much more arduous and lengthy work. In some kinds of therapy free associations over a considerable period of time may be required. Groups may find that they must be trained in methods of collecting data, and communities may be asked to undergo the often laborious task of a searching self-survey.

But perhaps the heart of the matter is that during this phase the client system is usually coping with a changing and broadening interpretation of the question at hand. As data are collected and analyzed, the problem which seemed simple at first is likely to take on the appearance of an intricate, many-faceted difficulty. This is the point at which vested interests—either particular pressure blocs within social units or particular segments of the individual personality—are likely to become aware of the threat which is posed by change, and their defensive reactions may smash the whole mechanism of collaboration between the system and the change agent. The client may begin to think that his problem, as it is newly defined, is too pervasive or too fundamental to be remedied, and he may decide to give up without a struggle. Or the client system may be hostile; even though it ostensibly continues the collaboration with the change agent, it may close up its sources of information and reject the agent's diagnoses. This is a trying time for both client system and change agent. Usually it is a question of attempting to strike some kind of balance within the client system between two extremes of inaction: the inability to do anything because of a helpless dependency and defeatism in the face of unexpectedly acute problems, and refusal to do anything because of a hostile rejection of all diagnostic interpretations.

Phase 4. The examination of alternative routes and goals; establishing goals and intentions of action

This is the stage in which the client system translates its diagnostic insights first into ideas about alternative means of action and then into definite intentions to change in specified ways. In the process both cognitive and motivational problems are likely to arise.

A committee which has been formed to study community problems, for instance, might acquire a clear understanding of the pathology of its community's illness—let us say it is a matter of noncommunication among conflicting groups—but this does not mean that ideas about what to do and how to do it will automatically follow. We have already noted this point in Chapter 5. In order to think clearly and realistically about targets and leverage points, the committee must pursue its processes of conceptualization beyond the merely diagnostic. The techniques for doing this will be discussed later, but it is generally recognized that the client and change agent cannot proceed intelligently in any problem-solving endeavor without considering the alternative possibilities of action.

Even more interesting are the problems of motivation which arise when the client system begins to consider its actual intentions. Among the alternative routes, which route shall be chosen? In most cases this is a specific question which demands a concrete decision, and the decision must be in the nature of an investment—emotional as well as material—in a certain plan of procedure. Naturally, problems of motivation—that is, problems of the client system's emotional and material resources—arise. For example, during this phase it often becomes clear for the first time that certain present satisfactions, such as the pleasures of pursuing traditional goals or behaving in accustomed ways, will have to be given up if the change to a more desirable level of performance is to be accomplished. This may serve to intensify the client system's inclination to continue what it has been doing. A case in point is the hospital afflicted with acute morale problems in its regular nursing staff. A survey showed that the problems were caused, at least in part, by certain types of authoritarian procedure practiced by the head nurses—and the head nurses themselves became fully aware of what they were doing. In a series of discussion groups they explored ways in which their procedures might be changed. But these discussions produced very little change. The discussions had given the head nurses a clear intellectual understanding of what was wrong but had failed to commit them wholly to the necessary change effort. In other words, the intentions of the head nurses were still indeterminate, and they needed to explore more deeply the question of precisely what would have to be given up in order to accomplish their ultimate aims.

Another type of motivational problem which is often revealed during this phase of the change process is the client system's anxiety about awkwardness or failure in attempting new patterns of behavior or new procedural techniques. Often these anxieties can be eased by providing ways for the client to test innovations before they are permanently adopted. If the client system is given an opportunity to explore tentatively the consequences of a new functional concept, some of the strangeness wears off and the client acquires confidence in his ability to do what is expected of him. Unfortunately, too many change relationships are broken off before this phase is reached, so that the client system is often left to cope alone with the diagnoses and recommendations which have been presented by the change agent.

Phase 5. The transformation of intentions into actual change efforts

The real success or failure of any change effort, so far as the client system is concerned, is determined by the degree to which the original ineffectiveness or stress within the system is mitigated and functional efficiency is achieved or restored. This means, in effect, that success is measured by the way in which plans and intentions are transformed into actual achievements. The active work of changing is the keystone of the whole change process. During this phase the client system faces a number of critical problems. One of the most common is that of eliciting support from the change agent while the movement toward change is beginning. As we have noted above, by this time the relationship with the change agent may already have been ended, in which case the best the client system can do is to imagine what the change agent might expect as the steps of the change effort are taken. In other cases the relationship with the change agent may still continue, but the actual day-to-day efforts of the client system to change its way of functioning may occur only in situations which permit no direct contact with the change agent. The therapist, for instance, may never see his patient in the very circumstances which produce the patient's maladjustive reactions. This means that the client system must derive whatever support it can from discussions after the fact, usually in brief and more or less formal meetings with the change agent.

Another problem, of course, is that of securing sympathetic acceptance of the change efforts from the various subparts of the system or from adjacent systems. A foreman who attempts to inaugurate new working methods in the face of fellow workers who are apathetic or hostile will usually sense failure and give up his change efforts.

Obtaining adequate feedback on the consequences of the change effort may also prove difficult. This is particularly true if the desired change affects primarily relationships external to the system. In such cases the system may be unable to find out what the results of its change efforts really are, and hence it may not know whether to continue the efforts, modify them, or abandon them altogether. Sometimes when a client system receives no clear information on the consequences of its change effort it interprets this as a sign of failure and gives up, even though the change effort may in fact be producing precisely the desired effect.

PHASE 6. THE GENERALIZATION
AND STABILIZATION OF CHANGE

One of the important questions about any process of change is whether or not the change which has been accomplished will remain a stable and permanent characteristic of the system. Too often change which has been produced by painstaking and costly efforts tends to disappear after the change effort ceases, and the system, which wanted to change, slips back instead into its old ways.

One critical factor in the stabilization of change is the spread or non-spread of change to neighboring systems or to subparts of the client system. If a community which has inaugurated a citizens' council finds that the idea has spread to several neighboring communities, there is a strong likelihood that the innovation will be esteemed and retained. Similarly, if a teacher who has adopted a new teaching method finds that others on the teaching staff have copied her, she will probably feel that this confirms the wisdom of her change and will be encouraged to continue her new practices.

Usually, however, more direct kinds of positive evaluation and reward are necessary. If an industrial concern has changed its personnel practices or its procedures of communication between departments, it usually wants to find out if these changes have actually affected the efficiency or productivity of the working staff. Confirmation, in other words, must come in the form of objectively significant data. In large social systems such evaluations are not always easily obtained. As a result, desirable changes may be rejected on insufficient grounds simply because no adequate means of evaluation presents itself and the people concerned assume that no evaluation means a poor evaluation.

As we observed in Chapter 4, many systems possess an inherent momentum which tends to perpetuate a change once it has attained a certain state of equilibrium in the system's normal operations. In effect, this is a process of institutionalization: certain changes tend to endure simply because the system's progressive movement is a stronger force than that of any of its incipient retrogressive tendencies.

Again, procedural change may become stabilized because it is supported by structural change. For example, in a small staff group that we have observed, the practice of reviewing and assessing the results of meetings became institutionalized because at one point in its history the group accepted a written agenda for all its meetings which included as a final item "the evaluation of the meeting's success." Community and organizational work offer many more dramatic illustrations of the way in which structural changes may support and maintain different procedural changes. The inauguration of a suggestion box for employees tends to assure the institutionalization of a practice of reviewing and considering staff suggestions. The development and acceptance of a new rate of production for the assembly line may serve to perpetuate a heightened level of activity in all subparts of the manufacturing system.

PHASE 7. ACHIEVING
A TERMINAL RELATIONSHIP

We shall see in Chapter 9 that there is a variety of terminal adjustments among client systems and change agents. And we have already pointed out that the end of the change relationship may come as early as the third phase of the sequence. The problems which arise at the end of the relationship often depend on the point in the change sequence at which termination occurs.

Some change agents emphasize the problem of dependency as the major issue of the final phase. If the client system has come to depend heavily upon the change agent for support and guidance throughout the processes of diagnosis, change, and evaluation, then naturally the end of the relationship is likely to be a somewhat painful affair. The way in which these problems are solved can be particularly important in determining how effectively the client system will incorporate the desired change into its permanent existence.

Other questions arise too. Has the client system learned problem-solving techniques well enough to cope with new and different problems when the change agent is no longer present? Will changes internal to the client system produce unforeseen conflicts with the environment? Will the client system acquire harmful and half-understood doubts from other change agents whose conceptions of change are different? And so on.

Sometimes we note a special effort to build a substitute for the change agent into the permanent structure of the client system. For example, one organization terminated its relationship with the change agent at the point where he had helped them to train and organize "a program development and evaluation unit" within the staff. In another case a community institutionalized an annual self-survey as part of its permanent program before it dispensed with the services of the change agent. Some of the same problems which occur in Phase 2 also occur in this final phase, and it is particularly interesting to note the difference between change projects which are expected to terminate in the complete independence of the client system and those which end in the assurance that the change agent will continue to be available for consultations or renewed change effort if the system's new equilibrium is threatened by new problems and stresses.

In this chapter we have amplified one of the aspects of the change agent's job which we mentioned in the last chapter—his need to understand the several phases of the process of planned change.

We have suggested, on the basis of our study of the work of various change agents, that it is possible to identify seven such phases and that it is important for the change agent to differentiate among them if he is to choose the helping techniques which are most appropriate. And we have noted again that at all times, during each phase, the change agent's job is to help the client system work at the task of changing. This means that the relationship between the change agent and the client system, the channel through which all the agent's knowledge and influence must pass, is the most important single aspect of the change process.

We should here say once more that our sequential order of phases is too logical to represent the change process as it usually unfolds. In any given case one is likely to see that the phases overlap and repeat themselves. Yet the seven phases, as we have derived them from our case materials, actually do seem to fit almost all of the examples we have examined, and we believe that they are useful not only for the purposes of systematic analysis but also for the purposes of professional change agents who want to clarify and understand the working requirements of their job.

In the next three chapters we shall refer to our seven phases of change process in describing the professional techniques of giving help.

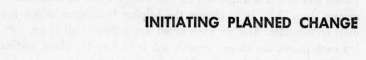

INITIATING PLANNED CHANGE

7

We turn now to the actual methods of giving help which have been reported by our sampling of change agents.

The literature of change reveals a considerable difference among change agents in respect to their awareness of the potential choices which can be made in the selection and application of working techniques. Some agents take pride in their professional ingenuity; they are at pains to perfect their choices of particular techniques for use at particular times and with particular client systems. Other agents seem to rely consistently upon the standard techniques which they acquired in their training or which have worked well in previous situations and which they assume to be generally applicable. Furthermore, even change agents whose work reveals a high degree of resourcefulness in the application of new and ingenious techniques are often unable to explain why a particular method seems appropriate to a particular situation. This inability to give explicit theoretical reasons for using one method rather than another makes it difficult for change agents to communicate effectively with one another about their significant experiences and inventions. As a result many change agents have difficulty con-

ceiving useful conditional generalizations about the helping techniques which they have created to meet the needs of particular
situations.

A few change agents seem to feel that to deliberate about one's
methods or about one's way of behaving toward the client system
reduces the spontaneity of one's good intentions and implies a
manipulative relationship with the client system. But most of the
professional helpers in our sample agree that the job of giving
help is a complex one and requires of the helper a high level of
awareness concerning the process of change and the choice of appropriate helping techniques. They realize that when one accepts
the responsibility of giving help a moral relationship is established which demands the helper's utmost purposiveness. This
means, obviously, that the change agent must give thought to
everything he does.

Change agents also differ greatly in the degree to which they
emphasize either the methods of maintaining and using the relationship with the client system or the methods of work used in
solving the problems of the client system. When we use the term
"helping method" we mean it to include both of these orientations
as well as any other activities which are conceived in terms of the
welfare of the client system. Thus helping methods include research, demonstration, role playing, free association, interpretation,
and in some cases even complete silence and inactivity.

Our description of helping methods in this and the two succeed-
ing chapters is not detailed enough to make this book a how-to-do-it
manual, and of course that is not our intention. Instead we are
trying to identify and classify some of the clusters of helping
methods that are related to certain change objectives and certain
phases of the change process. Our hope is that these categories
will provide suggestions and criteria for the selection of appropriate helping methods or the creation of new ones in particular
change situations. Much of what we hope to do is embodied in the
desire to make it easier for different groups of professional helpers to communicate with one another so that they may discover
how the techniques developed in one area of specialization or in
work with one type of client system may be relevant throughout

the province of professional help. We shall see, for instance, that change agents working with individuals and change agents working with communities can learn a lot from each other.

HELPING METHODS USED IN PHASE 1:
THE DEVELOPMENT OF A NEED FOR CHANGE

Our review of the reports written by change agents has led us to make a rough classification (see pp. 132-33) of three different types of starting points in the partnership between change agents and client systems.

First, the association may start when a change agent perceives a need for help in a particular client system and sets out to try to stimulate the system's awareness of its needs. His hope, of course, is that the system will decide to avail itself of his services.

Second, the change association may start when a third system, connected in some way with both the change agent and the potential client system, perceives the client system's need for help and takes the initiative in bringing the client system and the change agent together.

Third, the association may start when the client system itself becomes sensitive to its own malfunction and actively seeks help from an outside source. This is probably the most common type of starting point in work with personality systems, though not with larger systems. Some of the processes of Phase 1 in the change sequence may already have taken place when the first contact is made with the change agent in this type of initiation.

This classification of starting points into three types has been made so that we can use it as the framework for our consideration of helping methods which are relevant to the first stage of the change process.

Cases in which the change sequence
is initiated by a change agent

If our attention were focused solely upon the domain of the psychotherapists, we would soon conclude that virtually all change partnerships are initiated by client systems. Psychotherapists believe that the internal development of a need for help is a crucial element in the establishment and maintenance of a successful change association. In some recent literature, it is true, psychotherapists who are interested in preventive psychiatry have suggested ways of reaching out toward clients who may need help but do not seek it. As we look through the whole spectrum of change activity, however, we find a variety of situations in which the change agent takes the first step. It might be possible to construct a scale which would show, at the left end of the continuum, change agents who take the greatest initiative in organizing the change partnership and, at the right end, change agents who take the least initiative. If this were done, agents working with communities would be on the left and agents working with individuals would be on the right. Generally speaking, the larger a system is, the less organizational unity it demonstrates in recognizing problems and taking initiative to seek help.

It is interesting to note, though, that there are change agents working with each level of client system who have found it necessary to assume the initiative for beginning the change partnership. In each of these cases, however, they have also found it necessary to invent methods for doing this which would make their initiative an acceptable part of the change process. These agents have emphasized the need for stimulating a voluntary desire for help in the client system; the client should not feel that it is being forced to accept an influence relationship. Even when coercion has brought the agent and the client system together, as in the case of work with delinquent children, the agent's methods must usually be directed toward winning psychological acceptance and creating a desire for help.

In the last chapter we gave two illustrations of cases in which the change agent assumed the initiative for beginning the change association. The following are additional illustrations taken from our case materials.

A change agent is asked by an organization in Community X to speak at its annual banquet. He says that he would be glad to do so if the group would be willing to hear him talk on the subject of

"The Community Council Movement and How to Organize a Community Council."

The staff members of a university extension service invite leaders from a number of communities to meet together for a conference on community problems.

A change-agent team interested in community development recruits influential people in a number of communities to come together for a workshop on "Community Action Methods."

A university staff writes and distributes to community newspapers a series of articles on the establishment of a program of community consultation which is available to interested communities. This publicity is followed by letters to influential citizens.

A change-agent team persuades the management of a housing project to adopt a plan of desegregation and then to launch a program to interpret the new policy.

A child-guidance center and a county juvenile court collaborate in inviting the parents of delinquent children to attend a series of discussions.

The staff of a mental-health clinic organizes a social-relations training program for children who have been rejected by their classmates.

The chairmen of all program committees of organizations in Community X are invited to participate in a week-end training institute on program planning.

A management consultant asks the president of one of his client firms to introduce him to the head of another firm.

These illustrations show that in some cases the change agent's initiative consists of no more than telling people that his help is available, while in other cases he works actively to stimulate the potential client's awareness of a need for help. The range of initiatory activities is wide. Let us look in greater detail at some of the objectives and methods which have been most frequently reported by our sampling of change agents.

Methods by which change agents make known their availability and readiness to help. Two change-agent teams, both located at regional universities, have reported on their campaigns of newspaper publicity and their work in preparing descriptive brochures. Their object in conducting publicity campaigns was threefold: to describe their programs for giving help, to announce the facilities which they had at their disposal, and to tell potential client systems how they should go about asking for help. Another change agent, a training organization, has produced and distributed a report outlining the nature of its training program, the various types of client systems which have been helped in the past, and the ways in which previous clients have found their training beneficial. In preparing such literature, change agents have often received effective help from professional writers and public-relations counselors.

The staff of a county mental-health educational program has related the ways in which it has worked through organizational channels in calling attention to the availability of trained discussion leaders for community conferences on mental health. Another community mental-health group has reported that it made itself known chiefly by making the members of its staff available to community organizations which wanted speakers on the problems of mental health in modern life.

In another type of situation which has been described in our case materials, the availability of the change agent is announced after he has been employed by a whole system for the benefit of its various subparts. This is the case, for instance, in a school system which has employed a consultant. The consultant is then advertised as an available resource for each teacher in the system.

Other somewhat less direct ways for a change agent to communicate his accessibility are illustrated in the sections which follow.

Methods by which change agents stimulate an aspiration for improvement in client systems.   A fairly large number of change agents have described methods for stimulating new and more compelling "images of potentiality"—that is, new ideas about possible improvements—in the prospective client system. One worker has told about his insistence on choosing his own topics for after-dinner talks to community groups, a device which has allowed him to focus attention on successful changes which have been made in other communities. In his talks he emphasizes the good that can come from community development, with the result that his audiences often decide that they should emulate the success which has been achieved elsewhere. Another change-agent team prepares special case studies of significant change in other communities; these studies are then distributed to prospective client systems. One team of change agents has made motion pictures of cases of community development. Several change agents have emphasized the fact that such communications are most effective when they come not directly from the change agent but from the client systems which have already undergone a successful experiment in change. Pragmatic analyses of experience are more convincing than theoretical demonstrations of expertise. For example, one change agent uses a "workshop on wheels" to transport potential clients to other communities so that they can see what has been done and talk with participants in the change process. An industrial-consultant staff has described a similar operation: an industrial firm which had successfully completed a change process with the staff's help invited representatives from other firms to attend an open house, the purpose being to talk about the particular change processes in question and the agent's methods and objectives. In-service teacher-training units frequently report making use of demonstration classrooms where they can organize new and different teaching procedures and group activities. Unfortunately, however, the use of demonstration as a means of stimulating desire to change has been generally neglected in the areas of social relations and group dynamics. Workers in this area should study the techniques of demonstration which have been so carefully and skillfully developed by those in the fields of agriculture and technological change.

Methods by which change agents heighten or spread sensitivity to specific problems. Many of the change agents in our sample have recognized the necessity for taking steps to stimulate a keener awareness of problems within the potential client system. The chief objective in some cases is to obtain a more widespread awareness of the prospective client system's problem, especially where awareness is at first limited to a particularly sensitive subpart. The methods which change agents use to evoke a contagion of awareness might in many cases be called shock techniques. For instance, one team of community workers found that in order to actuate a community self-survey on the processes of intergroup relations it seemed advisable to dramatize the discrepancy between professed values and accepted practices in the community's routine activities. The change agent said in effect, "This is what you say you believe, but look what you are doing." Another change-agent team has written about its success in organizing feedback sessions to report the results of a survey to parents, teachers, and children. In the survey each group had been asked what it thought the other groups expected of it and what it expected of the others. The feedback sessions then showed what a wide variance there was between the expectations which each group actually held and the expectations which the other groups believed it held. Here the change agent said, "This is what you think you are expected to do, but *this* is what you are really expected to do. What do you make of the large discrepancy?" Another case study reports an instance in which the administrators of a company were given an opportunity to provide themselves with their own complacency shock. In this instance a procedure of role playing was set up in such a way that the administrators stepped into the roles of employees and experienced the employer-employee relationship from a new perspective. In the course of doing so they learned many things they had not realized before about their relationships with their employees. Again, a report by the staff of a leadership-training workshop describes a somewhat similar procedure of role reversal, used in this case to quicken sensitivity to the feelings and problems of others in intergroup relations.

The staff of one training program reports an experiment in which all the members of the group were told what the other members thought of their behavior and how the other members wanted them to change. The anonymity of all participants was of course preserved. All the information gathered was summarized and interpreted to individual members by a training leader. This flow of information resulted in a new sensitivity to interpersonal problems in members of the group who until then had been unaware of the group's complex relationships.

One team of community change agents reports an interesting method for evoking awareness of community needs. One of the team established himself in a small community as an observer. His job was to win acceptance from the citizens of the community but at the same time to be a persistent questioner making thoughtful inquiries about aspects of community life which seemed to need improvement. The result was that problems which the citizens had not recognized as such, because they were used to them, began to appear in a new light, and the community thus became aware of some of its needs.

Several change agents have described methods of inducing a spread of problem awareness throughout a client system by utilizing the system's more sensitive persons or subgroups in a kind of collaborating network. In one of the community mental-health projects, for instance, workers created a "referral network" throughout the community, using persons who were sensitive to the problems of mental health to stimulate sensitivity in others and to help locate sources of trouble. Another community program has developed a system for locating influential persons who are ready to receive training in the skills of stimulating community-wide awareness of common needs and problems.

What is called a "problem census" is an example of another type of technique which has been described by various workers. One team of community change agents, for example, held an "area conference" to which important citizens from a number of communities were invited; the discussion centered on points of trouble which could occur in any community. Thus each citizen could make a "census" of his own community's needs. Such discussions help people to think more clearly and specifically about the problems they face in daily community life. Other change agents have described a good many variations of the problem census, a technique which has proved exceedingly useful in provoking intelligent interest in the collective problems of a social system.

Methods by which change agents offer help in solving an acknowledged problem.   Often one encounters problem situations in which there is a high degree of sensitivity to the problem itself but very little impetus to seek aid in solving it. In such cases the change agent need not be concerned about arousing a heightened awareness of the problem; his job is to find some means of transforming the existing awareness into help-seeking action. One of the most frequent means of doing this, especially in the larger social units, is by telling one subpart that a comparable concern about the problem exists in another subpart and that the two subparts might profit by coming together to explore ways of solving their problems. Here the change agent functions as a liaison; he merely induces communication between the subparts of a system in which there has been blockage or apathy. A consensus then often arises within the system on the need for help. For example, one change agent has said that in beginning a particular community change process the easiest way to bring citizens together was to invite them to talk about a specific problem of intergroup conflict which was causing much anxiety but which evoked very little spontaneous communication. The desire to be relieved of their anxiety by sharing it with others led the citizens to accept the change agent's invitation to discuss this specific problem, and once they were together they went on to propose concrete solutions not only to this problem but to others as well. Another change agent, whose work was with industrial organizations, has described his method of bringing together the members of the top-level staff in the client system. Each of them individually was dissatisfied with discussions at staff meetings, but each also felt that the others did not share this dissatisfaction. When the agent brought them together and pointed out the mutuality of their concern regarding the quality of staff discussions, they were at first surprised, but they soon realized that by concerted action they could in fact do something to overcome their difficulties. This kind of mutual misunderstanding is exceedingly common in all types of social relationships and is called "pluralistic ignorance" (98) by social psychologists.

Another quite different orientation toward change is that of agents who work in terms of utilization of a power conflict. Here the awareness of the client system's problem is already acute; it has taken the form of a grievance toward vested interests outside the system. The change agent uses this grievance as a springboard for the change relationship by identifying himself strongly with the goals of the client system and offering his help as an additional source of strength in the conflict with the outside interests. Such partisanship is a departure from the role of neutrality which most change agents recommend in most situations. Sometimes the power conflict occurs wholly within the client system, in which case the change agent identifies himself with the aggrieved subpart and works toward a resolution of the problem through the settlement of the subpart's claims. We shall return to some of these problems in our analysis of the later phases of the change process.

Methods by which change agents create special social atmospheres in which the accepted standard is to recognize the existence of problems and the need for help.   One can acknowledge a problem and allow oneself to seek help in solving it much more easily if the social climate encourages this kind of self-awareness than if one feels isolated in one's difficulties. If the change agent can create a special social situation in which it is considered perfectly all right to have a problem and to want help in solving it, then the client system will probably feel much better about asking the change agent to help. One change-agent team reports at some length its attempt to create a training laboratory where the members of the team could illustrate by their own values and behavior the social acceptability and "normalcy" of the change process. The theory was that when potential clients were introduced into this atmosphere they would learn that the desire to understand their problems and remedy them was both natural and respectable. In such a social climate the person who asks for help is behaving according to the group standard; since others do not consider his behavior deviant, he does not do so himself. This technique of creating a "permissive atmosphere" will enter many points of our discussion of change techniques.

The variety of illustrations which we have used so far is by no means exhaustive. The number of specific techniques which have been invented by change agents who are interested in encouraging a desire for help in a potential client system is large and diversified.

Cases in which the change sequence is initiated by a third party

In our case materials there are a number of illustrations of change efforts which have begun when the change agent and the client system were brought together by a third party. Here are two examples:

> A mother whose son and daughter-in-law are suffering from marital difficulties asks a marriage counselor if there is anything he can do to help.

> The shopkeepers and citizens of a particular neighborhood ask a change agent—in this case a social agency—to make contact with a delinquent gang which has been disturbing the life of the community.

In addition, there are a number of cases which could be reported equally well in this section or in the next one. These are cases in which one subpart of a system comes to a change agent and suggests that he should establish a relationship with another part of the system. A representative of management in a particular company, for example, may attempt to bring about a relationship between a change agent and his company's labor force in order to remedy certain problems which management believes are interfering with the company's welfare.

Most of the cases we have reviewed seem to be illustrative of situations in which the third party experiences specific discomfort as a result of a malfunction in the proposed client system, sometimes only because the third party is closely identified with the client system and sometimes because the third party is itself suffering from the client system's disruptive activities or ineffectualities. We looked through our case materials to see whether or not we could find a case of a third party offering help for reasons other than self-interest, and we did find one or two examples. At a conference of organization leaders, for instance, the leader of one company reported to his colleagues the success which his organization had experienced in working with a particular change agent. He offered to introduce to the change agent any of his colleagues who were interested, and later several introductions were actually made. In such instances, rather than being driven by a need to reduce its own discomfort, the third party is motivated by a desire to help stimulate further development in the neighboring systems.

Most of the initiatory techniques used by change agents in cases where contact with the potential client system has been brought about by a third party are the same as those which we have already discussed in the previous section. Even when the first move is made by a third party, the change agent must win the confidence and stimulate the problem awareness of the client system. However, there are one or two special techniques which are worth mentioning briefly.

Clarifying the relationship with the third party. In the cases which we are considering now the change agent not only finds himself in a triangular situation, but he is always in touch with the third party before he is in touch with the client system. Hence he may be suspected of being in collusion with the third party. He may have to prove that he is not before he can win the approval of the client system. In the report on work with delinquent gangs, for instance, the change agent describes in great detail the suspiciousness of the gang and the extreme difficulty of proving that he was not in league with the police or the courts. It was a question of proving that he understood and sympathized with the gang while at the same time withholding approval of many of the gang's activities. This presented many difficult problems which could be solved only by the development of great skill in responding to delinquent sensibilities. In a situation of this kind the change agent must arrive beforehand at an agreement with the third party about the ways in which he will conduct himself in his dealings with the client system; this is especially true when the third party occupies a position of authority. In the case we mentioned earlier of the change agent who was invited by the management of a company to establish a relationship with its labor force, the change agent's first job was to come to an understanding with management. He needed to be sure that he was free to exercise his independent judgment in solving the labor problem; he had to extricate himself from any taint of partnership with management before he could take up his responsibilities as a professional helper with labor. Similarly, in the case of the mother whose child would not eat, the change agent (therapist) needed first of all to make it clear to the mother that he could not accept her goal of making the child eat more until after he had judged the child's problem on the basis of his independent and professional criteria and after he had obtained whatever help he could from the child in clarifying the nature of the problem.

Hence in cases which are initiated by the action of a third party, clarifying the relationship with the third party is a necessary precondition to winning the acceptance of the potential client system.

Using the third party as an aid in giving help. The example of the organization leader who introduced his colleagues to a change agent demonstrates one way in which the third party can often be more effective in stimulating the client system's readiness for help than the change agent himself. In this case the leader's friendly recommendation had already paved the way toward acceptance before the change agent had done anything at all.

Similar aid from the third party is illustrated in the examples of the delinquent gangs and the problem child. In the case of the gangs, for instance, one of the important aspects of the disruptive relationship between the gangs and the third party (that is, the surrounding community) was the feeling of mutual hostility which had developed and was being maintained. Recrimination and retaliation followed each other in a vicious cycle. The change agent was able to break this cycle by inducing the third party to make a friendly gesture, an offer of certain recreational facilities to the gangs. In this way the change agent used the third party as an important factor in the helping program for the client system, and this help had a good deal to do with the success of the change effort as a whole. In the same way, the change agent who dealt with the problem of the child who refused to eat used the third party, the mother, as an aid in his program to help the child to change; he persuaded the mother to change her attitude toward the child, thus facilitating the child's realistic adjustment to its own problems.

It is probable that a wider survey of the literature of change would reveal other ways in which change agents give help to a client system through using the influence of connected systems. By this means the change agent exerts his initiative indirectly, working through systems whose strategic position in relation to the client system is in one way or another more favorable than his own.

Let us turn now to our third type of change situation, that in which the potential client system acts independently to take the first step.

Cases in which the change sequence is initiated by the client system

In the terms of our sequence of change phases this third category represents a situation which is psychologically different from that found in the first two patterns of initiative. Here the potential client system has already negotiated at least part of the first phase in the sequence by the time the change agent appears on the scene. The system has already become sensitive to its need for help, has already discovered that help is available, has already turned to a source of help outside the system. Here are some examples:

The management staff of an industrial organization has become sensitive to interpersonal malfunctions which have created blocks and stoppages in the procedures of staff meetings; the staff members agree unanimously to seek the help of a consultant.

An individual feels that his internal tensions make it impossible for him to work productively, and he decides to see a psychiatrist.

The program committee of a parents' organization becomes more and more disturbed about the number of members who are not attending meetings. The committee makes an appointment with a social scientist from a nearby university and asks his advice.

The administrator of a hospital grows alarmed at the degree of intergroup friction among the various units of his organization. Points of disturbance have developed between the laundry and nursing staffs, the attendants and staff nurses, the nursing supervisors and the medical staff. The administrator seeks help from a group which offers training in human relations.

A number of fraternities in a university community feel under great pressure from the community at large because the citizens criticize their practices in admitting new members. The fraternities seek consultation with a research staff which can help them to diagnose their problem clearly and explore alternative courses of action.

The manager of an industrial plant becomes concerned over the rate of absenteeism among his employees and the consequent drop in the rate of productivity. He calls in the representative of a consultant organization.

In all these cases a rising level of "pain" has disposed the client system to seek relief. The symptoms are painful and help is needed. In the first two cases, those of the small group and the individual, the whole system has collaborated in the decision to seek contact with a potential change agent. In the other cases only a small part of the whole system took this first step, and this suggests a number of hypotheses which we shall explore later. Possibly in larger systems the subparts find it so difficult to communicate with one another on matters of this degree of delicacy that the initiative toward change can come only from a small segment of the whole organization. Or it may be that only certain subparts of large systems become sensitive to pain because they are the only parts in a position to feel pain, that is, they are in central or especially vulnerable locations within the system. And in some systems perhaps only certain subparts possess the means to articulate a need for help.

Another question comes up. Must a system be in pain to feel a need for help? The answer is no. We find a number of cases where the motivation to change seems to derive not from the need for relief but from the positive attraction of a potential improvement. Very often this aspiration toward improvement seems to be a symptom of health. We have called this an "image of potentiality," and it may develop in a number of ways. For example:

The executive of a manufacturing plant visits a neighboring plant and finds a higher rate of productivity than he has been able to achieve among his own employees. The mangement of the neighboring plant attributes its success to a profit-sharing plan. The executive seeks out a consultant and asks for advice on introducing such a plan into his own organization.

From her reading of professional literature a classroom teacher has acquired a number of clear ideas about things she would like to do differently in her own work, but she feels that she doesn't know how to make the changes. She enrolls in a summer workshop to learn how these changes can be made.

A particular industrial firm has enjoyed a good deal of success in the past and attributes it to a policy of keeping in close touch with new developments in technology. New machines and new inventions have been quickly introduced to raise productivity. By analogy, the leaders of the firm decide that they might extend the area of their success if they adopted a similar policy toward new developments in the applied social sciences, especially as they might affect employee morale, personnel practices, and so forth. The leaders agree to seek advice from a social-research institute.

These examples show that there may be a number of reasons for seeking help in addition to the need for relief from pain. Part or all of the system may aspire to become like some other system which has been demonstrably successful. The system may have acquired a rather concrete image of betterment without having learned the techniques by which betterment may be achieved. Or the system may be generally oriented toward improvement: past successes in change may have established a momentum toward continuous change, continuous readjustment to the possibilities of improvement which are offered by the advances of the physical and social sciences.

In trying to decide how to respond to such requests for help, a change agent must ask himself a number of questions. Is the system, or a significant part of it, really ready to accept help? Are my resources relevant to the process of improvement which the system wants to follow? Do I really want to help this particular system? Do I have enough time to devote to these new responsibilities? These are the questions which the change agent must at least consider—even if he does not answer them completely at the moment—before he can accept a working relationship with the client system. We have already said that such questions as these normally belong to the second phase of the change sequence: in cases where the client is eager for help the first phase has often been completed before the change agent is called upon. In cases where the change agent must exert himself to stimulate a need for change and a desire for help, he has at least by implication already committed himself to giving help if it is wanted, thus having put part of Phase 2 before Phase 1. The reader will remember that we have pointed out more than once the way in which our sequential schematization may be altered in the intricacies of actual change processes. This is a good example. But in almost all cases there still remains something for the change agent to do by way of defining the realities of the change relationship and establishing its limits. This is Phase 2. It calls for the use of a number of specific techniques, and these are therefore what we shall consider next.

HELPING METHODS USED IN PHASE 2:
THE ESTABLISHMENT OF A CHANGE RELATIONSHIP

In this section we shall scrutinize the problems which various change agents have reported they met in Phase 2 of the change sequence—that is, in establishing and defining the nature of the change relationship and in clarifying the mutual expectations of the agent and the client about what is to be done, how it is to be done, how long it will take, and the like. Many change agents have nothing to say directly about these questions. Others make only brief comments. Our comparative summary contains both our inferences about the orientations of various change agents and their explicit statements of practice.

Assessing the capacity to accept and use help

Most of the psychotherapists in our sample agree that a certain "ego involvement" is a precondition to the client system's assuming a responsible role in the change process. Clients must demonstrate a readiness to establish at least some kind of rapport with the therapist if there is to be any basis for communication. This is true even in cases where the therapist is prepared to work at nonverbal levels of communication.

The same type of problem appears in different forms as we turn to the work of change agents who are concerned with larger social systems. We can make the analogy between individual and larger systems by rephrasing the psychotherapist's problem of communication as a concern for the client's capacity to make "data from the inside" available to the change agent. Several of the change agents in our sample who have worked with organizations report that this has been the substance of their first question; in other words, they have asked the subpart which approached them (for example, the personnel department) whether or not its position in the total organization of the client system was such that it could provide the information about the total system which the change agent needed in order to make his diagnosis and recommend an appropriate change procedure. In the same way, the change agent needs to know whether or not the particular subpart which has approached him is representative of the total system and will be able to guarantee a continuing working relationship with him. Two reports, one on work with a group of hospital nurses and the other on work with the foremen of a factory, mention failure in this respect: although the nurses and the foremen had in each case been the first to approach the change agent, neither group was able to establish a sound link of communication with the total system. Hence the change agents were unable to obtain the information which they needed in order to diagnose the problems of the client systems.

Some of our community change projects seem to provide a rough parallel to psychotherapeutic problems of ego development; in a number of cases the community system suffered from such a lack of integration or cohesiveness that the change agents experienced great difficulty in sustaining a collaborative relationship. An interesting analogy is suggested between the efforts of Redl and Wineman (14) to support and stimulate ego development in such a way that it would permit the growth of an active working relationship with the change agent, and the efforts of some community change agents to stimulate the development of a cohesive corps of individuals with enough community awareness to collaborate in solving community-development problems.

Another question of capacity arises in work with larger social systems. Is the particular subpart with which the agent is connected able to change, and if it is, can it influence the total system to change? Examples have been reported in which the particular sub-group developed a strong motivation to change but was unable to effect the change because of the weakness of its position in relation to the other parts of the total system. In several cases organiza-tional problems of this nature led to completely negative results and an intensification of the system's basic difficulties. The change agents were able to conclude only that they had been mistaken when they entered into helping relationships with the particular subgroups without also establishing firmer connections with other parts of the total systems. We shall see that this problem recurs in each of the phases of the change sequence.

We have been surprised to find in our investigations how little of this kind of preliminary exploring many change agents have done. One might think that the potential client's capacity to change would be a basic question, yet many change agents seem quite willing to take on a new job without exploring the internal stresses and capacities involved. Perhaps the reason lies in the lack of ade-quate post-change evaluative techniques; most change agents are unable to tell after they have completed a project precisely how much influence they have had on their client system's course of change. Consequently, it is difficult for them to establish criteria for measuring a system's capacity to use help and to employ these criteria in work with the next potential client.

Assessing the motivation to accept and use help

The most frequent assumption in the work with individuals as client systems seems to be that a feeling of pain and the hope of securing some relief assure the necessary and appropriate motiva-tional conditions for beginning a helping relationship. The develop-ment of a cohesive relationship between the change agent and the client system, plus the assurance given by feelings of progress, will then provide the motive power for the continuation of the working relationship. Relatively few questions seem to be raised about the possibilities of inappropriate types of motivation for seeking help. Some of the change agents working in the field of leadership train-ing and human-relations training have attempted to formulate criteria for the assessment of appropriate motivation. The most frequent assessment question seems to go something like this: "Is this person who is seeking help motivated primarily by a desire to achieve more power over other persons or by an attempt to achieve more understanding of and power over himself?" Clearly, this is a very difficult question on which to get information. A little further probing makes the question even more difficult, because most change agents working with individuals recognize that it is not necessarily undesirable for a personality system to be motivated by a wish to acquire more effective means of influencing other persons. The problem becomes whether the newly acquired resources for influence are likely to be used in the interest of constructive or destructive means and goals, whether they will be used to achieve coercive domination or responsible leadership.

Change agents who work with organizations and communities raise the same kind of question. Is the subpart which is seeking help motivated by a desire to achieve a more dominant position within the client system? If the answer is yes, this need not signify merely a destructive ambition to rule. Many change agents who work with communities make it their explicit practice to assist the formation of new power centers which will promote the welfare of the total system rather than the vested interests of an entrenched subgroup. Here again it becomes a question of determining why a particular element wants to gain power, and to answer this the change agent must rely on his observations and insights.

Change agents working with industrial organizations also report a problem in the assessment of motivations. Some agents have shied away from jobs in which the vested interests of management appeared to ask for a change program aimed at countering the demands of labor and preventing the distribution of power and benefits. Other agents have maintained that it is impossible for any agent to take responsibility for judging motivations in cases of this sort. They feel that if they can enlighten any subpart of a system by conveying to it the best scientific knowledge about human relations, the entire system will be benefited in the long run. These questions of professional standards and ethics affect many aspects of the change agent's job, and we shall be returning to them later.

Assessing change-agent resources and motivation

Although few of the change agents we studied present explicit analyses of this aspect of beginning a helping relationship, a number of different assumptions seem to be clear from the approaches which have been described. Some change agents who work with all levels of client systems seem to make the assumption that the particular helping procedure which they have developed or which they have been trained in is appropriate for most of the problems of most of the client systems with which they work. The methods themselves vary greatly, of course, from the free-association and interpretation procedure of the psychoanalytic session, the group observer and feedback procedures of some of the workers with small groups, and the diagnostic-survey and recommendation procedure with organizations, to the community self-survey with working committees. The particular method used is the major resource of the change agent as a helper and is considered an appropriate contribution to the wide range of problems and client systems.

A second orientation emphasizes the amount of professional training of the change agent. The assumption here seems to be that if the change agent has had accredited training experience he has the resourcefulness to cope with the problems which will arise regarding a variety of client systems.

In some kinds of work, particularly with large client systems, agents are tending more and more to emphasize the need for a division of specialized services such as one finds in certain change-agent teams in order to provide the range of resources which is required for complex jobs. For example, some change-agent teams include members who never come in contact with the client system but instead apply their specialized knowledge to the processing of data; other members of the team specialize in collecting the data, and still others in interpreting and using the data after it has been collected and processed. Other teams may be divided into sections which can work effectively with different subparts of a large system; for example, in industrial relations some change-agent teams include both specialists in labor and specialists in management. In some community projects teams may make a geographic division of labor so that the helping relationship may be carried on on several fronts at the same time.

In this matter of commitments and responsibilities one of the greatest differences among change agents concerns their perspective on the amount of time which the agent and client must agree to spend in working together. Some agents organize their work in such a way that the change relationship consists of no more than a single consultation. Others think in terms of a more intensive but still relatively brief process; they make a diagnosis and recommend a course of action, but then leave the client system to carry on alone. Still other agents proceed in terms of a clearly delimited sequence of interactions in which the timetable itself controls the progress of change. This would occur in the fifteen weeks of a training course, for instance, or the twenty-two weeks of a community self-survey, or the three intensive weeks of a summer workshop. Some agents, on the contrary, say that the length of the change process must depend solely upon the dynamics of the change itself. These agents differ among themselves about the point at which the change relationship should end, but most of them have in mind a developmental sequence of change against which they can measure any particular case; each change effort must reach a certain point of completion before the change agent can consider his responsibility fulfilled.

In a series of interviews with a small sample of change agents we found that the problem which causes the greatest concern is that which arises when the original estimate of the time required for a given change process turns out to be too short. When this happens the change agent is often unable to give as much time and energy to the later phases of the change effort as he would like to, and he may suffer from feelings of guilt on this account. At the same time, the client system may grow discouraged as the time perspective is extended, and the whole change effort may deteriorate rapidly.

Beyond these questions of time, energy, and skill, the change agent must consider his own motives in entering any new change relationship. Some agents obviate any possible difficulty on this score by refusing jobs in which they cannot identify themselves completely with the goals and values of the client system. More frequently, agents emphasize the need for personal control over their inclinations to become involved in the conflicts or commitments of the client system; they believe that they must attempt to maintain an "outsider's" objectivity if they are to help the client system explore the realities of the problem situation. Psychotherapists have experimented for a long time in order to establish the kind of professional training which will give a change agent the necessary objectivity.

Another motivational problem arises for change agents who combine an interest in helping the client system with an interest in contributing to scientific progress. Some agents, for instance, collect data for research while the change effort is in progress. Agents must decide whether or not this divided loyalty to quite different helping goals will interfere with the helping relationship to the client system. As we shall see in a later section of this chapter, most change agents seem to agree that their responsibilities to the client and their responsibilities to science are not incompatible.

Obtaining a mutuality of expectation for the change relationship

In the second phase of the process of change there are often a number of subphases. Very frequently we find that the change agent and the client system agree to a trial period, for instance, during which they can test one another's attitudes and capabilities before they embark on a protracted relationship. The change agent may feel that he needs a closer look at the client system's problems before he can decide definitely whether or not he is able to help. The client may want time to satisfy himself about the agent's capabilities or motives, or he may want to test the acceptability of the agent to other subparts of the client system. But whether there is a specific trial period or not, most change agents describe the beginning of the change relationship as a time of testing and clarifying mutual expectations for the progress of the relationship thereafter. By a process of verbal communication and more or less covert observation, each party adjusts himself to the other, and the success of this adjustment—its reliability and durability—is an important determinant of the success of the whole change effort.

Usually the client system has definite preconceptions about the ease and speed with which his problems will be solved, and many change agents have emphasized the danger which these preconceptions present to agent and client alike. Above all, the client must not be allowed to fall into the trap of believing that his case will be solved more quickly or easily than it can be. Most change agents assume, for instance, that even though they may begin with the client system's definition of the problem, further diagnostic explorations will reveal more fundamental difficulties, more complex underlying problems. These must be solved if there is to be an effective change. Hence the client's original ideas about his difficulties and the length of time it will take to remedy them may be totally upset, with the result that the client becomes disheartened and inclined to give up. This means that from the very first, even before he knows what the client's problem really is, the wise agent will caution the client to expect hard work. He will do this in order to forestall the false optimism which the client is likely to feel simply because he has made contact with the agent and has derived a sense of reassurance from putting his problems in expert hands. If the client's false expectations are allowed to continue, the chances are the change relationship will break up before any real help can be rendered.

Another point which often must be worked on early in the relationship concerns the number and identity of the people who need to be involved in the change process. Such a question doesn't come up in most cases of individual psychotherapy, although sometimes in work with children or families several people may be involved in the therapeutic context. In these latter cases, for example, the therapist may be at pains to establish an expectation for the entry of a parent into the helping relationship between the therapist and the child. But usually in change programs occurring at the level of the larger systems a number of people or groups are involved. Research on community-leadership training, for example, has revealed that it is more effective to train teams than individuals.

Similarly, many agents who have worked with industrial organizations point out the necessity of establishing an initial expectation that both union and management officials will be involved in any change process. The reports of the Tavistock staff (36) put a heavy emphasis on the advisability of conducting rather detailed discussions among all the subparts of an organization in order to arrive at a consensus on the desirability of establishing a working relationship with a given change agent. Agents who have worked with communities point out that the change agent in this setting has especially difficult problems of deciding which groups he should begin to work with. He may work with a group which consists of representatives from the various subparts of the community, he may form a new group with a special interest in community welfare and improvement, or he may choose to start with one of the official or semi-official elements of the community, such as a community council. In any case, though the change agent hopes to work toward a broader involvement of community subparts as the change project moves along, he usually cannot expect a very broad base of contact or very formal contact with the community in the beginning. Usually he must develop his relationship with the community from small beginnings.

Clarifying expectations about the kind and amount of work which will be required

One advantage of having concrete demonstrations of change to review with a prospective client system is that the client can see for himself what types of effort he will probably have to make in order to accomplish the desired change. This avoids a good deal of misunderstanding about the respective responsibilities of the two parties to the change relationship. Some kinds of relationships are much easier to clarify in this respect than others. Some change agents who have developed community self-survey procedures are able to show in precise detail what kind and amount of work will be expected from the citizens of the community at each stage of the surveying process. Similarly, these expectations can usually be established clearly in training programs and workshops. But it is much more difficult to achieve this clarity of understanding in cases where the progress of change is determined very largely by the dynamics of the change relationship and by the way in which new problems and new facets of old problems emerge as the change process advances. In such cases new resistances to work are likely to develop in the course of the change relationship; new responsibilities will devolve upon both parties as unforeseen predicaments arise. In some cases, such as that of a group-development program in a school system, it seems safe to predict that the change relationship will last for a very long time and that it will be reviewed and renewed periodically.

The change agent must try to find a creative compromise between discouraging the client system and leaving it without any clear concept of what will be expected. If the client is too discouraged by the work prospect, he will abandon the change project before it starts; if, on the other hand, he is allowed to form his own conceptions of the work to be done, he is likely to create a falsely optimistic view, in which case his discouragement is only temporarily delayed. Where the compromise will fall in any particular case cannot be predetermined, of course. Everything depends on the change agent's ability to judge each of the factors of personality and capacity which are presented to him in the specific circumstances of his work.

Anticipating difficulties which will emerge in the change relationship

Here again the change agent must strike a balance between realism and optimism. He must help the client system to understand at least some of the problems which may come up in the course of their working relationship, but at the same time he must avoid giving the client system a view of the future which will be too discouraging at the outset. The change agent's job will be made easier or harder by the nature of the individual case and the kind of client system with which he is dealing. It is probably a good deal easier, for instance, to help a citizens' committee anticipate some of the problems of blockage and resistance which may be created by other parts of the community in the course of the change effort than it is to help an individual understand the kinds of internal conflict which will develop in the course of psychotherapy. A typical example of change strategy is provided in the case of the agent who was working with mothers of feeding-problem children. He told the mothers at the outset that there would be no immediate reward for their changes in behavior toward their children; in other words, he established a "pain perspective." We are not told how much this pain perspective helped the mothers to carry on during the difficult period when their change efforts seemed to be useless. However, it was probably an important factor in supporting their change efforts.

Several change agents whose work has involved intensive therapy with individuals and small groups have emphasized the importance of telling the client system at the beginning that the change relationship will probably encounter severe strains as the therapeutic processes unfold. The object in so doing is to help the client system realize that these strains are quite normal and should be expected. The agents report that by establishing this expectation of strain at the outset they have helped their clients to maintain a working relationship even during periods of strong resistance or ambivalence.

Defining the influence relationship

Many change agents emphasize the importance of clarifying the relative positions of influence of the change agent and the client system at the beginning of the change relationship. In many coercive relationships, for instance, in which the change or treatment has been ordered by an external authority, all power may appear to reside solely with the change agent. This is the case when delinquent children are committed to a welfare agency by the courts or when the board of directors of an industrial firm orders the administrative staff to reorganize. Without exception, change agents who deal with these types of cases agree that somehow, in spite of the coercive nature of the initial situation, the client system must be helped to develop a voluntary readiness for change; otherwise the change relationship cannot succeed. The client system must willingly accept the influence of the change agent. But this means that the client system must believe that it also possesses influence over the change agent and over the course of the helping process. Change agents seem to agree that the client must never feel that it is the object of a one-way power relationship. Some client systems want to lean heavily on the change agent, want to develop a relationship of dependency. Change agents differ a good deal among themselves in their ideas on the value of allowing such a dependency to occur. In some kinds of change efforts a dependent client system may be desirable, at least in certain phases of the change relationship; in other kinds of cases dependency should never be allowed to occur. But even change agents who emphasize the importance of a dependency relationship usually also emphasize the importance of allowing the client system to set its own pace and end the change process whenever it wants to. The main point is that the early association of the change agent and the client system will establish the tone of their working relationship. Consequently, the change agent has the job of making the reciprocal-influence situation as clear as possible early in the change relationship.

Clarification of special goals of the change agent

A fairly large number of change agents report that in much of their work they have been guided by additional objectives beyond the needs of the client system. They have wanted to help the client system, but they have also wanted to do something else. Some have been interested in research which would contribute to general scientifically validated knowledge. Others have used the particular case on which they were working as a demonstration in which they could exhibit their specialized change techniques for the benefit of other, potential client systems. Most change agents agree that it is exceedingly important to tell the client system about these additional objectives and to obtain the client's acceptance of them. This should be done at the beginning of the change relationship. Change agents report that many client systems are actually pleased to know that their change experience may be a contribution to other systems as well as a help to themselves. In some cases clients have voluntarily taken a good deal of extra trouble to provide the records and other data which were necessary for research or demonstrations. On the other hand, clients have sometimes objected to a demonstration which required that they, as participants, should be kept in the dark about the progress of the change experiment even while they were being asked for their full co-operation. But, on the whole, clients have often been helped and encouraged by the knowledge that their change effort was a contribution toward a larger objective.

So far in this chapter we have reviewed briefly some of the considerations which change agents have discussed in their reports on the methods of establishing an effective change relationship. Most of the change agents give very little explicit description of the techniques which they use at this stage. So far our aim has been to show the kind and quality of thought which goes into the first stages of the change relationship. The giving and accepting of help is not just a spontaneous matter of good will, not simply a question of offering help or asking for it. Even before he makes a specific offer, the change agent must know his own capacities and objectives, and from the first moment of contact with the client system he must devise a dynamic *modus operandi* and guide it as it evolves. He must establish the expectations with which both client and agent face forward into the days or months or years of their association. Unfortunately, we lack full reports about failures which have occurred in this early stage; most change agents have not reported on cases where the client system withdrew before the actual work of change had begun or where the change agent himself decided not to pursue the relationship. We need much more information of this type before we can create a really satisfactory theoretical analysis of these first stages in the change process.

SOME COMPARATIVE OBSERVATIONS
ON CHANGE METHODS

In this chapter and the next two we are trying to determine whether or not the methods of giving help which are used by the various types of change agents are similar enough in their range and variety to allow us to talk about them within a common conceptual framework. At the same time we want to learn as much as we can about the differences among the methods used in work with individuals, groups, organizations, and communities. It is these differences upon which we should like to concentrate now. Let us stop, therefore, in our sequential analysis of the phases of change and consider the differences among methods which have appeared so far in Phases 1 and 2.

We have already pointed out certain obvious differences in the source of initiative for establishing the change relationship. We showed that the initiative shifts from the client to the agent as one progresses from small to large units. Agents who work with individuals typically rely on the spontaneous awakening of problem awareness within the client system. (The exception, though it is just beginning, occurs in certain community mental-health programs where the staffs have attempted to generate public sensitivity to certain kinds of mental-health problems.) Furthermore, agents who work with individuals have tended to rely on their conspicuousness as members of an established profession to provide potential client systems with sufficient information about where to seek help.

So far there is no well-defined corps of professional change agents who work with face-to-face groups as client systems. Often such small groups are parts of larger organizations, that is, staff units, work groups, or committees. Generally speaking, small groups do not seem to acquire a spontaneously articulated desire for help. The small group probably has more difficulty than either the individual or the organization in taking the initiative to establish a relationship with a change agent. This may be because a face-to-face group is sufficiently small as a unit to need unanimity before it can act in such important matters, yet large enough to encounter resistance and ineptness of communication when matters of delicacy arise. In the few cases of work with small groups which we were able to include in our study, the change agent usually found it necessary to take a great deal of initiative. He called attention to other groups which had found ways to improve their efficiency, or he pointed out that a self-survey might be a safe and interesting thing to do. Small groups, perhaps simply because they are small, are vulnerable to many threats, internal and external, and they proceed with great caution. In a few cases, however, the group's power figure (for example, a chairman or classroom teacher) may feel free to seek professional help without first securing the consent of the entire membership.

At the level of work with organizations, change-agent teams occupy a much more prominent professional role. They are likely to be visible on the horizon of the potential client system. These teams often communicate their availability by active demonstrations of their past successes, and they are usually quite ready to show any potential client system the ways in which they can help it. In other words, the initiative for establishing the change relationship exists almost palpably in the atmosphere of business, industry, governmental units, and the like, and many organizations are made highly aware of their own potential difficulties by the publications, demonstrations, and advertisements which are initiated by the change agents. Often the awareness of a problem and the desire to seek outside help are generated more or less spontaneously in the executive echelon of an organization; leaders can think freely about improvements in their organizations because they as persons are usually affected only indirectly by any changes which may be made. Another factor which may compel a system's readiness to change is its competitive business relationship with other systems. Competition makes it easy for organizational leaders to think in terms of improving their competitive status without any connotation of present weakness or failure.

Perhaps the patterns of initiation in the change relationship are most strikingly different in the case of work with communities. As we have already noted, most change efforts in communities are originated by change agents whose motives derive from a sense of mission and a belief in the human values of community development. Here, clearly, initiative belongs to the agent. But the agent's target is seldom the individuals or groups at the top of the community's power structure. Often agents have concentrated on finding or engendering a new group, a new center of "community awareness." The agent sees his job as one of releasing this new social energy and channeling it toward the specific problems that need the community's attention. These change agents assume that the official leadership in the community will resist proposals of change. Where the impetus to change has been provided by a community group, the group has almost always been a voluntary organization belonging to the informal structure of the community, seldom an official part of the community's political or administrative hierarchy.

Naturally, we expect these differences in the source of initiative to affect the change relationship as it is defined through the mutual expectations of the change agent and the client system. Yet what impresses us most is the fact that change agents working with each type of client system seem to use the same wide variety of approaches to the working relationship. Whether the client system is an individual, a group, an organization, or a community, we can find change agents whose roles in the change relationship range from one extreme to the other—for instance, from active teacher to nondirective consultant, from the expert whose diagnostic skill derives from previous experience with other systems to the investigator whose diagnosis depends entirely upon research into the problems of the present system, from agents whose time perspective is indefinite and depends on the dynamics of the change process itself to agents whose time perspective is established beforehand in preplanned sequential units. These common varieties of skills and orientations were the most striking feature of our analysis, and they suggest that change agents working with the various types of systems face the same types of action-decisions in deciding how to work with their clients. Nevertheless, certain differences are perceptible—differences in emphasis which are observable in the change relationship as it is typically organized by agents working with the different types of client systems.

In the first place, change agents who work with individuals are on the whole clearer and more precise in their conceptual descriptions of the change relationship than are the agents who work with other types of systems. They rely heavily on the interpersonal dynamics of the agent-client relationship as the chief context of change, and they are consequently aware of minute shifts in emphasis and content which seem less important to those agents whose work involves a less intensive relationship. Most change agents who work with individuals know that the change process will extend over a relatively long series of work sessions, each of which will be a direct confrontation of agent and client.

On the other hand, no clear pattern of change relationships has so far developed among change agents who work with small groups. Here one encounters every kind of orientation. Sometimes the change process is limited to brief diagnostic procedures; sometimes it is an extended form of group therapy. Perhaps the most common change pattern in work with small groups is that in which the agent observes the group in action for a given period of time and then interprets the group's processes to the group as a whole, sometimes adding recommendations for ways in which these processes may be improved.

Work with organizations seems to fall into three divergent patterns. First, some agents follow the model of dynamic therapy in which the client's problems are worked through in a process of self-regulating and analytical interaction. Such an orientation is illustrated in the reports of the Tavistock group (36). Second, some agents, particularly those who are concerned with rates of productivity, are oriented primarily to the diagnostic survey in which an attempt is made to assess causative factors such as workers' morale, supervisory attitudes, and so forth. Third, still other agents offer a specified "package of help"; such packages are intended to effect a general improvement in unified areas of structural or functional scope and may include such devices as supervisory training programs, executives' seminars, or work-system analyses. Another point worth noticing is that change agents who work with organizations have acquired a much greater sensitivity to the problems of achieving an integrated relationship with the various subparts of the client system than have those who work with individuals and small groups.

Change agents who have attempted to define a working relationship with a community have been much more aware than other agents of problems of fragmentation and faulty communication within the total system. What this means, in effect, is that they have very often been required to deal with problems which have arisen out of the indifference or ignorance of subgroups in matters concerning the welfare of the whole community. These agents have been particularly impressed by the problem of obtaining a dispersion of influence within a social system, especially when there is a low level of interdependence among the subparts. The problem is complicated even further by the fact that very often the subparts with which it is possible to establish a relationship are not those which can exert an influence in the power structure of the system. This means that very few change agents who have worked with communities have been able to establish an operable relationship with the whole client system. As we shall see later, this creates a multitude of relational problems which appear much less often in work with organizations and hardly at all in work with face-to-face groups and individuals.

SOME COMPARATIVE OBSERVATIONS
ON CHANGE FORCES, RESISTANCE FORCES,
AND INTERFERENCE

In Chapter 4 we distinguished between initial and emergent forces toward or away from change, and we also defined interference forces as the components of any client system's existence which compete with the change forces for attention and energy.

At this point we want to review briefly some of the most significant differences, as they have appeared in our study, in the initial forces for and against change in the different types of client systems. In later chapters we shall consider the differences between emergent forces in the different types of systems.

Forces toward change

The reports of work with individuals make it clear that in contrast to larger systems the personality system is quite sensitive to disruptions in internal dynamics and is also active in setting its own standards for achievement, which means that the individual is often the first to become aware of his need for self-improvement.

In contrast, work with small groups seems to reveal that the lower cohesiveness of the total system and its failures of internal communication result in uncertainty about criteria of achievement and therefore in a deficiency of self-awareness. In other words, the small group is much less likely than the individual to recognize its own need for improvement. On the other hand, the small group, like the individual, is sensitive to internal disruptions; the throes of interpersonal conflict can be particularly painful in a face-to-face situation. In several studies of group change, we find that significant forces toward change have arisen from external pressures, for example, from other parts of the organization. That is to say, although the small group's internal change forces may be weak, it is particularly susceptible to change forces exerted from the outside. As we noted before, the small group in our society is often in situations in which it is highly vulnerable to social pressure.

Our reports of work with organizations seem to indicate that productivity is the main criterion of success, even in organizations which are not explicitly motivated by the need for profits. That is to say, organizations are more sensitive to the need to produce, whether the demand arises outside or inside the system, than they are to problems of communication or conflict between subparts of the system.

Community systems, on the other hand, seem not to be sensitive to problems of productivity. Problems of internal disruption—delinquency, poor schools, inefficient community services, and the like—provide the main forces toward change. In addition, communities are sometimes provoked into seeking help when the evidence of intergroup conflict, particularly racial conflict, becomes inescapably flagrant. It is notable that this kind of "pain" is usually associated with moral standards.

Forces against change

Perhaps the four most frequently noted sources of resistance to the idea of help are (1) reluctance to admit weaknesses, (2) fear of failure or awkwardness in trying to initiate a new practice or behavior pattern, (3) a fatalistic expectation of failure instilled by previous unsuccessful attempts to change, and (4) a fear of losing some current satisfaction (for example, power, dependency, and so forth). A given time or place may also make many competing demands on the client system's resources, and these may interfere with the drive toward change. In fact, the tempo of modern life with its manifold pressures and demands may make it very difficult indeed to find a good time and place for the kind of reflection and intense self-awareness which is required for the processes of assessment and change. In the next chapter we shall observe the way in which some change agents have tried to overcome this problem of interference by creating special "cultural islands" or "analytic hours" in which the client can work without interruption on problems of achieving change.

Perhaps the greatest resistance force operating in small groups is the members' imperfect awareness of their own interpersonal processes and their lack of a frame of reference in which to judge their performances and their possibilities for improvement. Coupled with these factors is the insecurity which we sometimes find among group leaders who feel that any diagnosis of group functions is a threat to the stability of their own roles. In some groups, moreover, one finds an ideological resistance to self-appraisal: members feel that the techniques of social science are a waste of time when applied to small groups. Paradoxically, small groups such as school boards and executive committees are often prey to "anti-intellectual" elements. In addition, interference forces may be particularly strong in small groups which have busy agendas; ordinary responsibilities to a larger system may preclude attention to internal processes.

In the case of organizations, we again encounter the criterion of productivity as a main factor in motivations toward or away from change. The principal resistance force in any organization may be a fear that change will adversely affect the organization's productivity. Another frequent source of resistance in organizations springs from conflicts, which may be only latent, between the various strata of authority or between subparts. This often means that one subpart's effort to obtain help is viewed by other subparts as an attempt to buttress a particular vested interest. Such a misunderstanding leads naturally to resistance by the rest of the organization. Two frequent sources of interference in organizations are provided by the primacy of production schedules and the commonplace belief that it is improper to spend "company time" on theoretical, rather than productive, operations.

Perhaps the most conspicuous resistance to seeking help which arises in communities is that which stems from the community's lack of mechanisms for making decisions. This is a kind of negative resistance. Because communities usually possess a low degree of organizational unity, there may often simply be no readily available means for deciding that help is necessary. This means that the change agent is forced into the difficult position of having to build a new subpart or identify himself with one or another existing subpart of the community, in which case the rest of the community is likely to resist him and reject his proposals. Or, especially in large communities, the subpart with which the agent establishes his relationship may be so inconspicuous that it affords virtually no influence over the rest of the system and no spread of involvement in the emotional commitments to the change objectives. Another aspect of the community's negative resistance is simply the low degree of responsibility for the general welfare which exists among the fragmented subparts of the community system: no subpart is closely enough identified with the public weal to risk its limited power in the cause of general change. These are very broad statements, of course, not intended in any way to deprecate the many splendid examples of disinterested community service which can be found in every American city. As for interference, its sources in community life are manifold. The active citizen is subjected to the demands of dozens or hundreds of competing goals and "causes." In many large communities the confusion is increased by the inadequacies of communication among subparts. Thus many different change goals may be pursued at the same time by different and competing interests. In a sense, then, our cities are afflicted with too many change efforts

WORKING TOWARD CHANGE

8

We are ready now to focus on the central part of the helping process—the job of assisting the client system to achieve an understanding of the problem situation and to convert these insights and understandings into goals of change and courses of action toward the desired improvements. In working toward change there are many different patterns of collaboration between change agents and client systems. At the same time, many helping techniques are held in common by different types of helpers.

In Chapters 2 and 3 we noted that every change agent has a characteristic orientation toward diagnosis. Some approach the problem of diagnosis largely in terms of preconceived judgments; they apply to their particular client's problems notions of process and structure which they have derived from their previous experience. This helps them to make a quick diagnosis without engaging in lengthy or experimental investigations into the particular conditions of each case. Examples of this diagnostic orientation appear frequently in work with industrial organizations. The key to low productivity often lies in poor communication between first-line supervisors and their work groups. This is a pattern of weakness which is inherent in our typical managerial con-formation. Change agents know this, and consequently, when they are called upon to help with a problem of low productivity some of them feel that they can safely turn to this area of com-munication and apply to it their proved remedies without gather-ing much new information about the particular conditions of the individual company which has asked for help.

Other change agents take the opposite tack. They rely heavily upon processes of research, and in diagnosing a particular client's problems they prefer to use as much new information as they can get about the history and present circumstances of the particular client system. They differ greatly, of course, in the extent to which their diagnostic orientations lead them to look at one or another aspect of the client system's organization or operation (for example, human relations or work flow, power structure or communications, emotional problems or study habits, and so forth). There are wide differences also in the kinds of research which these agents pursue; some concentrate on specific areas, others seek more general information. Some agents can obtain the kind of information they need directly from the client system simply by asking questions and soliciting reports. Other agents feel that they need information which lies deeper in the client system, that is, below the level of conscious awareness, and that this information can be obtained only by indirect means.

Change agents also vary greatly in the extent to which they feel it is necessary or desirable to share their diagnostic insights with the client system. An effective collaboration between agent and client may require complete candor or just the reverse. Some agents believe that the client's work toward change in some cases can best be sustained by a policy which withholds some of the agent's information and analysis. At the opposite extreme, other agents think that clients should always participate fully in the fact-finding processes and that their diagnostic understanding should emerge spontaneously from their own analysis of the facts as they are revealed. These agents emphasize the client's emotional commitment to change goals which the client himself has formulated.

We shall see that these various diagnostic orientations determine to a large degree the change methods which are used by agents during Phases 3, 4, and 5 of the helping process.

CHANGE METHODS USED IN PHASE 3:
DIAGNOSIS OF THE PROBLEM

The methods used by change agents during this phase of the change process—which we have defined as the process of diagnosing the problem of the client system—can be classified under four headings: (1) obtaining information, (2) processing information or formulating a diagnosis, (3) stimulating understanding and accepting diagnostic insights, and (4) imparting diagnostic skills. Using these classifications, let us look at some of the change methods employed most frequently by the various agents encountered in our study.

Obtaining information

Methods of direct questioning. The majority of change agents, no matter what type of client system they are working with, try to find out what the client thinks about his own problems by questioning him directly. Most of the change agents who have worked with face-to-face groups report that they have tried to obtain this kind of information by questioning the members separately; several agents have suggested that the best way to do this is by using post-meeting reaction sheets on which the members can indicate their satisfaction or dissatisfaction with the group's operations and their views of the problems which need to be solved. Some agents have used information gathered in this way as the basis for group interviews in which the agent's questions were refined to a point of greater precision and sensitivity. From analyzing questionnaires and rating scales these agents develop hypotheses which are then used as probes to stimulate further reactions in group meetings.

In work with organizations and communities three methods

of direct questioning seem to be used most frequently. First, there is a widespread use of the sample-survey procedure. In this method, a sample of the individuals who comprise the client system are interviewed and asked questions about the system's problems. Sometimes the sample is selected at random, sometimes it is spread representatively over all the subparts of the client system, and sometimes it is drawn from the various levels of a status or power hierarchy. The attempt is to obtain information about the total system by obtaining information from an appropriate sample of the units in the total system.

Second, change agents may employ a method analogous to that of using post-meeting reaction sheets with small groups. Questionnaires may be given to all the members of the organization or community. This approach is particularly valuable in obtaining information about conflicts between subgroups. In such cases agents need more information, more different reactions, than they can get by questioning simply a few members from each subpart. Third, agents use what may be called the self-questioning technique. This method is emphasized particularly by agents who believe that the client should participate as fully as possible in the fact-finding processes. Usually the technique employs a self-survey team composed of representatives from the client system. These team members collaborate in preparing a questionnaire or an interview schedule. Then they are trained by the change agent in the skill of using the particular survey tool which has been chosen (interviews, questionnaires, or the like). For example, in one of our cases the client system was a school community consisting of children, teachers, and parents. Here three survey teams were established. One, composed of student leaders who had been nominated by their fellow students, conducted interviews among the student body. The second, made up of teachers, interviewed the faculty. And the third, composed of parents who had been selected by the PTA, interviewed a sample of parents. Each team had been trained in interviewing techniques by the change agent.

Some of the change agents who use these procedures for obtaining information directly from the client system acknowledge in their reports that this method taps only one of the important sources of information. They use other methods to reach the important, more private, levels of experience in the client system. However, many agents feel that direct questioning is enough if adequate skill is used in the questioning process.

Methods of seeking information from neighboring systems. In Chapter 3 we noted that the change agent's diagnosis may lead him to the area of interaction between the client system and its environment rather than exclusively to problems within the system. This means that the change agent may need to uncover diagnostic information outside the client system. It is often important, for instance, to find out what effect the behavior of the client system has on other systems with which it comes in contact. Our case materials yield two examples of work with individuals which illustrate this point. In one case the change agent collected information by asking all the members of a group to rate each other on certain behavior scales (for example, a scale ranging from "tries to influence others too frequently and aggressively" to "does not offer his ideas often enough or with enough confidence"). Each member of the group indicated on the scale, by drawing an arrow, how much change he would like to see in the behavior of each other member in order to improve the group's interpersonal processes. In this way the change agent was able to secure information about the person he wanted to help from all the people who were associated with him; the information included not only evaluations of the client's present behavior but suggestions for ways in which his behavior might be improved. The second case involved a program to help individual children win acceptance from their schoolmates. Again, the chief source of diagnostic information was a questionnaire which asked for a sociometric rating. All the children in a given class were asked to tell what status they gave each other in the group and to give their reasons for accepting or rejecting each person.

In our case materials we came across only one instance of work with an organization or community in which external views of the client system were solicited on the basis of intergroup sociometry.

Methods of eliciting a demonstration of the problem. Several change agents have pointed out that frequently client systems may be aware of their problems but unable to give verbal descriptions of them. What is needed sometimes is a procedure which will allow the client system to point to its problem or demonstrate it in some way, thus furnishing diagnostic information by non-verbal means. In such circumstances a number of agents have resorted to techniques of role playing. When the nurses of a hospital staff, for instance, were unable to explain their conflicts with ward attendants, they were asked to act out several actual incidents of conflict. The change agent reports that he received by this means a much more objective and substantial representation of the problem than he had been able to derive from direct interviews. In reports on work with small communities we find references to a related procedure whereby the change agent asks a representative of the community to be his guide in a survey of the community's problems. The guide is requested to lead the agent to the points where the symptoms appear and point them out to him.

Methods of participating as an observer in the client system's routine activities. The three ways of gathering information which we have considered so far have this in common: they have depended upon some means of direct communication between the change agent and the source of the information. But there are other methods by which the change agent depends less upon procedures of direct reporting. Participation as an observer is one of these.

In much of the work which is done with individual children the therapist tries to obtain information by a direct observation of the child's behavior in a variety of life situations—at home, at school, and at the playground. Sometimes the agent tries to get his information from the people who are normally in a position to observe the child, such as the parents, the teacher, or the play supervisor. In other cases a trained observer, such as a visiting teacher or social worker, functions as a member of the change-agent team and reports his observations on various aspects of the child's life. In two of the cases which we studied, the change-agent team developed a battery of standardized activities for use in a normal classroom period. Representatives of the team then reported their observations of these diagnostic activities in terms of a series of standardized behavioral criteria.

Agents who work with small groups frequently ask permission to join the group's meetings so that they may observe at first-hand the group's regular procedures and operations.

Frequent mention is made of this observing procedure in reports of work with organizations and communities. However, the observer who deals with these larger units faces a good many difficult problems in obtaining an adequate sample of observations from which to make a diagnostic judgment. He must be sure, in other words, that he has seen enough to know what the organization's or community's processes really are; yet it is always impossible for him to see everything. Furthermore, many problems which are typical of communities and organizations—for instance, the inappropriate concentration of power, conflict between sub-groups, or ineffective methods of communication—are not easily accessible to direct observation. This is why many agents place so much emphasis on the importance of good informants, people who have had long experience in the client system and who have direct access to the positions from which the system's problems must be observed, but who also possess a certain degree of objectivity in reporting what they see and know. Another procedure is to "observe" the products of communication in a large system by studying memos, correspondence, records of meetings, and so forth.

Many change agents have pointed out that one of the most significant sources of diagnostic information is the change relationship itself. The sensitive change agent can observe the behavior of the client system during the early stages of the change relationship and discover much of what he needs to know in order to diagnose the client's problems. This kind of observation is emphasized particularly by psychotherapists who regard interpersonal relationships as the main locus of individual problems, and it is also helpful to agents who are working with individuals in group environments, as in human-relations training and group psychotherapy.

Methods of projective communication.   Many change agents assume that in spite of good will and a readiness to give information most client systems are organized in such a way that they naturally conceal certain kinds of information which would be helpful in making a diagnosis. Consequently, a number of methods have been developed to help the client system divulge information which is not easily communicated. The outstanding example of these methods is, of course, the free-association technique which is one of the important tools of psychoanalysis. The client is asked to make available to an outsider a spontaneous flow of mental activity. The change agent, as a skilled observer of these internal events, is able to interpret them diagnostically, thus arriving at hypotheses about the client's interior predicament which could not be reached in any other way. In psychoanalytically oriented work with children, where actions offer a more differentiated medium of communication than verbalizations, freedom of "utterance" is encouraged by the use of contrived play situations in which the children are invited to play with psychologically significant materials. The observing therapist can then "participate" in the inner life of the child. This is a device—the psychodramatic stage is another—for assisting the client to project his inner experience in outward forms, thus providing the change agent with material for diagnosis. A wide variety of projective tests has been developed for work with individuals, all of them designed to give access to the internal processes of the client through means which the client himself cannot consciously control.

Several attempts have been made to develop projective devices of this kind for use with small groups. In one type of test, for instance, the group is shown pictures of group situations and is then invited to make up stories on the basis of the pictures. The change agent can derive important data from the content of the stories and from the processes by which the group has created the stories. One change agent who was working with a staff group reports his use of role playing as a projective device. He asked the members of the staff to enact several scenes which were different from their regular activities but which were devised to present the staff with significant opportunities to display its interpersonal and problem-solving routines. The agent was able to use his observations of these dramatic episodes in diagnosing the staff's difficulties. We know of no fully developed attempt to use this indirect approach with organizations or communities, although several of Moreno's (29) applications of sociodrama to community contexts illustrate one method that might be used.

This brief review of the methods used to gather diagnostic information, though incomplete, is illustrative of the rich variety of interview procedures, observation procedures, and projective techniques. Our purpose has been to suggest some of the points of comparison in the work of the various types of change agents and to intimate the possibility of a conceptual framework within which batteries of methods could be organized.

Processing information or formulating a diagnosis

The purpose of collecting information about the client system's functional processes is to give the change agent, or the change agent and the client system acting together, an opportunity to diagnose the nature and cause of the problems which have led the client system to ask for help. Once the information has been gathered, change agents make their diagnoses in a variety of different ways.

Diagnosis from assumption of generality of problem. We have already pointed out that some change agents believe they can make a diagnosis in certain types of cases without gathering specific, new, local information. These agents are ready to assume, on the basis of their previous experience, that certain types of problems are virtually universal with certain types of systems. Some agents, for example, assume that any hierarchical organization suffers from a major inefficacy of upward and downward communication, that supervisors invariably need training in the skills of understanding human motivation, and that any large organization will be improved by clarifications of status and responsibility. Some change agents who work with communities are ready to assume that any community is afflicted with such problems as the need to involve more citizens actively in the general welfare or the need to form a citizens' council. Obviously, such assumptions permit the change agent to cut short the diagnostic phase of his work and move rapidly into the area of active change efforts. But these agents are likely to encounter an additional problem when it comes to making their kind of help specifically applicable to the needs of the particular client system.

Diagnosis by change agents acting independently.   Many change agents hold themselves fully independent of the client system during the time that they are processing the diagnostic information and arriving at a judgment on the nature of the client system's problems. This is true of some work with all types of systems. In work with individuals, both children and adults, some change agents review the information they have been able to gather and make their diagnoses without collaboration with the client. Others may impart only a few of their diagnostic conclusions. In such cases as these diagnosis frequently is a joint undertaking of several agents; it may, for instance, result from the discussions of a clinic staff. Similarly, a team working in a community or organization may arrive at a completely independent judgment. The members of a team engaged in a sample survey, for instance, may code their interviews, process the data with an IBM machine, complete certain cross-analyses which are suggested by their previous experience and training, and arrive at a series of interpretive judgments about the major problems of their client system. Many community surveys have followed this pattern.

Diagnosis by change agents and client systems acting co-opera tively.   Other change agents report diagnostic procedures which are a collaboration between agent and client. Together they study the data which has been collected and try to understand its meaning. In individual psychotherapy, for instance, the diagnostic phase may involve much interaction between agent and client. First the client furnishes a certain amount of data by means of free associations of ideas and images; then the agent suggests an interpretive hypothesis, whereupon the client may differ with the interpretation and suggest another one, or he may produce additional data which help to verify or invalidate the agent's interpretation. This process may be repeated many times as the agent and client together arrive at diagnostic insights. Comparable patterns of work with small groups have been reported by several change agents. For a time the change agent may sit in the group's meeting, perhaps taking notes on the flow of events. Then during a special period at the end of the meeting, or in some cases at any time during the meeting, the change agent offers to the group a summary of his diagnostic interpretations, suggesting hypotheses or questions about the symptomatic meaning of certain events which have occurred in the meeting. These hypotheses and questions may lead some members of the group to furnish additional information about the events in question or about their perceptions of them. These in turn may lead to the discussion of alternative hypotheses, and in this discussion the members of the group may reveal themselves in new ways which will tend to confirm or refute the agent's original suggestions. A similar procedure has been described by several of the agents who have conducted surveys in organizations or communities. Here the data were collected by members of the change-agent team, and the findings were processed for graphic presentation to various subgroups. During these presentations the meaning of the data was discussed, and the discussions themselves proved helpful in amplifying or correcting the team's diagnosis. How far the change agent himself will go in suggesting possible interpretations of survey data depends upon the agent and the circumstances of the case.

Self-analysis. We have encountered a few, though very few, cases of work with individuals in which the client was asked to analyze his own problems. In each of these cases the client was given a kit of diagnostic tools (tests) to apply to himself and instructions for scoring the results and preparing a diagnostic "profile" from the data. In these cases the client may be asked to interpret the results of his analysis and diagnose his own problems; his interpretations can then be examined in discussions with the change agent. Self-surveys are, of course, a common procedure in work with organizations and communities. The change agent may merely train the self-survey team in the skills of collecting data and processing it. The team may be left to make its own diagnostic interpretations, or the change agent may remain as a consultant to give his advice or to suggest interpretive techniques. For example, a committee of social-agency executives undertook a self-survey to find out why so many members were dropping out of the groups under the executives' direction. The committee itself took a major role in interpreting the data and presenting it to fellow executives as the basis for further discussions and interpretations.

Stimulating understanding and acceptance of diagnostic insights

Some change agents feel that they have done most of their work when they have brought the client system to the point of a genuine insight into the nature and cause of its difficulties. Other change agents think that this diagnostic phase is merely preliminary to an extended program of giving help and working toward specified change goals. But in either case the agent must be sure that the client system understands and accepts the diagnosis. This demands, in many cases at least, a process of elucidation or stimulation. Finally, there are some agents who feel confident in proposing a program of change without a major phase of diagnosis. These various orientations underlie the great differences of emphasis which we find in the reports of change agents when they speak of their means of communicating diagnostic insight to the client system.

In much of the work with children, change agents have apparently decided that it is unwise to attempt any very complete discussion of diagnostic interpretations, and for obvious reasons. In one program, a case involving work with second- and fifth-grade children, the agent reports that most of the change activity occurs in the context of a game; the agent and the child do not talk about the existence of a problem. Nevertheless, here, as in most work with children, the agent tries to share his understanding of the problem with the child whenever the child seems ready to take on a new responsibility of insight.

There are a number of cases in work with organizations and communities in which change agents have worked by themselves to prepare the interpretations of diagnostic data and have then undertaken to present the results in such a way that they were understood and accepted by the client systems or by the particular subgroups in the client systems with whom the agents were working. Almost all agents agree that a written report is not enough. Clients must be given a chance to allay their anxieties by asking questions and posing objections. This means a consultation of some kind, probably a series of consultations.

A fairly large number of change agents have pointed out that the self-survey technique is particularly useful because the survey team usually comes to understand and accept the diagnostic data which it is collecting, simply by virtue of being so closely associated with it. This does away with the need for "selling" the diagnosis to the client. The survey team not only accepts the data but develops a strong interest in doing something about the problems which the data reveal.

One of the chief problems which is emphasized in the organization and community studies is that of dispersing diagnostic understanding to the whole client system. It does not do much good if the particular subgroup with which the agent is working accepts his diagnosis and the rest of the system rejects it. Yet this is precisely what happens in a good many cases. The subgroup attempts to launch a campaign of change and finds that the rest of the system will not even acknowledge the need for a change. Naturally, this is not likely to be a problem when one is dealing with individuals or small groups, because then the total client system is in direct contact with the change agent.

Imparting diagnostic skills

A good many change agents have said that they aim to help the client system in two ways: they want to help solve the particular problem which is causing trouble, and they want to give basic training in skills which can be applied in the future when new and different problems arise. They believe that the client system should become able to cope with more and more problems without seeking outside help. Hence many agents try to train their clients in the procedures of collecting and processing diagnostic information. But it must be emphasized that this kind of learning is not easy. In cases of psychotherapy it may involve a complete revolution in the client's attitudes and habitual ways of comportment. In cases of work with organizations and communities it may involve the creation of a new and special department or team which can specialize in the skills of diagnosis and interpretation. Actually, this whole region of change theory is relatively unexplored. Much more work remains to be done.

CHANGE METHODS USED IN PHASE 4:
ESTABLISHING GOALS AND INTENTIONS OF ACTION

Our everyday experience tells us that often our insight into the cause of a problem leads us spontaneously to take the right remedial actions. But the literature of change shows that this is far from being true in most efforts of social or psychodynamic change. More often than not diagnostic understanding alone fails to provide a sufficient base for establishing the direction of change, which, as we have seen, is the concern of Phase 4. This is equally true in matters of individual behavior, interpersonal relations, organizational operations, or social processes. A child, for instance, may come to understand that other children don't like him because he is too bossy, but this insight in itself does not tell him how he should behave differently. A group may have been helped by a change agent to discover that its work is impeded by the withdrawal of many of its members from the processes of making decisions, but this knowledge alone does not automatically give the group adequate techniques for involving all its members in the patterns of group responsibility. Again, the community self-survey team may have discovered that one of the main causes of tension in the community is a lack of contact among various subgroups; the team is still faced with very intricate problems in deciding how to bring about more normal relations among the subgroups in question. There is plenty of evidence from the past to show that simply bringing people together is as likely to stir up more tension as it is to restore social equanimity.

A number of change agents hold the optimistic belief that if the process of working out a diagnosis has been satisfactorily completed, then the positive forces toward change which had been blocked will be released and the client will spontaneously perceive new and more appropriate modes of action. These perceptions will result in definite intentions to adopt the reformed modes of action. No doubt this is what actually happens in some cases. Unfortunately, the assumption that diagnosis leads automatically to change has seldom been tested by studies which might show whether or not the change has been stabilized and permanently adopted by the client system. However, the literature on work with groups, organizations, and communities indicates that we need to study carefully the movement from diagnostic insight to change, with particular attention to the matter of helping the client system to establish change goals and develop change commitments. There are some cases in which diagnostic insight has appeared to release tension toward change without any effort of translation. In other words, abstract understanding in itself channeled the impetus toward change into the available lanes of action. But in other cases the relationship between the change agent and the client system in the diagnostic phase seemed to offer no springboard to the phases of intention and action. Sometimes the change agent has been able to help his client convert diagnostic insights into a recognition of goals but not into a plan of action. In other words, the client's understanding of the cause of his problem has shown him what should be done to remedy it but not how to do it. The needs, choices, and contingencies which appear in any consideration of this linkage between insight and action indicate how crucial this point may be in the change process and how inadequate to it many of our change techniques are. This is one place where change agents ought to concentrate their inventiveness. Many of them seem insufficiently aware of these problems.

We have organized the relevant procedures in Phase 4 of the change process under four headings: (1) defining the directions of change, (2) arousing and supporting intentions to change, (3) providing opportunities for anticipatory testing, and (4) developing and mobilizing competence in action.

Defining the directions of change

In Chapter 5 we discussed some of the theoretical and strategic aspects of the problem of locating a leverage point at which to begin the change process. The chief consideration in the selection of a leverage point, of course, must be whether or not it leads ultimately in the direction of the major goal which the change agent or change agent and client system have established. But in one sense the leverage point itself is a goal, a limited and immediate objective which the agent and client must achieve as the first step in their actual process of change. Thus change can be viewed as a scheme of tactical and strategic goals, and this is the way some change agents prefer to think of it. A number of agents, particularly those working with communities, have emphasized the part that this choice of an immediate objective plays in their work. They point out how important it is that the agent and client agree realistically upon an immediate goal which will bring about a reasonably quick experience of success. Such a success will launch the change program smoothly and give it an immediate impetus. Several of the change agents who have worked with survey data on organizational or community problems stress the importance of organizing the data for clear visual presentation so that it will serve as a good basis for discussion meetings on ways to attack the problems which the data have revealed. Such meetings are really mind-stretching techniques; they often serve to wake up the client and excite him to the possibilities of change. In connection with such meetings one or two change agents have spoken of the value of a "brainstorming" technique: in a meeting all the members of the client group list as quickly as they can the ideas which occur to them about possible courses of action. A kind of mutual free association results in which it is important that no member should challenge or censure another member's ideas, although sometimes questions which aim at constructive clarification serve to stimulate further ideas. One case report tells of work with a large group composed of several hundred members. The members were divided into "buzz" groups or small committees of six or seven, and each little group was asked to list on a card all of the means which it could think of for achieving the goal which the larger group had just agreed upon. (The problem was that of improving the educational facilities in a certain neighborhood.) The cards were then collected and immediately tabulated by a summary committee. Meanwhile the meeting of the larger group continued; then, when the summary committee had finished its tabulations it made a report on all the courses of action which had been recommended by the small committees. A general discussion followed, during which a number of decisions were reached concerning the most feasible and effective plan of action. In other words, immediate goals and plans were adopted in an atmosphere of enthusiasm which had been brought about by the close participation of the whole group in the process of reaching a decision.

Another way to help the client system establish its goals is to secure information about the ways in which other systems have successfully met comparable problems of change. The traveling workshop described by the Ogdens (69) is one illustration of this technique, and there are many others. The aim is to bring representatives of the client system into communication with other systems. The result is a kind of demonstration of success, a proof that particular kinds of problems can be solved by particular kinds of change techniques. Another example of this procedure by demonstration is provided in the report of work with a staff committee. The group had already completed a diagnosis of its problems, and the need for improving its decision-making processes was quite clear. With the help of several members of the committee the change agent set up demonstrations of alternative paths of action. By direct observation the members of the committee were able to compare these alternatives and discuss their relative merits. Here the change agent was functioning primarily as a resource. Out of his previous experience he drew a map, so to speak, of the possible routes and destinations. But the committee was left to make its own itinerary.

Often one of the change agent's most important jobs is to impress upon the client system the futility of hoping for a single, quick, and easy solution to the client's problem. Instead he must usually encourage the client to think in terms of a series of goals extended over a long period of time. This allows the client system to achieve success in stages or to enjoy a more or less continuous experience of success. Many change agents find that the opposition between the client system's desire for early success and the change agent's realistic expectation of an extended effort forms the context within which the change agent must try to help the client system arrive at a feasible choice of goals and a reasonable definition of methods. Part of the agent's help may be a scheme to test tentative goals ahead of time. This will be described below.

Arousing and supporting intentions to change

One might think that every client system demonstrates its intention to change when it accepts the relationship with a change agent. But this is not the case. Many factors within the system or in the system's environmental circumstances may inhibit the movement toward change even after the client system has come to a clear understanding of its problems and needs. In fact, as the client system achieves a keener insight into the dynamics of its problems, it may acquire an increasing burden of pessimism and anxiety which virtually blocks off any possibility of constructive action. This is why many change agents have stressed the importance of giving the client system actual proof that other systems, in circumstances just as unpropitious, have conquered the difficulties of change and have solved their problems successfully. Success stories, in fact, are a stock in trade for many change agents. Often they are incorporated in documentary films or printed case studies.

Most of the research which has been done on the processes of decision making and public commitment has concentrated on this phase of the change process, that is, on the movement from an understanding of the need for change to an actual intention to make a change. These studies have emphasized the importance of group standards and public commitment to them as the basis for a real motivation to change. Several of the change agents whose works we have studied show that they understand this aspect of social dynamics. For example, several agents who have worked with organizations and communities stress the importance of cohesiveness as a factor in the success of teams or committees organized within the client system. If the committee is closely knit, so that it is in effect a network of interpersonal commitments, the motivation to change will be a multiple force in which each component supports the rest. Cohesiveness results in a concentration of motives, which is just what the change agent wants to bring about. Other agents have emphasized the role of leadership in group discussions; the leader must spur and channel the energies of the group toward a group decision to change. In this way the decision itself becomes a commitment to change which supports and expresses the intentions of the group. One change agent has reported on the meetings of a group of nurses. At each weekly meeting the nurses were encouraged to form active goals for that week's work so that the success in achieving each week's goal could be reported at the next week's meeting. This kept alive the nurses' intention to change and created a visible program to which the nurses felt committed. However, there is a danger in any procedure which elevates the change agent to a position of active leadership: the change relationship may become coercive rather than voluntary, in which case the goals of change will no longer enjoin the commitment of the client system.

Two change agents have described the methods by which they attempted to mobilize the client system's feelings of aggressiveness or competition toward other systems as a basis for a motivation toward change within the client system. One can see how this might be done, but at the same time one can see the danger. A change agent who has stimulated his client system's feelings of hostility in order to mobilize emotional energy for the accomplishment of an immediate change objective may find that the feelings of hostility persist after the immediate change has been brought about. This could lead to obvious complications.

It was pointed out in Chapter 4 that the force of inertia which militates against change at the beginning of the change process may become a force of momentum which keeps the change effort going after it has once begun. "Now that we've started, let's keep going"—this is what the client seems to say. Some change agents who have worked with self-survey procedures suggest that involvement in the processes of gathering data creates a desire in the members of the self-survey team to use the data which they have collected. They want, so to speak, to get their money's worth or effort's worth. This is one of the psychological meanings of involvement; it is one of the change agent's most useful tools.

Some of the projects which we have studied—for instance, the summer training laboratory and the program to retrain German leaders—have encountered problems of what we call "anticipatory anxiety." Often when individuals or groups are asked to commit themselves to change, they hesitate because they fear the consequences of altering stable procedures or patterns of behavior. They fear especially the reactions of others who are not connected with the change agent. The individual asks himself what his friends will think if he suddenly begins doing thus or so. The group fears that its place in the larger social context will be disturbed if it adopts a new program or alters its traditional policies. We have discussed this problem of anticipatory anxiety with many different groups, and we are led to conclude that almost everyone anticipates a negative rather than a positive response to any change effort which impinges on other people who have not been directly involved in the change. Some of our colleagues have suggested that this may be because in our childhood years we were punished more than we were praised for our experimental attempts to practice new modes of behavior. Or it may be that we derive comfort from a familiar, predictable mode of existence.

Another kind of anticipatory anxiety which afflicts some client systems is the fear of what will happen when the change relationship ends and the change agent withdraws. The client may hesitate to commit himself to a process which he knows will leave him in the end without the support of the helper.

Providing opportunities for anticipatory testing

Some psychoanalytically oriented change agents emphasize the importance of the dynamic relationship between change agent and client system as offering the client a chance to test new techniques before he puts them into general effect. The transference projection especially offers this kind of opportunity; the individual patient can use the security and experimental freedom of the relationship with the therapist as a safe area in which to practice the new patterns of behavior which he will later adopt in other social contacts. Change agents who work with transitional or therapeutic communities, such as Jones (10), Bettelheim (1), and Redl and Wineman (14), are particularly interested in this question of anticipatory testing. They have created special social environments in which the patient can feel safe in his attempts to try new modes of behavior. They assure the patient that he is not playing for keeps, that he can practice without danger the techniques which he will later use in the "real world." With the support and encouragement of the change agent, the client tests and practices his skills until he wins confidence enough to use them in other life situations.

Other change agents, those who have worked in special educational programs such as summer workshops, supervisory training programs, or cross-cultural programs of acclimatization point out that the client system must be taught to think about the applications of his new-found skills to the situations he will encounter in his nontraining environment. He must find ways of adapting the general values, goals, and skills which he is learning in the classroom, workshop, or training program to the specific situation in which he is involved at home or on the job. An example is provided by the work of training leaders of the Mutual Security Agency program which helps teams from other countries to learn from American methods of production. The leaders found it necessary to encourage frequent discussions of productivity problems "back home" so that the visitors could think through ways in which the American examples could be adapted to a different setting. Similarly, the National Training Laboratories found it advisable to institute special periods of consultation each afternoon; the trainees are invited to ask the consultants about the problems they will find when they return to their own organizations and communities. These consultations frequently lead to general discussions of the means by which new skills and ideas can be translated into practice in the specific environments from which the trainees have come. In some contexts change agents have found it useful to establish clinics in which the individual members of a training group can raise questions about the practical application of their new skills or about their own plans to change when they return to their home environments. These questions can then be discussed in critical terms either by the change agent or by the other members of the group. Change agents who work with training programs often make a considerable effort to give trainees a broad and flexible conception of the problems of initiating change back home rather than allow them to develop a rigid and narrow plan of action. The rigid *a priori* plan may break down; the broad understanding of means and ends will permit a flexible attack on a variety of unanticipated problems.

Some change agents have gone even further in providing opportunities for client systems to rehearse their plans and intentions to change. Several agents report that they have assisted individuals or groups to set up replicas of real situations so that the process of real change could be enacted experimentally beforehand. Thus, through an exercise of role playing, a particular community action committee enacted ahead of time the "drama" which would probably develop when the members of the committee introduced certain new proposals in the community council. By so doing the committee discovered a number of points of resistance which had not been anticipated, and consequently more realistic plans were laid for the forthcoming encounter with the community council.

These are a few of the devices that can be used for reality testing in the process of developing plans for change. There are many other relevant techniques which we do not have space to discuss. However, it is worth noting that many client systems cannot proceed into change until some kind of testing or rehearsing has been permitted, and almost all systems benefit from it.

Developing and mobilizing competence in action

Another source of anticipatory anxiety for client systems is fear lest the change program require operations which the system is not competent to perform. What skills, what abilities, are needed for this job? The client system is naturally apprehensive about the answer. Connected with this fear is the concern—particularly evident in organizations and communities, though its analogue exists too in work with individuals—to develop or locate the sub-part of the system which can assume definite responsibility for performing the actions of change. Most of the change agents who work with community systems indicate that one of their major problems in starting a change effort is to mobilize a particular subgroup which can actually do the things that have been judged as good to do. One change agent speaks of the importance of or-ganizing *ad hoc* action committees to work on particular action problems. Others advocate an executive committee which can rep-resent all the subparts of the system and take action as an organ of the whole system. One problem in community change efforts is that the subpart of the community that has the motivation and plans for change is often different from the subpart which has official power to act. As a consequence, new change efforts must usually be localized in new subparts of the community, subparts which somehow wrest power to act from the community's vested authorities or, failing that, act outside the normal power structure.

Change agents who work with individuals in small groups em-phasize the importance of skill training as a means of helping the client system to improve its capacity to act. Skill-training ex-ercises, for instance, are used in a number of the summer train-ing laboratories. In a typical practice session the trainees are given a chance to put a particular intention into effect. For ex-ample, trainees might practice techniques for showing disapproval but not rejection to a subordinate. Comparable techniques of skill training have been used in work with various social systems. For instance, different agents have used skill training in work with supervisors in organizations, with community leaders in inter-group relations, and in work with children in classroom groups.

As we have already noted, skill training is also a prominent factor in the work of transitional communities and therapeutic institutions where an effort is made to duplicate, in the hospital or at the camp, many of the aspects of the real-life situation, but with a more permissive climate and with encouragement to try out new techniques of interpersonal relations.

There are also a few reports of the use of skill training in work with whole groups, such as organizational staffs, where the skills in question are those of operating or making decisions as a unit. Maier (28), for instance, has described his technique for demonstrating the place of leadership in a group. He poses two different kinds of leadership, two different roles, two different skills. Then he asks members of the group to use these two different skills in conducting a discussion so that the group can see what effect the skills have upon its ability to make decisions and carry on business. The demonstration itself constitutes training in leadership skills.

All of these change agents realize, of course, that problems of understanding, incentive, and intention come first and that skill training is only one aspect of the process of change. Nevertheless, it does appear that change agents often neglect their responsibility for imparting the skills which change effort demands. This can mean nothing but failure and frustration for the client system, particularly as the change process advances into its final stages.

SOME FURTHER COMPARATIVE OBSERVATIONS
ON CHANGE METHODS

At the end of the last chapter we reviewed what seem to us the most interesting similarities and differences among the methods used by change agents who work with the different types of client systems. Now we should like to continue these summary observations with particular reference to Phases 3 and 4 of the change process.

It seems clear, first of all, that the size of the client system has an important effect upon the way in which the change agent sets out to gather diagnostic information. Change agents who work with individuals obviously cannot make direct observations of internal processes, and hence they rely heavily upon various kinds of reports from the client. But clients are biased. They create various subconscious mechanisms to defend themselves, and consequently the change agents must often use indirect or projective techniques to obtain information which the client cannot give directly. Various projective devices have been invented to accomplish this end. In addition, of course, the agent is able to observe the client directly during the interchanges of the therapeutic session, and the data obtained by this means is often exceedingly valuable to the agent when he attempts to interpret the material contained in the client's verbalized reports.

In work with small groups the emphasis shifts to methods of direct observation, and because the groups are small and can be seen all at one time, this is an eminently satisfactory way to gather information. The agent who is present at a staff meeting, for instance, can see very well for himself how the staff conducts its affairs, especially if the relationship is such that the members of the staff can behave naturally while he is there. Unfortunately for those who work with organizations and communities, this kind of direct observation is virtually impossible when one is dealing with large and complex systems, and hence the change agent must have recourse to other approaches. Agents have contrived various ways of looking at the cross section of a large system. In most cases they rely upon a sample of informants. Because the individual in a large system is likely to feel somewhat more detached from the total system than does the ego from the rest of the personality system or the single member from a small group, it is more possible to rely on direct interviews as a source of objective information about an organization or a community, at least if enough such interviews are conducted and correlated.

An analogous point appears when one considers the use of self-analysis or self-surveys. It is almost impossible for an individual to be entirely objective in conducting a self-analysis. But self-surveys in large systems can be made with reasonable objectivity because it is possible for the individual within the large system to look more impersonally at what he sees around him. Even though he is a participant in the system, he can conduct interviews and observe events with at least a moderate degree of objectivity because he does not feel that he as a distinct person is responsible for the system's problems and failures.

Another interesting point of contrast between work with small and large systems lies in the extent of the data which the change agent attempts to collect on matters concerning the interaction between the client system and other, neighboring systems. As we have seen, agents who work with individual personality systems often consider this a prime source of diagnostic information. The client system is clearly revealed in the patterns of action and response which appear between the system and the environment. Consequently, it is rather surprising that agents who work with groups and organizations make so little effort to obtain comparable diagnostic information about their clients. This is another direction which needs to be explored.

To us, one of the most striking points which emerged from our examination of the case materials was the fact that the same variety of techniques is found among all the different types of change agents. That is to say, agents working with each level of client system exhibited the same range of diagnostic procedures. We found that change agents working with individuals, groups, organizations, and communities all have practiced diagnostic procedures based on no new information, on independent diagnostic research, on collaboration with the client system, or on self-analysis.

There does seem to be, however, significant difference in the methods by which different change agents attempt to share their diagnostic insights with the client system. In work with individuals this sharing is a more or less continuous process which is part of the interaction between agent and client. In work with small groups, on the other hand, agent and client tend to join in more or less limited and formal discussions of diagnostic problems; such discussions may take place during special evaluation periods at the end of group meetings or when reports on post-meeting reaction sheets are presented at later meetings. Still more formalized methods of presenting diagnostic data are used in work with organizations, and agents who deal with communities are usually forced to rely chiefly upon written reports which can be circulated within the client system. Obviously, in work with organizations and communities the change agent faces the special problem of insuring a spread of information throughout the client system's various subparts.

As one might expect, change agents working with client systems of all sizes are aware of the problem of locating a leverage point or immediate objective as the first step in the actual process of change. The difference appears in the kind of leverage point which is usually chosen. Agents working with organizations and communities typically look for structural leverage points—that is, subparts which are especially accessible or which possess a particular strategic value by virtue of their location in the total system. Agents working with individuals and small groups, on the other hand, tend to look for functional leverage points—that is, parts of the system's regular operating mechanism which it is safe to start with, assuming that the change process may uncover more serious and fundamental problems as it goes along.

Similarly, change agents who deal with all types of systems recognize the importance of establishing realistic expectations for change and of attempting to insure an early experience of success. In other words, all agents face the problem of keeping the client's motivation toward change alive and vigorous. The problem of co-ordinating the mechanisms of decision and action is more troublesome for agents who work with large systems. That is to say, a linkage between the decision to change and the actual motion toward change may be more tenuous in large systems, where the two functions may lie in separate subparts, than it is in small systems, where the two functions are likely to be performed by the same subparts. Again, when it comes to the problem of assuring the effectiveness of the contemplated change action, agents who work with individuals tend to rely on various kinds of skill training, while those who work with groups concentrate more on "methods" and "procedures."

Finally, we find that change agents who work with the larger types of systems often tend to shorten the working relationship with the client system, frequently ending it with the diagnostic phase. Perhaps this is because the difficulties of developing a genuine relationship with a large system are so great, although there are examples of a complete "working through" relationship. It may also be that a large system, with its greater objectivity toward its own processes, can accept a diagnosis and act on it without needing the continued presence of the change agent to reinforce the diagnosis.

SOME FURTHER COMPARATIVE OBSERVATIONS
ON CHANGE FORCES AND RESISTANCE FORCES

The resistances to forward movement in this stage of the change process may originate from a number of sources. As in the other phases of the process, resistance may stem from the dynamics of the client system's internal operation, from the environment, from the behavior of the change agent, or from the nature of the change relationship.

One important source of resistance or blockage in the diagnostic phase is the conceptual or intellectual difficulty which arises, for both change agent and client system, in converting diagnostic insights into projections of possible goals and means. This is a trying effort for everyone concerned and is often the source of misunderstandings.

The stage of diagnosis and interpretation is also likely to be a period of particularly acute emotional stress for all types of client systems. Diagnosis often reveals the true extent of the sacrifices which change will require. The client system may grow discouraged to learn that accustomed and gratifying patterns of behavior or procedure must be given up if the change is to be successfully accomplished. Resistance to these sacrifices usually lasts throughout the rest of the change process, of course, but it is likely to emerge during the phase of diagnosis and goal setting. A corollary to this type of resistance is that which develops when the client system becomes aware of the discrepancy between conscious intention and current actual behavior. The client system may be dismayed to discover what its own habits actually are, and the change which is needed in order to remedy these habits may suddenly appear too great to attempt.

Another frequent source of resistance at this stage is conflict between the influence of the change agent and the influence of the client system's "operating group." The expectations of the change agent, for instance, may be considerably at odds with the expectations of the client's friends and relatives. The client may fear that the changes which have come to seem desirable and reasonable in the course of the change relationship will in fact evoke a negative response from the other systems in whose orbit the client exists. The resistance that derives from this fear is likely to grow stronger as the change process nears its end and the time comes for the client system to adopt a new mode of behavior.

A somewhat similar resistance often springs from the client system's fear that it actually does not possess the strength or skill which is required for the contemplated change. These feelings of inadequacy very commonly develop at the same time as the client's increased diagnostic sensitivity toward the source of its problems.

Occasionally the change agent's own behavior during this stage creates a justified resistance in the client system. Agents are not always as perceptive or skillful as they ought to be. When an agent insists on a change which is actually not feasible in the client's circumstances, the client naturally objects, and this has been known to happen more than once. Moreover, the change agent may make a mistake through unavoidable ignorance. In many cases the agent simply cannot tell what the reality of the client's day-to-day existence may be; the change relationship is often restricted to rather formal and special occasions and does not give the agent an opportunity to see the client in normal circumstances. In spite of his efforts to overcome this ignorance by many different means, the agent may ask the client to do something which simply cannot be done in the client's real mode of existence. When this happens the client will resist, and the agent can only do his best to recognize his own errors of judgment with promptness and good grace.

We have already mentioned the positive, or change, force which often emerges during this stage as a kind of momentum or desire to get one's money's worth. Trainees who have already learned various new skills, or the members of a self-survey team who have already compiled a certain quantity of data, feel that they have accumulated an investment in the change process, and they want to see it through to the end. In addition, a similar change force is often provided simply by diagnosis: when the client system becomes fully aware of its problems, its "pain" often seems to increase so that there is an intensified desire to do something about it. At this point a very important emergent force toward change may be the change agent's assurance that the client system really does possess the ability to carry through a successful change. If a good working relationship has developed between agent and client, the agent can do a good deal to assuage the self-doubts and ambivalences which naturally attack the client when he begins to understand the dimensions of his problem. The agent can help by offering verbal reassurances and by reinforcing these gestures of understanding with demonstrations of actual past successes in other client systems. Yet the fact is that not many change agents have reported their observations on this delicate phase of the change process. The motivational problems which may arise as the client system moves from diagnosis to intention remain largely unexplored, or at least unreported, in most fields of change specialization. Here is an area which needs much research.

THE TRANSFER AND

STABILIZATION OF CHANGE

9

Acquiring new self-understanding and developing new intentions and skills are important aspects of the change process. But the main test of the change agent's help remains the stability and permanence of the client system's changed behavior when the agent is no longer actively working with the client. The change process must equip the client system to carry on effectively in a wide range of day-to-day activities after the initial change project is over.

The change agents whose work we have studied ask themselves such questions as these: Do the first change efforts result in success and a continuation of the change or in failure and an abandonment of change? Does the change diffuse throughout the client system, or does it remain a relatively isolated and minor phenomenon in one subpart? Is it necessary to give the client system special support for a while in order to assure the permanent penetration of change into the system's internal dynamics?

This business of transferring change skills and motivations from the area of the helping relationship to other areas where help is not present constitutes one of the most crucial and least studied aspects of the helping process. Probably more time, money, and effort are lost at this point in the change process than at any other. When they begin to work with a new client change agents often discover that there is a long history of failures in previous change efforts. A client who has gone through this experience of trying, failing, and giving up, views new proposals to change with caution and even distrust. In fact, as our researchers are discovering more and more clearly all the time, a client's expressions of intent to change and even his ability to grasp new concepts and acquire new skills are not safe indications that an actual change will occur. There is even evidence which shows that many clients who respond most eagerly to the change agent's offer of help and who seem to be the most changed in fact often revert very quickly to their familiar, "normal" patterns of behavior in situations outside the context of the helping relationship. In other words, there has been no transfer of change. In addition, there are cases in which the transfer effort has been too complete: the client has rigidly held to new concepts of behavior even in situations where they were inappropriate and where he should have recognized the need for further change in order to adjust to unforeseen circumstances. This raises the problem of what we might call the changeability of the system.

In this chapter we want to explore various helping techniques which change agents have developed in order to support the successful transfer and stabilization of change in contexts outside the helping relationship. And we shall also look briefly at the concept of changeability as distinguished from change itself. Our discussion will progress in terms of the three final phases of change as we outlined them in Chapter 6: the transformation of change intentions into change efforts (Phase 5), the generalization and stabilization of change (Phase 6), and the ending of the change relationship (Phase 7).

But before we summarize the various helping methods which are used in these three phases, we should like to offer a few observations on the situational context of the helping relationship. This is particularly relevant to problems of the transfer of learning.

THE SITUATIONAL CONTEXT
IN WHICH HELP IS GIVEN

One of the most interesting questions you could ask a professional helper would be whether or not his problems of transferring and stabilizing change couldn't and shouldn't be solved by working directly in the life situations of the client system rather than in the removed situations which circumstances force on most agents. Wouldn't it be better for the therapist, for instance, to stand at the elbow of his patient in a variety of social confrontations rather than to meet with him solely in the confined context of the therapeutic session? The fact is that the majority of change agents whose work we have reviewed believe it is important to establish a special work situation removed from the pressures and demands of the client system's normal routine. Such a work situation may be an office for consultations which is completely private and pervaded with an atmosphere of relaxation, thus encouraging the client to explore his feelings and ideas freely; or it may be a workshop which allows the client to escape from family and vocational routines so that he may concentrate without interruption on problems of analysis and planning; or it may be simply a limited and temporary isolation such as is sought by a business group or government staff which moves to a secluded conference room for its weekly meetings. The staff of the National Training Laboratory in Group Development has specifically formulated its recommendations for creating a "cultural island for change":

> In most situations some set of forces—e.g., tradition, red-tape procedures, expectations of others, fear of failure, fear of loss of status—blocks the individual (or group) from making many changes or improvements in the way he works, thinks, and values. . . . Sometimes training can organize most of the forces on the job so that they encourage the individual (or group) toward change. But often the individual or group of individuals needs to be removed to a helping climate where the forces are designed and applied to encourage change. After the change is initiated (in the learning situation), and after plans for introducing the change on the job have been tested, the individual can move back to the job where further help may need to be given.

Training frequently requires the creation of a "cultural island" to initiate change. On this cultural island, separated from the mainland of conflicting and precariously balanced forces, as many forces of the helping culture as possible can be so planned as to encourage change. . . . Here forces of encouragement, permissiveness, understanding, reassurance, and assistance can be established to make change possible. If the change objectives are in the area of human relations and other "touchy areas" of the individual's personal structure (or the group's interpersonal structure), forces of resistance to change are undoubtedly great, and the value of the cultural island as a more comfortable place to consider and try out possible changes becomes very significant. (3, pp. 15-16)

Our review of work by various change agents does reveal a few cases where the agent has from the beginning established himself and his services as an integral part of the client's normal existence. For example, the report by Jaques (36) on his work with an industrial organization describes such a procedure: a psychiatrist from the change-agent team sat in on the regular meetings of various management groups and labor-management committees and offered comments and interpretations whenever they seemed relevant to the groups' ongoing processes. Thus the discussions of group problems which resulted became an integral part of the groups' normal problem-solving activities. In other situations, such as those described by Hogrefe (23) and Alinsky (52), the change agent has attempted to win acceptance as a temporary but regular constituent of the client system in order to be continuously present in the life of the group and to make his contributions from the inside. Some change agents who work with communities place great emphasis on being present in the community so that help can be given in the real "action situations" as they arise. In actual practice, however, most community change agents find that this is not feasible. Instead they work with a small subpart of the community and try to establish a working context in which analysis and planning can go forward freely and reflectively, apart from the press of regular community events and the influences of various community groupings.

Even where the helping process is to a large degree concentrated in the current life situation and where, therefore, transfer is not a major problem, there still remain serious problems which have to do with starting the actual change work and stabilizing the patterns of change after they have been learned. In large systems this involves the spread of the change pattern to all subparts, even though many of the subparts have not been immediately touched by the change relationship. All of these problems, of course, involve the change agent in a choice of working techniques.

CHANGE METHODS USED IN PHASE 5:
THE INITIATION OF CHANGE EFFORTS

Readers will recall that in discussing Phase 4 we described some of the methods which change agents use to prepare client systems for taking action toward change. We considered the various techniques for stimulating and supporting the client's intentions to change and his plans for changing; we examined the means of testing the client's change goals; and we looked at various methods for providing opportunities to rehearse new skills and procedures before they are put into general effect. In some cases the change agent need go no further; these kinds and amounts of help will be enough to let the client system transfer its tentative changes to the other areas of its existence, where the change agent will not be present. Once the management of a company has become convinced, for instance, that a profit-sharing plan would be desirable, the change agent may be able to withdraw. His support is no longer needed, because as soon as the plan has been put into effect—that is, as soon as the change has been made—the client will derive all the support it needs from the various subparts which are affected by the change. Similarly, the citizen group which has once clearly arrived at an intention to establish a community council may no longer need the change agent's help in winning official acceptance for the change. But we estimate, on the basis of our examination of the case materials, that in a majority of cases the relationship between the change agent and the client system must continue at least through some transfer efforts. The agent's support is needed if the client is to put its aims into effect successfully.

Methods of giving direct support to the client system during the initiation of change

Here one of the most common procedures which change agents use is the establishment of a situation in which the client system may move alternately back and forth between the context of help and the context of general reality. In other words, the change agent tries to see that the client will carry into his normal existence the skills which they have developed together and that he will then return with a report on his success in using the new skills. Consultations with the change agent may occur once a week or several times a week over a period of many months or even years. In many cases the change agent has made the report on the client's success in trying his new skills an established part of each meeting. Such a technique is used not only with individuals but with organizations and communities as well. A report on the training program for the nursing staff of a hospital, for instance, emphasizes this aspect of the agent's role. It points out the dangers of pushing the trainees into making commitments. Instead, the agent tried to create a situation in which the trainees would want to experiment with their new concepts of behavior and voluntarily discuss their experiences. These discussions, from session to session, seemed to sharpen the trainees' understanding of what was required on the job and clarified the next steps of change effort.

In another project, where an effort was being made to help improve the social relations of a number of rejected elementary-school children, the change agent obtained the permission of the children to observe their regular participation in group activities by using a one-way observation screen. What the agent saw was then made a basis for periodic discussions of the children's success in carrying out their change intentions. These discussions served a twofold purpose: to help the children understand more precisely and intelligently just what they were doing, and to give them emotional support and assurance for carrying out their change intentions.

An even more intensive supportive device of this type has been described recently in reports on a program for training and supervising graduate students who were in training to become professional counselors. The object was to bring the trainer into as close a relationship as possible with the trainee while the trainee was practicing his newly learned skills. The trainer sat in an observation booth from which he could observe the trainee in consultation with a client. By means of an electronic device the trainer was able to talk to the trainee without the client's being aware of it. Hence, whenever the trainee attempted a new mode of dealing with the client the trainer could immediately offer criticism, instruction, or support. But change agents emphasize that all of these procedures demand a warm and voluntary relationship between the change agent and the client system; otherwise the attempt to be helpful may merely be irritating.

A second type of directly supportive technique has been described in a number of reports on training groups. Each member of a particular group, for instance, invited a fellow trainee to accompany him and observe his efforts to practice a changed mode of behavior. At the end of a week the trainees exchanged their observations, using them as the basis for evaluating their own change efforts and as objective data for further group discussions. In work with groups and organizations the change intention often is not to adopt new modes of interpersonal relations but to attain a mutual agreement on the advisability of trying some new procedure or practice. Here the agent may offer a different kind of direct support. The report of the change process in the Seattle school system (46) is a good illustration. Several times over a period of years members of the change-agent team were invited as distinguished outsiders to come to meetings in which decisions were made concerning various innovations. The purpose was to allow the members of the change-agent team to support and sanction the proposals which were being offered by the particular subpart of the system with which the team was in contact. There could scarcely be more direct support than this.

In the description of the Scanlon Plan (48) for improving labor and management relations one sees a similar technique at work. Probably Scanlon's background of labor leadership and his prestige with management groups often made it possible for him to exert an especially strong influence on proposed innovations in organizational procedures.

A third type of direct support is illustrated by cases in which the change agent as a member of a team has entered actively into the client system's normal processes in order to carry through the first step of change.

There is, for example, the case of the change agent who met with a staff group to demonstrate the role of observer in the group's staff meetings. His object was to show how an observer would function if one of the group were trained to undertake this role. Similarly, in a fairly large number of community programs we find change agents who have become active members of small groups which are trying to put into effect a change plan that has been developed in collaboration with the agent. In other words, the agent gave up his role as impartial helper and joined in the actual efforts to initiate change.

A fourth type of direct support, exercised from a distance, is illustrated by reports of consultations by telephone during the client system's efforts to put changed concepts into practice. There is an additional case of a group which was experimenting with new leadership practices and which mailed tape recordings of its meetings to the change agent so that he could study them and offer pertinent suggestions.

The concept of direct support from a distance, admittedly rather paradoxical, leads us naturally toward an even less direct kind of supporting procedure which we might call "imagined audience support." This occurs in cases where the relationship between the change agent and the client system is characterized by closeness, willingness, and mutual understanding. In such cases we can assume that the client wants to live up to the expectations of the change agent even when the latter is absent. The psychological presence of the change agent is a source of support and encouragement.

Methods for developing support within the larger client system for change efforts by a subpart

We have seen many reports of failure and frustration caused by the unreadiness of a whole system to support the initial change effort made by one of its subparts. A number of the change agents whose reports we have studied offer suggestions for ways to support a change effort in a particular system by encouraging the whole system, or at least the important parts of it, to sympathize with the intentions of the individual subpart in which the change will occur. For example, some agents have induced the total organization to adopt an experimental attitude toward a proposed innovation by emphasizing that changes in operating procedures or problem-solving methods are not irreversible but can be abandoned if they prove unsatisfactory after a trial period.

Another illustration is provided by the case of a change program in a hospital staff. The nurses wanted to make an innovation in their working procedures but were uncertain whether or not the plan would be approved by the doctors. The change agent met with the doctors, explained the nurses' plans, and obtained the doctors' support for a tryout of the new procedures during an experimental period. The change agent was able to tell the nurses that the doctors were ready to support the change effort, and this provided the necessary backing for the first step in the change program. A similar method was used in a government change project where the change agent acted as an intermediary among several subgroups in a particular bureau. He was able to create an atmosphere of mutual understanding which allowed each subgroup to pursue its part in the planned change with the support of the others. Thus the agent stimulated a kind of reciprocal initiative within the total system. Another project is described in which the change agent prepared a classroom of children to support the change effort of their teacher and also encouraged the parents to look favorably upon the change efforts which were being initiated throughout the school.

The use of a "sanctioning committee" is reported in some cases of work with communities. Here the change agent helps to organize a committee of influential citizens who will give public support and sympathy to the change efforts which are beginning in the community.

When the change effort occurs in a unit which consists of more than one individual, the people who are making the change effort can derive a great deal of support from one another. Some of the research on community and organizational change, for instance, indicates that change can begin most effectively when a team of strategically located individuals has worked in close collaboration with the change agent. This collaboration develops common insights and intentions which provide mutual support and reinforcement when the change program enters the stage of innovation.

In our sample of change projects many agents do not speak of their efforts to provide either direct or indirect support for change efforts in the client system's sphere of existence. As a result, we can report here only a limited variety of methods appropriate to Phase 5. Much creative work remains to be done in developing methods for use in this crucial part of the helping process.

CHANGE METHODS USED IN PHASE 6:

THE GENERALIZATION AND STABILIZATION OF CHANGE

The chief functions of the change agent during Phase 5, as we have described them, are to give support and guidance to the client system during the initiatory steps of actual change and, secondly, to discover ways of assuring a positive response to change throughout the total client system. The chief function of the change agent during Phase 6, on the other hand, is to insure the generalization and the spread of a change effort which has already begun. This involves not only giving the change effort itself a certain prominence or visibility but also providing the means by which information about the consequences of the change can flow easily to all parts of the system. In many cases the means may already exist, of course, but the main point is that there must be a fair and intelligent evaluation of the change by the whole system in which the change effort has occurred. Only in this way can the change, if it is a good one, be incorporated systematically into the client's structure and ongoing processes. Two illustrations will help to clarify this difference between the helping methods of Phase 5 and those of Phase 6.

A change agent was working with the policy staff of a large organization to help the members improve their methods of reaching decisions. It was a question of group problem-solving procedure. The agent and the staff worked together through the phases of diagnosis, examining and interpreting their current procedures, and as a result of this the staff arrived at a number of intentions for change. One of these was the adoption of a technique for slowing down the interaction of the group during its meetings so that the more reflective members would have a chance to contribute to the consideration of each point in the staff's agenda. In other words, group discussions had been too impulsive and had tended to become cursory because some of the more thoughtful members could not be heard. The staff decided to change this by adopting a new and purposely slower, more deliberative procedure. During Phase 5 of the helping process the change agent sat in on a number of staff meetings as an observer and helped the group to scrutinize and appraise its efforts to use the new technique. But he also was involved in efforts to help the group collect specific data which would show whether or not the new technique was working; in other words, he participated in the activities designed to facilitate the flow of information about the consequences of the change (an aspect of Phase 6). For example, he helped the staff members develop and use a post-meeting reaction sheet on which each member of the staff was asked to evaluate the meeting in terms of his own opportunity to participate. That is, each staff member was asked whether his opportunities to express his ideas were greater or fewer than formerly and whether he thought the new processes for reaching group decisions were better, worse, or about the same. In addition, the change agent worked with two members of the group in making a study of the group's efficiency in reaching decisions. The study concerned such questions as the number and kinds of decisions which the group had made before and after the procedural innovations. The change agent helped to process these data so that the group could look at them easily and discuss the findings intelligently. These discussions of the subjective and objective evaluations of the change effort were the primary factor leading the group to accept and institutionalize the new procedures.

In another case a change agent was working with an individual, helping him to improve his social effectiveness so that he could win acceptance from others in interpersonal situations. After a series of consultations, the client arrived at an intention to give freer expression to positive feelings toward others. The change agent tried to support the client's initial efforts (Phase 5) by giving him an opportunity, during the weekly consultations, to talk about his efforts during the past week and to act out verbally a number of episodes which had occurred during the week. The client and the agent agreed that they could see certain clues which seemed to indicate success. Apparently the client's changed behavior toward others was evoking a positive response. But at the same time they both knew that in adult interpersonal relations it is often exceedingly difficult to find out precisely what people feel and think. Consequently, the change agent took direct action (Phase 6) by inviting a number of persons in the client's daily orbit to confer informally with him on their reactions to the client's changed behavior.

Obviously, in many cases the results of change will be so conspicuous that the client system will need no further help in interpreting them. It is clearly evident to the mother of the feeding-problem child, for instance, whether or not the child begins to eat more food when she changes her behavior toward him. And it is probably equally clear to the management of a factory that certain changes in production methods lead or do not lead to consequent changes in production figures. It is our observation, however, that in most cases involving intrapersonal adjustment or interpersonal relations, including changes of social process or structure, the consequences of change are not immediately or clearly visible, with the result that the client system frequently fails to find the support it needs in the success of its own efforts. Therefore, the change agent must provide help in finding and interpreting data on the consequences of change, and he must see that the data are made available to everyone concerned. Here are a few approaches to this problem which have been reported by our sample of change agents.

Methods for assessing the effects of change

The client's experience of new and highly gratifying satisfactions as a result of his efforts to change should be one of the major factors in the acceptance and stabilization of change. But often the effects of change are not immediately perceptible. Those who have participated in the evaluation of research projects know how difficult it often is to identify and appraise the effects of a given change effort. Most client systems larger than a single individual need help in locating and understanding the effects of change.

In a number of cases we find change agents helping their client systems to evaluate change by recalling the pattern of functioning at an earlier time, thus furnishing a means of contrasting the client's state before and after change. Has the change corrected the problem which was uncovered in the diagnosis? This is one way to tell whether or not the consequences of change are worthwhile. Mann's report (44) on a program of research feedback is a good example of this kind of help. Data from an interview study of changes in morale before and after feedback and discussion of diagnosis were collected and presented for interpretation as the basis on which the client system would be able to reject or accept and stabilize certain innovations in procedure.

Again, in a certain community program an annual self-audit was established with the help of a change agent so that progress on a number of change efforts could be periodically surveyed and recorded. The audit covered a number of the community's problems, such as delinquency, intergroup conflict, inadequate recreational facilities, and so forth.

In work with small groups a number of change agents have described techniques for regular evaluations of group progress toward change. Usually these are special meetings or special periods in regular meetings during which various methods of collecting and interpreting data on the effects of change are employed.

In work with individuals we have one example of a case where the change agent helped the client to establish a procedure of periodic and systematic self-interviews or self-evaluations. The object was to increase the client's sensitivity to indications of success or failure. This same client was also helped to develop a means for collecting evaluative information from his associates so that his interpretations could be based on reasonably objective data.

Similarly, a staff group made arrangements for a change agent to return at intervals of several months and observe the group in action. Here the group wanted an "objective mirror" in which it could observe the real value of the changes it was making.

Only a few of the cases we have studied have given evidence of the change agent's attempt to provide the client system with a means for checking the continued consequences of the change effort.

The momentum of change effort as a stabilizing factor

We noted in Chapter 4 that many of the sources of resistance to change in a given system may become stabilizing factors and sources of acceptance once the system has successfully moved through the process of change. We noted also that the general forces which make for stability in any large interdependent system often become factors in the maintenance and stabilization of change. A changed state of affairs produces changed expectations and satisfactions, and these in turn tend to maintain the change. In addition, a system which has already gone through the often painful process of change will probably want to keep the fruits of its labor; it thinks that it should get its effort's worth, so to speak, from the hard work of achieving a new pattern of function or structure. Frequently the client's expense is literally a financial one since most change agents must charge a fee. Consequently, the client feels quite naturally that it should keep what it has paid for. And what it has paid for is the change. Gradually the change will become such an accepted part of the client's normal mode of existence that it will lose its unfamiliarity.

New pride of status as a stabilizing factor

A frequently reported observation is that a client system which becomes involved in interpreting or "selling" its change effort to a neighboring system is likely to become more fully committed to the effects of change. The process of communicating one's satisfactions makes the advantages of change seem more real. For example, a community which had inaugurated a new community council was rather ambivalent toward the value of the new feature until representatives from neighboring communities began to ask questions about the advisability of establishing similar councils. Then, of course, the citizens became aware of their status as the possessors of a new and valued facility. The result was that their indecisive feelings about the community council vanished, and they became fully committed to the usefulness and value of their change effort. Several change agents have described methods by which this type of communication between client and neighboring systems may be encouraged. The Ogden (69) workshop on wheels, for instance, brings teams from other communities into contact with the host community and provides an excellent means for the host community to demonstrate its achievements.

Methods of encouraging a spread of change through demonstration

Change agents who work with communities and organizations are particularly sensitive to the fact that a change in one subpart of a system may be viewed with suspicion and caution by other subparts. The agent must furnish opportunities for the other subparts to learn about the change and accept it without loss of face.

An illustration is provided in the case of a small group of teachers who had developed, with professional help, a new teaching procedure which would improve classroom morale and help children to participate actively in various learning activities. Other teachers were curious about the new procedure but on the whole remained cautious and aloof. The change agent helped the client team develop a demonstration-report in which the teachers could show clearly what they were doing, and the agent supplemented the report with objective interpretations of the reasons for the change effort and what its real meaning seemed to be. The client teachers were not forced to sell or defend; they merely *showed*. The rationale was provided by a neutral outsider. This is essentially the same process as that described by the Tavistock consulting team in its report on the "budding-off conference" in work with an industrial client.

Methods of helping to allay resistance to spread

One of the most discouraging moments in many a process of change comes when resistance to change suddenly appears in an important subpart of the system. Usually the initiating subpart responds by being intensely angry or painfully disheartened. Often it seems incomprehensible to the proponents of change that this kind of resistance should occur. "Why are they resisting something that will benefit them as much as it does us?" "Can't they see that this will be an advantage to the whole community even if they have to give up a little bit?" At such times these and similar statements are what one is likely to hear.

This is the point in the change effort where the professional agent's help is often indispensable. His objectivity can help stimulate an effort to analyze the difficulty intelligently. Sometimes only he can prevent the client from giving up altogether or attempting bullheadedly to push the change through against insuperable opposition. In addition to giving his help with an objective analysis of difficulties and strategies, the agent can often act as a mediator or liaison among the conflicting subparts, and he may be able to bring about a modification of the resistance. In a large government bureau, for instance, a change agent had helped the first-line supervisors to develop a new procedure for planning work assignments within the group. The people at the next level of supervision resisted the new procedure until the change agent met with them and told them how the new plan had developed, how it would work, and how it would benefit them as well as other parts of the total system.

The institutionalization of change as a stabilizing factor

We have already referred to the fact that once a new practice is adopted or a new pattern of behavior is fully accepted, forces for the maintenance of the new state of affairs—and against additional change—begin to arise. In Chapter 4 we spoke of opposition to change as resistance forces, but there we were speaking primarily of forces which come into operation at the beginning or during the process of a change. Once a change has been successfully completed, the forces which resist tampering with it or abandoning it are in effect forces against changing a change.

This raises a number of problems for the change agent. Naturally it seems desirable for a new procedure or mode of behavior to be fully accepted and "internalized" by the client system, but at the same time there is a danger that the new practice will be embraced so eagerly as an answer to all problems that it will produce a wholly undesirable rigidity in the system's conceptual outlook toward further change. No single change can equip a system to meet every problem that may arise in the future, unless it is the change from unwillingness to willingness to change. An important part of the change agent's job is to encourage both enthusiasm for the present change and a realization that every change, including the present one, is more or less tentative and never final.

CHANGE METHODS USED IN PHASE 7:
ACHIEVING A TERMINAL RELATIONSHIP

In the discussion of Phase 2 (establishing a helping relationship) we noted that one of the important aspects of entering and remaining in a helping relationship is a mutual understanding about the length of time the relationship will last and the kind of work which each partner will be expected to do. As the helping relationship passes through its various phases, two conflicting tendencies manifest themselves within the client system, one or the other being dominant at any particular time. Sometimes the dominant tendency is to seek a termination of the change relationship and to regain autonomy or at least freedom from the restrictive association with the change agent. At other times the dominant tendency may be to seek a closer and more dependent relationship with the change agent and to resist any possibility of a break in the association. Most change agents, whether they work with individuals or with larger systems, report this same pattern of internal conflict. Moreover, they report such conflicts within themselves. Sometimes the change agent feels that the client system cannot possibly function without help and guidance. At other times he feels that the relationship with the client system should be ended, either because he himself has been rejected or because the client has reached the point where help is no longer needed. We shall not analyze here the ups and downs of these competing forces. Instead, we want to look at the methods which change agents use to assist the process of arriving at a mutually satisfactory terminal relationship. We use this phrase "terminal relationship" advisedly, because we do not mean "termination of the relationship." We have observed that in many cases of change there is some kind of a continuing relationship between the client system and the change agent even after the initial change has been achieved.

All of the change methods which we have described in the preceding chapters can be viewed as the attempts of the change agent to help the client system acquire the use of resources which have been hitherto blocked, unco-ordinated, nascent, or only potential and to deploy these resources in such a way that they will contribute to the controlled efficiency of the system. The job of the change agent in Phase 7, on the other hand, seems to be to help the client system assess its achievement in the change effort. The client system must decide whether or not its resources have been successfully mobilized and secured, and it must decide whether or not change is in general a successful way to solve its problems.

Much depends, of course, upon the client's experience in the preceding two phases; if this experience has been satisfactory, then
the client's decisions will be affirmative. It will be apparent that
the change effort was indeed a feasible means of dealing with the
problems of one's existence in reality, one's "life situation," and
that change effort can produce positive consequences. But there
are a number of other interesting questions which arise at this
terminal stage.

Has the helping relationship been specific only to certain types
of problems, or has it provided a basis for attacking a variety of
new and unpredictable problems? Has there been any provision
for incorporating the kind of function performed by the change
agent into the permanent structure of the system, and can such a
provision be made? Is there a need for periodic examinations of
the system's ongoing operations to identify new sources of difficulty and dispose of them before they become serious? Has the
client system been helped to learn how to identify problems which
are beyond its resources and how to obtain help if such problems
arise?

Here are a few illustrations of the methods which change agents
have used in dealing with these questions of the terminal relationship.

General preparation for changeability

At several points in our discussion we have noted that some
change agents, instead of solving problems directly, prefer to give
their client systems training in "problem-solving methodology."
For example, some of our change agents who have worked with
organizations and communities have trained the systems to carry
out diagnostic self-studies and have not attempted to make their
own separate and independent diagnoses.

Some change agents stress collaboration in the processes of
diagnosis. They ask the client system to participate actively in
the work of gathering and interpreting diagnostic data so that
both members of the partnership can work together toward an understanding of what the trouble is and how it should be remedied.
Change agents have explained their insistence on this kind of

participation by saying that it lowers the client's resistance to change. But there is an even more significant reason: in most cases the involvement of the client in the processes of diagnosis affords a training in the general methodology of problem solving which will serve in the future to help the client meet the problems which will continue to arise as long as the client, whether individual organism or social system, exists.

Methods by which the role of the change agent may be permanently incorporated in the client system

We have noted already a number of instances in which small groups have established a permanent group observer by delegating this function to one of their members. The purpose of such an innovation is to provide a means by which the group may continue to collect diagnostic data on new problems whenever they arise; the device makes self-diagnosis and problem solving a regular part of the group's routine. Similarly, in reports of work with larger organizations and communities there are several cases in which one of the changes introduced in the structure of the client system was a permanent operational research unit staffed by trained personnel. Such units are designed to furnish the organization or community with a continuing flow of information about operational efficiency, the assumption being that areas of difficulty will show up in the unit's data before they become critical. In effect, any community which conducts a self-survey automatically receives into its structure a more or less permanent change agent. Whenever a self-survey team is trained, its members presumably retain their skills and continue to afford the community a source of self-help.

Conducting periodic examinations

So far the notion of periodic checkups to prevent problems or catch them at an early stage has not made much progress in the fields of professional help we have studied here. Even the annual audits which have been instituted in communities and the procedures of periodic self-interview for individuals are intended primarily to keep track of progress in solving problems which already exist, not to discover new problems or potential problems. True, some work has been done with preventive psychiatry, especially with children, but virtually nothing of this sort has been attempted in larger systems. It would seem worthwhile for communities, organizations, and groups to investigate the advisability of establishing procedures for periodic examinations of some kind, either by external change agents or by specialized subparts of the system.

Learning when and how to ask for further help

In our world of rapid change and growing complexity it seems rather unrealistic for any change agent or client system to think that a brief period of professional help will ever equip a client to continue completely alone from then on. Outside help may never again be needed to meet the particular problem which has caused difficulty, and perhaps after a given change effort the particular kind of outside helper from whom assistance has just been secured will never be needed again. But it seems safe to say that any client system will need help of some kind from time to time. The conditions of individual, corporate, and social life today are such that single systems can almost never protect themselves against all the contingencies for which professional help is the only rational answer. Consequently, many change agents feel that they are responsible for teaching their client systems to adopt appropriate attitudes toward seeking outside help. Clients need to know in general what kind of help is needed for different kinds of problems and where it can be obtained. The agent must make known his own future availability as a source of help, but in a way that avoids creating feelings of dependency, and he must tell the client how to go about finding other kinds of help. None of the change agents whose work we have reviewed has described specific procedures for meeting these problems, although some have shown that they are aware of them. The literature on human-relations training, however, does contain a number of illustrations of ways in which people have been trained to approach consultants and to define the need for help effectively. We have not been able to find any material on ways to differen-

tiate between the need for outside help and the need for mobilizing internal resources. Some attention has been given by professional groups such as the American Psychological Association
to the problem of providing materials which will help a prospective client system to appraise the professional competence of
change agents and suggest ways to locate appropriate sources of
help. But even this aspect of the problem is largely untouched.

SOME FURTHER COMPARATIVE OBSERVATIONS
ON CHANGE METHODS

During these final phases of the change process there are striking differences among change agents in respect to their ability to
enter or observe the client system's sphere of action. Agents who
work with individuals have relatively little opportunity to observe the day-to-day actions of the client, and they must rely chiefly
upon the client's reports of his success in applying new skills to
the exigencies of daily life. In addition, of course, therapists can
learn a good deal by observing the behavior of the client during
the actual episodes of the helping relationship. Agents who work
with individuals in group-training sessions must depend almost
solely upon the clients' reports of their out-of-training experiences.
Agents who work with small groups are much more likely to be in
direct contact with the client's sphere of action. Acting as immediate observers of group actions and techniques, these agents can
offer direct support and prompt evaluations of the client's attempts
to initiate new procedures. Change agents who work with organizations and communities usually participate to some extent in the
ongoing life of the system, but the change efforts (for example,
new procedures, new channels of communication, new structural
arrangements, and so forth) are often so spread out in time and
space that the change agent cannot serve as a direct observer and
supporter of the specific actions of the client.

In addition, change agents who work with individuals and small
groups can interpret the effect of change much more quickly and

easily than can agents who work with organizations and communities. It is much easier to collect information about the consequences of change in a small unit than it is to find out precisely
what has happened when the change is spread over many parts of
a large unit.

When we turn to the question of procuring the support of other
subparts in a system for the change effort which is being made by
a particular subpart, we find that agents who work with clearly
hierarchical systems have been the most active. They are frequently called upon to assume an intermediary role between the
hierarchical levels of a client system, their task being to win approval on one level of authority for a change which is desired on
another level. However, we do find that therapists working with
children sometimes take on a similar role in relation to parents,
and the "sanctioning committee" which has been used in some
community programs to win support in the community at large for
the change effort of a particular subpart also seems to fill an essentially meliorative role.

The technique of stimulating mutual support among the members of a client team is seen most frequently in organizational
and community programs of change. Occasionally, however, in
groups such as Alcoholics Anonymous and in other programs of
group therapy, an atmosphere of common experience produces
mutual support for individual attempts to accomplish behavioral
innovations.

On the other hand, agents who work with all types of client systems use the device of demonstration to stimulate enthusiasm for
change in a client system. In work with individual trainees a number of agents have pointed out that one of the easiest ways to be
sure that a given change will be thoroughly "internalized" is to
get the trainee to become a trainer. As educators have often said,
"The best way to learn it is to teach it." And we have already
noted how some change agents working with organizations and
communities induce their clients to demonstrate their change techniques to neighboring systems, thus acquiring a kind of investment in their own success.

One of the greatest differences among agents who work at the various levels of client systems seems to occur in connection with the problem of assuring a spread of change throughout the client system. As we have seen, it is usually a question of winning acceptance of a given change from all the important parts of a system so that the change will not remain isolated in one subpart but will become ingrained in the whole structure. The agents who work with large systems are the ones most concerned about this problem, for obvious reasons. Usually change in a large organization or community is instigated by a particular subpart. If it remains solely in that subpart it will probably become a focal point for resistance. Hence before the change can be stabilized it must spread throughout the system. However, this is a problem which occasionally comes up in work with individuals too. Here it is a question of bringing into play the whole personality of the client. A patient who has consciously learned a new technique of behavior may still resist it subconsciously. It would be interesting to explore more systematically the differences and similarities between processes of spread and resistance in highly interdependent personality systems and in large, less cohesive organizational and community systems.

Another basis for comparisons among the different kinds of systems is the ease with which they can absorb a permanent "mechanism of changeability." By this we mean their ability to build into their permanent structures a mechanism for performing the function of the change agent after the change agent is gone. Probably large systems can do this more easily than small ones can, or at least more easily than individuals can. A division of labor is required; one subpart must be appointed or created to play the permanent role of the change agent. This is often a fairly simple matter in large organizations or communities where the system as a whole can command a wide range of resources. When the client is a single person, however, the problem is much more difficult. Techniques for self-assessment are never wholly satisfactory, because the individual cannot remove his assessing faculties far enough from the rest of the system to collect objective data and interpret them dispassionately. In other words, it is virtually impossible for the individual to be detached, in any practical sense of the word, from himself. In the larger client systems, such as organizations and communities, there are not only specialized subparts of the system which can take on this kind of responsibility, but there are very often persons whose professional skills equip them for precisely this kind of work. Small groups fall in between. Agents who work with small groups have often mentioned this problem and have complained about the difficulty of finding a member of the group who is equipped to become a group observer. Nevertheless, many small groups have attempted to assure the continuity of change by adopting some such structural mechanism.

Finally, there is the business of ending the change relationship completely. Agents who work with individuals find that this is a phase of particularly delicate emotional problems, while agents who work with larger systems are more concerned about questions of spread and stabilization. The individual whose change effort has been thoroughly successful will be able to give up his relationship with the change agent without suffering unduly the loss of the agent's stabilizing influence, and the organization or community which has fully accepted the results and methods of change will be able to continue on its new course without the agent's direction or advice. But most important of all, it seems to us, is the client's ability to face new problems and new changes, and this is true whether the client is an individual or a large social system. Many change agents feel that they must inculcate the right attitudes toward change and if possible arrange for the establishment of an actual "mechanism of changeability" before they can safely say that a terminal relationship has been achieved.

SOME FURTHER COMPARATIVE OBSERVATIONS
ON CHANGE FORCES AND RESISTANCE FORCES

In addition to the forces facilitating and blocking change which we have previously discussed (and which continue to occur throughout the change process), there are several new dynamic factors which become particularly apparent during the later phases, the phases of application, stabilization, and termination.

Emergent forces toward change and the stabilization of change

Probably the most significant emergent force toward change is that which arises from the acceptance and approval of the change effort by the rest of the system or by neighboring systems. In almost every case we have analyzed we have seen the crucial importance for the client system of the anticipated response, and then the actual response, to its change. Nowhere else is the function of status anxieties more obvious. Acceptance and approval are strong additional incentives to intensify and sustain the change effort.

The client's motivation in many cases is further shaped and strengthened by the praise and active support of the change agent, especially when actual steps are attempted in practicing new techniques. This is a particularly important factor in cases where there is no other immediate reward or where there may be a negative response from other systems not engaged in the change process. The client obviously can cope with external resistances much more easily if he feels that the change agent at least is on his side.

Even in cases where the change agent is not actually present or the helping relationship has been ended early in the change process, the image of the change agent's expectations may exert an important force toward continued change. The client can draw strength from the thought of what the agent would do and say if he were on hand.

The importance of mutual support and a mutual commitment has been mentioned also. Where individuals are working together as a team they gain a sense of mutuality from their joint commitment and shared experience, and this may be true even if they are each working toward different goals (that is, toward personal, individual changes in individual life situations). The members of a program in group therapy can face their individual frustrations and awkwardnesses with a much stronger faith if they know they are all going through virtually the same ordeals.

Another very important source of motivations toward change

may be the appearance of evidence that the change effort is actually producing the desired effect. The evidence may consist of internal cues, a slackening of pain or tension; or it may be external to the system in the form of higher rates of productivity, more effective communication with other systems, and so forth.

Finally, we noted that during these phases of change the desire to attain the full benefits from effort expended—or money spent—may exert a powerful stimulus toward continuing the change effort until the end. Any expenditure of time, money, or effort signalizes an investment in the success of the process at stake, and this creates a momentum which carries the process onward. Sometimes this momentum is institutionalized, as it were, in actual structural changes within the client system, and these changes make it difficult to give up the change effort.

Forces toward giving up
or reversing the change effort

Probably the emergent resistance to change which is most common is that which arises from the negative responses of other parts of the client system or of neighboring systems. When one's experiment in change is derided or ignored there is pressure to abandon it. Frequently a vested interest, either inside or outside the system, will offer such strong resistance to change that it cannot be overcome. Sometimes, on the other hand, resistance springs from the unsuitable methods which the client system and the change agent have used in introducing change, and this kind of resistance may be overcome by adopting more acceptable tactics.

The blockage which occurs when unsuitable methods have been used may be evidence of a lack of skill in communicating or demonstrating change intentions. Sometimes the subpart of the client system which is active in change becomes alienated from the rest of the system, and the resulting conflict in values leads to an unwise choice of change techniques—unwise, that is, from the point of view of winning acceptance from the rest of the system. Paradoxically, the development of a close relationship with the change agent may lead the active subpart away from the rest of the client system, a situation which the change agent himself must do his best to correct if the total change effort is to succeed.

A third type of blockage may result from the return of the client subsystem to active contact with the rest of the system after a period of relative isolation in a "cultural island." When the subsystem returns to the parent system, the old pressures of conformity and tradition may reactivate former resistances to change.

Finally, in many kinds of cases the people who are making a change effort experience great difficulty in obtaining reliable information about the effects of their change. Often this may lead them to fear that their efforts are producing a weaker or different effect than they had expected, and they may therefore decide, on insufficient grounds, that their efforts are not really worthwhile.

Special forces toward a continuation or termination of the change relationship

As we indicated earlier, very few of the change agents whose reports we have studied offered helpful observations about the process of terminating a change relationship. However, we can infer from the little material we have seen that the most common source of a desire to continue the change relationship is the client system's wish to go on receiving the rewards which the change agent, as a source of support and approval, can offer. In other words, the change relationship has developed into a relationship of emotional dependency which may persist beyond the end of the actual change effort. In addition, the client system may experience a kind of technical dependency; the skills needed to carry on the change may not yet be fully developed in the client system, thus prolonging the need for outside help. Sometimes the client system may anticipate the emergence of new problems which it will find difficult to solve without the help of the change agent.

Beyond these motivations which arise from the client's dependency, the change agent himself may feel that the relationship should be continued beyond the point of normal termination. He may want to continue enjoying the emotional rewards of his dominant position, or he may simply feel that the client still has a lot to learn.

But the contrary desire to break off the relationship is often just as strong. Most client systems want to prove that they can stand on their own feet and that they are capable of carrying through the planned changes. Often the change agent can heighten this motive by saying that this is precisely what he expects; that is to say, he reinforces the client's pride in independence by establishing an expectation of strength and success.

As we have seen, the change agent can often assist the development of a desire to end the change relationship by arranging for periodic consultations or examinations for an indefinite time after the end of the change effort. Similarly, the end of the change relationship can be made easier for the client system by the development within the system of specific mechanisms to substitute for the role of the outside change agent.

SOME UNFINISHED BUSINESS

10

The comparative analysis which we have offered in the nine preceding chapters leaves us with a rather insistent sense of unfinished business, both for ourselves and for the helping professions. It seems that we end up with many more questions and problems than we had at the beginning. Perhaps, then, there will be some value in stating some of the general problems which still demand attention.

1. Does our tentative framework for describing and generalizing the change process and the role of the change agent stand up when it is applied to the work of a larger sample of change agents and to a wider variety of cases of planned change? Very likely our own provisional analysis of the present sample of change cases needs modifications. In what areas should these modifications be made, and what directions should they take?

2. What problems stand out as priorities for research and for theory development? Does the framework we have constructed help us to locate these priorities?

3. What are some of the important methodological problems of research on the processes of planned change? (We shall attempt

some answers to this and the previous question in this chapter.)

4. What clusters of data and theoretical insight have already emerged in the behavioral and social sciences which may now be integrated in a comprehensive theory of change? What help can we obtain from personality theory, learning theory, role theory, social-structure theory, from group dynamics, and so forth? This task of translating relevant concepts and data from the behavioral sciences into insights about planned change and the technology of giving help presents an exciting challenge, but it is one that is outside the scope of this book. However, we believe that some of the current work on the utilization of the behavioral sciences by the professions (82, 84, 88, 89, 93) is moving in this direction.

5. What does our analysis of change procedures suggest for the scientific and professional training of change agents? Is the time ripe for giving a broader interdisciplinary cast to professional training? Precisely what would be the ingredients of such training? (These questions will be explored in Chapter 11.)

As noted above, this chapter will be devoted to a consideration of some possible directions for future research, to some of the chief methodological problems of research on change, and to a few observations on the development of a theory of planned change, which will be made at random throughout our discussion. Researchers and theorists in the various disciplines are working constantly to improve our general understanding of personality structure and function, the dynamic operations of small groups, and the social dynamics of organizations and communities. And each year we see more and more fruitful generalizations which cut across these areas of theory. Our special focus here is on the need for a unified theory of change and changeability and on a number of priorities for research and experiment which are indicated by our analysis.

CHANGEABILITY WITHIN THE SYSTEM

The need for an objective view of the system's life history

Every type of client system has characteristic patterns of growth and development. For the individual there are both physical- and mental-growth cycles as well as characteristic sequences of psychological development. Groups, organizations, and communities all reveal at least three distinct phases: periods of growth and expansion, periods of stability, and periods of decline. There may also be transitional periods when the system's modes of operation and organization are undergoing significant changes.

It seems probable that the kind of change which any client system can undertake at a given time depends upon what phase of development the system is in. Consequently, the change agent needs to know what the significant phases are, how to identify them, and how to adapt to them in helping to conduct a program of planned change.

An interesting study by Long which is now in progress (90) illustrates the possibilities for research in this area. The study is part of a larger project which is being carried out by Blocksma, Fox, Lippitt, and others (2) to help elementary-school children improve their skills and sensitivities in social behavior. Long has been able to collect data on the mental and physical development of these children since they entered school, and he has located each child on a physical- and mental-growth curve. He hopes to use the position of the child on this curve, together with information about the slope of the curve, in attempting to understand the ability of the child to benefit from help in changing his patterns of social relations.

There is another kind of historical data which is important for the change agent. This is information about the past successes and failures of the client system. Individuals and groups tend to dramatize their past experiences, insisting that something which has failed once can never succeed again or that something which has succeeded once must be repeated over and over. Yet conclusions derived from the past are often not in accord with the present.

We need further research to help us understand the conditions in which a client system is able to break free from its past, as contrasted to the conditions in which the system is a victim of its past and unable to commit itself to something new.

The parameters of change-potential

As we learn more about any particular kind of system, we tend to develop certain assumptions about ways in which it can or cannot change. At the level of the individual, for example, many different techniques can be used to define the capacities of a client, specifying the typical levels of performance which he can be expected to achieve. The intelligence test was one of the earliest of these techniques, but it has been followed by personality tests of all kinds, vocational-preference inventories, marital-adjustment inventories, and many other measures of personal predisposition and competence. In industry we find assumptions about what constitutes a "reasonable" rate of production. Groups and communities, too, share certain assumptions about what is a reasonable amount of work or a reasonable level of aspiration.

The change agent is of two minds about these assumptions and classifications. To the extent that they are valid they help him to make realistic plans with the client system for future goals and programs of change. On the other hand, he has seen many cases in which they have proved invalid. Faced with the right challenge, individuals transcend their measurable potentialities. The "incurables" of yesterday are being cured today. The Scanlon Plan in industry (48) serves as one example among many of the way in which a new approach to the organization of work has resulted in important changes in "normal" production rates. Occasionally groups and communities also have surpassed the highest hopes of their members.

Here, then, is another area in which research is necessary. Assumptions about the capacities or limitations of a client system, or a group of client systems, can be tested only by change efforts which challenge them. In the face of such challenges probably some of our present assumptions would hold up, others would fall. But in either case it is important that the challenge be made.

Interdependence as a factor in the change process

Our interest in the client system as a system has led us repeatedly to focus our attention on the relationships between the parts of the system and between the system and the environment. We have been especially interested in interdependence and in the process by which change in one part of a system or its environment leads to change or counterchange in another.

A good deal of information about sequences of cause and effect within a particular kind of system has been obtained by investigators in the particular scientific specialties, and more is being added all the time. Consider, for example, the question of how an individual learns. Educators know a lot about how he learns in school. Social psychologists and specialists in communication know how he acquires attitudes and beliefs and how these may be changed through indoctrination and new experience. Psychologists have developed several different theories of learning, and they are finding out more and more about the conditions in which each is applicable. All of this helps us to understand something about what sequences of events will lead to a change in an individual. Similarly, specialists in other fields can make a number of significant "if-then" statements about sequences of cause and effect in the systems which they have studied.

In many cases the change agent can use this information as a guide when he is planning new change projects. In some cases, however, he finds that the theorist who is concerned with the system per se treats it as if it existed in complete isolation. Statements of cause and effect are valid only if there are no "external" forces at work. Yet the change agent's objective may be to set up precisely such an external force. Then new research is required to find out what happens to the internal dynamics of the system when an external change force is introduced.

A recent study of attitudes in fraternity houses (25) illustrates the error of assuming that ordinary patterns of organization and interdependence will determine what happens in critical or extraordinary situations. The study was conducted on a campus where there had been some fairly vigorous agitation to do away with discrimination in admitting members to fraternities. Some of the

fraternities argued that it was impossible for them to change because they were chartered by national organizations whose constitutions required discrimination. It might have been expected that
the attitudes of fraternity members toward admitting newcomers
from minority groups would be the same as those reflected in the
laws of their respective national organizations. But this was not
the case. In fact, there was no relationship at all between the attitudes of fraternity members and what their national constitutions
said (or did not say) on the matter of discrimination. Rather, the
important determinants of fraternity attitudes seemed to be the
needs which individuals were attempting to satisfy through their
fraternity memberships. This is a perfectly reasonable finding,
but it probably would not have been scientifically observable except
under conditions of stress. If the conventional fraternity views had
not been under attack, then very likely the fraternity members
would have been willing to accept the guidance of their national
officers and it would have been impossible to differentiate the other
factors which affected their beliefs.

Many more examples could be cited from practical experience
as well as from research to show that a system engaged in change
will exhibit unusual patterns of interdependence, either between
parts of the system or between the system and the environment.
Discovering the nature and determinants of these relationships is
an important part of research on changeability.

One reason why it is so important to clarify patterns of interdependence both within the system and between systems is that
this knowledge is crucial for the change agent in deciding how
large a unit he shall accept as a client system. As we have seen,
the change agent sometimes makes mistakes and accepts as client
a system which cannot possibly achieve the goal that has been
agreed upon. For instance, he works with one level of a hierarchy
when he ought to be working with three, or he works with a child
when he ought to be working with the peer group or the parent.

Motivation and readiness to change

We have noted before that we seem to know very little either
about the development of pain or about the development of "images

of potentiality" in systems larger than the individual. Brim (4) found that the basis of a motivation toward change is significantly related to the acceptance and use of the change agent's help. In other words, the capacity for change may be great, but the readiness to change may be very little. There is practically no research on the "natural" development of a need for change and not much on what kind of stimulus situation will lead to an awareness of pain, a higher level of aspiration, or a desire to seek outside help. Here are a number of questions that require investigation. The whole subject of motive and readiness is obscure. Readiness for what? What different objectives and procedures are suitable to different types of readiness? How does readiness shift as the change process develops? What are the symptoms of readiness to accept and use new insights into the nature of problems within the system?

The resolution of conflicting loyalties

A great deal of research evidence indicates that attitudes and values tend to be anchored in the relationship between one person or group and another. This fact is important for both change and resistance to change. As the relationship with the change agent develops and as change goals are defined, the client system usually finds itself in a situation of conflicting loyalties. On one hand is the change agent with his demands and expectations, on the other is a complex of reference systems which has largely determined the client's status and conventional attitudes. The client is tempted to be loyal to the change agent when he is present and loyal to the other systems when they are present. But the need for a continuous self-identity and the fact that these opposed loyalties usually overlap create conflicts which must be resolved somehow—by giving up one relationship, by finding a compromise, by changing one set of allegiances to make them compatible with the other, or perhaps, in dire cases, by the client's removing itself from the disturbing situation. Ways of handling conflict between opposed loyalties are an important part of the change process. If we had a better understanding of this conflict and possible ways of resolving it, we would know more about planned change. Basic and applied research are much needed.

WHAT DO CHANGE AGENTS ACTUALLY DO?

Much of what we know about planned change comes from the reports which have been made on actual change projects either by the change agents themselves or by co-operating research teams. It is this variety of case studies which gives us insight into the details of change and makes it possible for us to distinguish between the techniques which have led to success and those which have led to failure. But there is a great need for more systematic and detailed reports of success and failure. Every point of decision in the change process sets up a new research problem: What is the most effective and satisfactory way to proceed, given these specific conditions? Or, putting it another way, what consequences would follow from taking each of the alternative choices of action which appear at this point in the change process? The number of research problems which would follow from this approach is enormous, and we cannot hope to discuss them all. However, we shall try to examine some of the chief areas in which more research is needed.

Conditions in which the assistance or intervention of the change agent is indicated

In our discussion we have tended to assume the presence of a change agent who is working with a client system to achieve the latter's change goals. But it is important to remember that in many circumstances the client system may be able to work without a change agent and may prefer to do so. One of the questions that concerns both parties, therefore, is the question of determining in what conditions the assistance of the change agent may be useful or necessary and in what conditions the client system can do better working alone. These conditions may have to do with the nature of the client's problem, the client's skills and past experiences, the client's readiness or unreadiness for change and his expectations for the change process, the accessibility of the change agent, and many other things.

A related question is whether the client system should depend upon its own observations in diagnosing its problems or call in outside help. What kind of diagnostic assistance will be most useful to the system? The problem is always one of how to obtain for the system the best view of its own needs and difficulties in terms of its power to act. Too much information, by presenting a range of problems too great for the system to solve, may be as damaging as too little information or information which is distorted.

Once the helping relationship has been established, questions continually arise concerning the appropriateness or inappropriateness of the change agent's intervention at each stage of the change process. Ezriel (86) has proposed an ingenious model for research on questions of this kind. He develops the reasons why "psychoanalytic literature is exceedingly poor with regard to criteria for correct interpretations, or with regard to a theory of predictable responses to interpretations," and he then suggests and illustrates a procedure for predicting what the client's response should be if a diagnostic interpretation is correct and appropriate. A large number of checks on the correctness of predictions, and hence on the theory of dynamic processes being studied, can be made in each sequence of interaction between the change agent and the client system. Great strides could be made toward a theory of the process of change if a few change agents working with various types of systems at each of the four levels would begin to explore such prediction designs and to think seriously about the data which would emerge.

Problems of getting started

If a change agent is committed to a working relationship with a client system, he will want to create an understanding of the discrepancy between the way things are and the way they might be, and he will want to amplify the reasons which lie behind existing pains and dissatisfactions. Both of these aims can be sources of discouragement, particularly for the client system but also for the change agent. Certainly a very important problem for study concerns the means by which a change agent can stimulate aspirations for the future and insights into the present without creating acute feelings of hopelessness or frustration. In effect, this means that ways must be found which will make it possible for the client system and the change agent to live with frustration, to accept it as a challenge rather than an insurmountable obstacle. This is a perennial problem for change agents, and it is not easily solved. Two different approaches to it are suggested by current practices. Some change agents focus attention on the immediate next steps in the change process, depending upon constant activity and a succession of minor successes to prevent the client's withdrawal. Other agents assume a responsibility for progress, thereby fostering a sense of confidence in the client, based either upon the agent's past successes with similar systems or upon a personal relationship in which the client is encouraged to become emotionally dependent upon the agent. Research could help to investigate the effectiveness of these two approaches and their effects upon later stages of the change sequence. A point which certainly needs to be explored is the possibility of developing more refined techniques for making frustration more of an asset and less of a liability.

The growth of the relationship between the change agent and the client system offers another important opportunity for research. We need to know more about the decisions which establish the quality and atmosphere of the relationship and how these decisions are put into effect. Does each change agent have preconceived definitions of the roles which are to be played by himself and the client system, definitions which are reapplied in each new case, or does he vary the pattern of the relationship to meet different conditions? If the latter is true, what conditions influence the agent's decisions? For each kind of relationship, how are expectations established? What is the process by which the client learns and accepts his role and his relationship with the change agent?

A recent study by Polansky and Kounin (96) is directed toward this last question. Interviews were conducted with one hundred and fifty persons who had just come from their first consultations with a professional helper. In these interviews each person was asked about his reactions to the consultation and to the helper. When the results of the interviews were analyzed, they showed that during the consultations the clients had been engaged consciously or unconsciously in making two kinds of judgments: first, an appraisal of the change agent's ability to help with the specific problem, and second, an estimate of how much satisfaction could be expected from a relationship with the change agent. The first judgment is associated with the client's willingness to follow the agent's advice, the second with his willingness to return and see the agent again. Both factors, of course, are involved in any final commitment to a working relationship with the change agent. It would be interesting to see what could be done if the ideas suggested by this study were explored in research with other types of client systems.

Another part of getting started which lends itself readily to research is the problem of bridging the gap between the original points of view of the change agent and the client system. Agent and client are likely to view the client's difficulties in different ways, each starting with a different set of premises and assumptions and each convinced that his own interpretation is the more accurate one. When a working relationship is established the client usually moves toward the view of the change agent. Often the problem of reaching agreement on the client's difficulties is defined in terms of the client's readiness or resistance, but in actual practice there is likely to be give and take on both sides. The research problem, therefore, is how to expedite communication between two persons who possess contradictory views of the same situation and how— assuming that sometimes communication is impossible—to tell in advance whether or not efforts to develop a common frame of reference will be successful.

Another area for research involves evaluation of the effectiveness of different techniques which the change agent can use to stimulate change. Thus, for example, there have been a number of investigations of the effectiveness of different techniques in changing attitudes. Comparisons have been made between factual reports, emotional appeals, and direct experience. Other studies compare different methods of presentation such as lectures, printed materials, movies, and radio. Another comparison is between change agents who present a candid explanation of all factors in a given change program and those who withhold certain kinds of interpretations from the client system. At the community level there have been studies comparing the effectiveness of demonstration (what others have done) with that of consultation (what you might do), and comparisons of the results achieved by change agents whose contact with the community varies from immediate and direct to distant and indirect (for example, the work of the Ogdens). Another contrast suggested by parts of our analysis would be between techniques which concentrate on creating pain or awareness of difficulty (shock techniques) and those which focus upon trying to raise the client's level of aspiration.

Other studies are concerned with the process by which a change stimulus is introduced. The series of experiments on group decision enter in here, as do the experiments on different ways of reporting research findings back to groups and organizations for their use in making decisions.

Although some research has been undertaken on problems of initiating the change effort, much more remains to be done before we can fully understand all aspects of this stage of the change process.

Transforming diagnostic understanding into path-goal images

Once a change agent has formulated his idea of what is wrong and what has caused it, how do he and the client system decide what to do about it? Though it seems to be taken pretty much for granted in the case reports of many change agents, this crucial step is by no means obvious. The principles which govern the transformation of diagnostic insight into change goals and intentions are a very prominent part of the theory of planned change. How does one differentiate ahead of time, for instance, between change objectives that are within the range of changeability and those that are impossible or improbable? How does one select the right leverage point? What kind of testing is possible to make these decisions more reliable? A study of the ways in which change agents, or change agents and client systems acting together, reach these decisions would add considerably to our understanding of the agent's role. Perhaps the most common single source of failure in change efforts is the difficulty of converting information about a given problem into strategic and tactical projections of what should be done about it.

Evaluating the progress of change

Many change efforts must be kept going for a comparatively long time before there is any clear success. Things may get worse before they get better. An important question for the change agent is: "How can I give the client system information, or techniques for obtaining information, which will show that progress toward the change goal is (or is not) being made?" Later in this chapter we shall discuss some of the methodological problems of evaluating change. At this point we want only to emphasize the importance of developmental research on techniques for ensuring this flow of information to clients. In some of the work with small groups a post-meeting reaction form (PMR) is used at the end of each meeting to collect information on feelings about relationships as well as opinions about group decisions, group efficiency, and so forth. These data are graphed and reported back to the group as a developmental chart of certain changes that are taking place. The change agent himself often acts as a source of information on progress, but there is still need for a variety of means of assessing progress at each stage of change. Here, then, is another point where the invention of new professional practices would be greatly welcomed.

The supportive context for change

The context in which change occurs is, of course, a matter of interest to theorists. Change agents have tried to find ways of setting the change activity apart from ordinary events in order to maximize the client's freedom to learn. Thus workshops are located in remote and attractive parts of the country, the participants in the workshops are discouraged from bringing their families, and the activities of the workshops are designed to occupy the full attention of the delegates during their waking hours. Similarly, individual therapists create special environments through the use of furniture, lighting, and the carefully scheduled fifty-minute hour. There has been less research than one might expect on the effects of these environmental variables, perhaps because the creation of a special environment is too big an operation to be made the subject of comparative study. The work of Lippitt (12) which showed that delegates attending a workshop as members of a team changed more than delegates who attended as individuals serves to illustrate the way in which a single environmental variable may be isolated and studied. However, much more could be done to specify the effects of different environmental variables on the entire change process.

In all of these studies of technique and procedure the nature of the contrasting alternatives tends to be specific to the particular kind of client system and the particular kind of change. Generalizations which extend to other systems or to a general theory of change are therefore difficult. In fact, before such generalizations become possible it will be necessary for more research workers to define their alternatives in terms which are conceptually as well as practically significant.

Perhaps the most critical question one asks in connection with problems of context is how much of the social system must be included in a given change effort in order to assure success. Is it enough to work with the child, for instance, or should the agent bring in the teacher and the family? Can one work with the personnel department alone, or must one work with the whole company? If it were necessary to designate one problem on which change agents most need help from research and theory, we should select the question, "How shall I determine the right client system with which to work in order to achieve the desired change goal?"

The transfer and generalization of change

In our discussion of Phases 5 and 6 of the process of planned change, we indicated our belief that the techniques of transfer are radically neglected by many change agents. There are a number of problems here which need extensive research. How can the client's dynamic and total sphere of action be kept "present" in the often restricted or removed context of the change relationship? On the other hand, how can the pressures and expectations which derive from the client's total sphere of existence be kept from dominating the relationship and restricting freedom to explore new ideas and patterns of action? How can the client be helped to introduce changes smoothly into the established rhythm of his existence instead of expressing his new insights and change plans too actively and aggressively? How can the client be prepared to meet the resistances which will emerge as his change efforts spread to other systems and affect other vested interests? The problem of studying the transfer and spread of change is a hard one. We shall look at some of the measurement difficulties later. The change agent has a unique opportunity to study the processes of transfer because in most cases his relationship with the client system continues, or could continue, through a period when the client is testing new insights in a variety of situations. One challenging research question is the extent to which skill training is needed to supplement cognitive insights and motivational changes in order that behavior change successfully.

The timing of change processes

Time provides the compass within which all change occurs. The change process divides into episodes or phases which occur successively through time, and each episode carries its own demands, limitations, and potentialities. Every change agent knows the impossibility of going "against time." Yet there is still much that we do not know about the significance of timing in the change process.

We have distinguished seven phases of change as one way of beginning a study of the time sequence. We have pointed out that such a sequence is often far from orderly and that the timing of the phases is very different in the different kinds of change. The research problem here, we think, is to specify the things which must happen in each of these phases in order to make a smooth and steady progression from the beginning to the end of the change process.

A second way to look at the problem of time is to divide the change sequence into periods or units which are based on the various problems with which the client system is occupied as change evolves. This approach is illustrated by Powdermaker and Frank (30) in their discussion of the techniques of group therapy. They have described a therapeutic method by which the group moves from one common theme to another. They find that when a group "picks up" a theme, several of the patients will associate personal problems with it, and the group will be unwilling to pay attention to anything not related to this common theme. Similarly, in individual analysis a patient may be expected to approach his problems at one period from the point of view of oral tensions, at another period from the point of view of anal tensions, and so on. Again, any interpretation by the change agent which is out of touch with a salient organizing focus can be of little help to the patient. It is possible that this way of thinking about time is primarily important for change agents who work at the level of the unconscious. Unconscious processes are notably intractable to external divisions of time and space; in other words, they tend to provide the organization for any change process in which they are involved—they are not organized by it.

Several different research problems are associated with the division of the change process into phases, whether the phases are defined in terms of unconscious preoccupations or in terms of the sequence of work steps. First, there is a need to test the general applicability and flexibility of our division of the concepts of change into various phases. Does the process of moving toward a given objective always involve the same phases? Do processes moving toward different objectives encounter the same phases? What happens if one of the usual phases is omitted or passed over superficially? What happens if the change effort is highly concentrated in one or two of the phases?

Second, we need more thorough investigations of the means by which change advances from one phase to another. Is it possible to speed up the change process? What can the change agent do to expedite movement from one phase to the next? How can he tell when "enough" work has been done in one phase and the next one should be entered? Is there such a thing as retrogression to an earlier phase or too long a continuance in one phase? If so, how can these things be prevented, or how can their effects be remedied? In short, what kind of control should the agent exert over the phasing of change, and how can this control be accomplished? Much of our research so far has unfortunately stopped with a description of what "normally" happens, leaving us with the implicit assumption that whatever happens is inevitable. But this assumption should be tested explicitly.

METHODOLOGICAL PROBLEMS
OF RESEARCH ON PLANNED CHANGE

The student who engages in research on planned change encounters a number of extremely puzzling problems to which there are no easy solutions. We shall not try to offer solutions in this discussion but shall content ourselves instead merely with setting out some of the difficulties. Each worker must find his own way to meet them.

Defining and measuring the dependent variables—
the phenomena being changed

Our interest throughout this report, as we stated in Chapter 1, has been in the analysis of change in psychological processes, social relations, interpersonal processes, problem-solving procedures, and social structures. Setting aside for a moment the problems of measuring change, we still find many difficulties in the way of obtaining *any* kind of measurement for these variables. What, for example, is a good measure of mental health? Is it how well the individual feels? How others feel about him? What his therapist thinks about him? Can mental health be measured by verbal instruments, calibrating, so to speak, the words which the individual uses about himself and his world? Or by projective tests which solicit his perceptions and interpretations? Or by various techniques of role playing? Or by direct observations of his behavior? Do we need information about his conscious processes, his unconscious processes, or both, or neither? Similar questions can be asked about groups, organizations, and communities. What do we need to know about them in order to make the relevant social and psychological evaluations, and how can this information be obtained?

The crux of the problem is that many social-psychological variables are internal-process phenomena without clear external symptoms, causing difficult measurement problems. Attempts to redefine them in terms of public symptoms for measurement may reassure the researcher, but they do not alter the nature of the subjective experience.

Let us consider a few examples. Mann (42) reports that the results of a training program for foremen may be viewed very differently by the foremen themselves and the men under them. Verbal questionnaires given to a foreman before and after training may show that he has changed his attitudes and skills as they are related to his role as supervisor, but at the same time reports from the men he supervises may indicate no change in his behavior. Has the program, then, succeeded? Before answering this, we must know the reason for the discrepancy and we must know what the program was designed to change. The skills and attitudes of the foreman himself, his behavioral practices, and the perceptions of these practices by the men below—all these are aspects of the supervisory relationship. It is true that change in any one of these may occur without change in the other two, but this does not make the change any less valid. It may be important and in the long run effective to change the attitudes of the foreman, even though there is no immediate extension of this change to his behavior. How can we tell whether a change which extends only to the verbal statements of a foreman is superficial and transitory or whether it is the first stage in a sequence of change which will eventually affect his behavior?

To take another example, consider the problem of evaluating the change which occurs as the result of training in human relations. The staff of the National Training Laboratories reports the use of a number of different techniques for evaluating change at the summer Laboratory in Group Development. Judgments on the extent of change were obtained from the trainee himself, from his fellow trainees, and from the training leader. Then the individual was asked to give a more detailed description of the ways in which he thought he had changed. Before and after training, "objective" measures were obtained for such factors as ideology, values, and ways of perceiving the home situation. This was done in part by constructing a hypothetical problem which trainees were asked to discuss before and after the training period. The individual's responses to the problem were coded for factors such as insight, sophistication, and breadth of understanding, and his before and after scores served as a measure of his change. The puzzling thing, however, was the lack of relationship between these various measures of change. It was obvious that different variables were being reflected in the different measures. Judgments by peers, for instance, reflected their relationships with the individual and how they had changed during the course of time. The judgments of the leader seemed to reflect a more comprehensive insight into the readiness of the individual to learn from the training experience. The trainee himself was most familiar with his changes in perspective or emotional tension, less aware of the operations of these changes in his interactions with others. The various interviews and tests, in other words, each sampled a different area of value or belief or understanding. Follow-up interviews told something about the meaning which the training experience had assumed in the memories of the trainees.

Once again it is impossible to say that any one of these factors alone is the object of human-relations training. They are interrelated in such a way that a change in one of them might lead to a change in the others. Together they provide a rough definition of the area in which learning should occur. However, they are not so closely linked that measurable change of one kind implies measurable change of another kind. How, then, do we obtain information about how much a person knows about human relations or how much he has changed? The different measures seem to be relatively independent of one another, each valid for some aspect of what we want to know but none valid for all. We are left with the suggestion that the "phenomenon" may be as heterogeneous as the measures we use to look at it; it is a complex of values, skills, and feelings characterizing the individual himself and the responses of others toward him, and it has no simple unity.

Similar difficulties arise when we try to assess other kinds of change. In psychotherapy it has become conventional to accept the therapist's judgment as the valid criterion with which other measures must be compared. Again, however, we must raise questions about whether or not the sample of behavior and experience to which the therapist is exposed is necessarily a better source of information, for all purposes, than the sample of experience available to other people, to a psychometrician, or to the patient himself. Each different vantage point yields different observations; each is a good source of information about some things and a poor source of information about others.

In work with communities there is likely to be somewhat more external evidence of achievement or the lack of it. Even here, however, there are intangible factors such as morale, a commitment to participate in the apparent gains already won and to continue working for further gains, and feelings of belonging to or being identified with the community. Public and less visible factors are both real, but neither automatically implies anything about the other.

The research problem therefore is to define and limit the variables as clearly as possible and to find the best way to measure the aspects of a given change situation which are judged important, without losing sight of the larger complex of variables in which the particular factors of interest are embedded.

Obtaining information about the process of change

It would be pleasant for research workers if they could assume that change proceeds along a single straight line in one continuous movement as the position of the mechanical hare changes during a dog race. Unfortunately, everything we know indicates that this is not the case. Change does not follow any single course, and the movement is never continuous.

Consider first the matter of direction of change. Each system must start where it is and move to another point. Thus each traverses a path which is in some way unique. We can see this most clearly in the case of a workshop which is trying to help a number of individuals at the same time. Some trainees may want to work on improving their skills in interpersonal relations; others may concentrate on understanding their private feelings and reactions. A person who is unfamiliar with the language and point of view of the workshop may want to begin by learning new terms and attitudes; someone else who is familiar with the words may want to set them aside and learn through emotional experience. The workshop can be considered as a kind of cafeteria in which each individual selects the kind of learning experience that will help him most, passing up the others. From this point of view, it is obviously futile to arrange the trainees in a single hierarchy ranging from the one who learns most and best to the one who learns least and worst. Each learns according to his needs and interests. The learning of each concerns what is relevant to him; his path of learning (direction of change) is not directly comparable to that of anyone else.

The irregular pace of the change process complicates the problem even further. The most common pattern of movement seems to consist of occasional spurts of learning or change, separated by longer periods of apparent stability. It is clear that something is happening during the periods of apparent nonchange—something which prepares the system for its subsequent spurts of movement—but what it is precisely we do not know. Nor do we know how to obtain reliable information about these latent or concealed elements of change.

One model for our thought about the relationship between latent and manifest change is the theory which views the change process as a succession of insightful reorganizations. During the learning period the system accumulates a number of new facts or ideas which are stored away, as it were, for further consideration and are not allowed to exert an immediate influence on ways of thinking or acting. But sooner or later the system undergoes a period of insight and reorganization. The new ideas or skills or feelings—whatever has been accumulated—are integrated with the old. A new gestalt is created which carries the system beyond its previous state of awareness and being. The formation of this new gestalt is what forces the system to move; the formation of the new gestalt is what we mean by change. The entire cycle, of course, may be repeated many times before the desired change objective is reached, and the change process may consist of a long series of reorganizations. The research problem is to determine what reorganization will follow from any existing accretion of new and unassimilated material.

Sometimes a system must move backward before it can move forward, and this adds another dimension of complexity to the problem. The overinhibited child, for instance, may need to become aggressively antisocial before he can learn to be truly and spontaneously social. The married couple which has come to a point of marital impasse may need to separate, thus putting the marriage in jeopardy, before they can find a new and more satisfactory way to adjust to each other. The industrial firm whose management policies have been paternalistic may need to undergo a period of violent labor conflict before a productive relationship between management and labor can be developed.

On the other hand, negative behavior is not always a sign of progress. Obviously, it may often mean a genuine and irremediable disintegration of the relationships in which the system is involved. The problem is to tell what place the current change will have in the long-range development of the system. Naturally, this is a problem for positive change too; an apparent change may be quite illusory and ephemeral, just as an apparent lack of change or a negative change may produce salutary effects.

The appearance of resistance raises similar problems of interpretation. Many psychotherapists report that they consider resistance a sign of progress; it means that important parts of the present (unsatisfactory) defense structure are weakening. But how does one distinguish between resistance which is an attempt to defend unsatisfactory elements of the status quo and resistance which is an attempt to protect necessary and satisfactory elements of the status quo? In the first case, resistance is a sign that the change process is moving in the right direction; in the second, it is a warning that change may be moving in the wrong direction.

We have been discussing the problems of predicting the future, of knowing what the ultimate effect will be of certain observed movements in the course of change, whether the direction is positive or negative. A similar problem arises in connection with the establishment of a base line or starting point. How does one measure a situation which existed before the measurements were taken? Partly this is the old dilemma which all scientists face: How does the process of measurement affect what is being measured? But partly it is an accidental difficulty which arises from the fact that a social scientist with a plan for research usually arrives on the scene only after the change process has been put into motion. Furthermore, there is a problem of selection. Systems which select themselves or are selected by others to participate in a change activity are often already different from other nonselected systems—and how can this be taken into account in assessing their starting positions? We have already mentioned the fact that different systems may want to move in different dimensions and change in different ways. This, too, can increase the difficulty of deciding what kind of base line measure is relevant.

The problem of separating the effects of planned change efforts from the effects of other "natural" forces is so well known that we do not need to labor it here. There are various techniques for estimating the extent of nonplanned change—the use of control groups in experiments, investigations of systems which wanted to begin a change but were unable to do so, and so on. But our main point is that it is not enough to know that some kind of change would have occurred without the introduction of a deliberate effort. The plan for change is only one of the many forces which affect the client's situation. What we really need to know is how this one force interacts with the others to advance or impede the movement toward a desired change objective.

Integrating the research function in the change process

A number of investigators—Polansky (97), Mann (43), Luszki (91), Lippitt (12)—have discussed the problem of co-ordinating the activities of a research team and a change-agent team. This ought to be, one should think, an easy and natural partnership, yet it often proves unexpectedly difficult. If it is to succeed, both parties must give it their serious attention. Mutual good will,

thoughtful planning in advance, and plain hard work are all pre-
requisites to a sustained co-operative relationship.

The benefits for both parties are easy to describe. For the researcher the chief gain comes from his closer association with the
processes which he is trying to understand. Many of the things he
wants to know can be learned only from the change agent. The
change agent alone can describe his own responses to the client and
the client's problems and explain his own thought processes in
making decisions; furthermore, the agent is usually in the best position to point out the cues which indicate how the change process
is developing. Other kinds of information must be obtained from
the client system, but even here the researcher must usually rely
on the change agent to arrange the necessary interviews. The researcher who works in busy and objective isolation may find himself cut off from important ideas and improvisations which develop
in the context of the change work itself, with the result that his
concept of change will be unrealistic and stereotyped.

The change agent also has much to gain from a close alliance
with research. If he can accept the researcher as a friend and col-
league, he will find many opportunities to acquire new insights
into what he is doing. Day-to-day discussions of events as they
transpire—discussions with a third party who is interested and informed—will often place instances of routine work in a sharper
focus so that details which might otherwise be missed appear in
their true significance. Moreover, the researcher's effort to gather
all the relevant information about a particular phase of the change
process may show up certain factors which the agent could not see
from his position in the thick of things; thus the agent's perspective will assume a more correct and balanced proportion.

The difficulties are not so easy to anticipate. Perhaps one of the
chief sources of trouble lies in the many compromises which both
the researcher and the change agent must make. Sometimes, for
instance, they don't know what would be best to do, but they must
do something, and so they gamble and hope for the best. Sometimes they think they know what the ideal course of action would
be, but limitations of time, money, or opportunity force them to
settle for something short of this. Sometimes, like all human be-

ings, they simply make mistakes. When these things happen, each person—agent and researcher—is likely to be placed on the defensive. The agent does not want a research person snooping around and showing up his mistakes. The researcher does not want a change expert looking at his research design and calling it impractical or unrealistic. Consequently, each is inclined to erect a protective barrier around himself and his work.

The maintenance of these defenses is made easier by the fact that each approaches his work from a special point of view. The change agent wants to understand the uniqueness of the client system and what this means in terms of the specific change project. The research worker, on the other hand, usually wants to generalize beyond the particular system to a comprehensive notion of one kind or another. He wants to find the ways in which the particular system is like all systems, not the ways in which it differs. Hence the research worker and the change agent may each feel that he has the best understanding of what is going on and that the other, from a biased or incongruent position, cannot tell what is really important. This only makes it harder, of course, for either one to get effective help from the other.

Another source of tension is competition for the time and attention of the client system. At a workshop, for example, trainees have only a certain amount of time. An hour that is used for research cannot be used for training, and vice versa. If both the research staff and the training staff want to do more than time permits, then every demand for the time of the trainees is a signal for mutual resentment and frustration. Every refusal to give up time becomes a potential occasion for guilt. These reactions, together with the demands of a close working schedule, serve only to drive the research staff and the training staff farther and farther apart. The results may be felt by the trainees, who, sensing a conflict between training and research, usually throw their favor to the side of training. This only intensifies the self-righteous indignation of the training staff, deepens the guilt feelings of the research staff, and leads to general alienation and discontent.

We have been talking about cases in which training and research are represented by different people. But the same conflict can appear even in cases where both functions are performed by the same person. The agent who doubles in research may feel that he is doing two different and contradictory jobs, and he may see no effective way to reconcile the demands of the two.

The best protection against a conflict between training and research is a unified plan which has been worked out in advance. If the plan is well made, training and research will not compete but will complement each other. This demands co-operation from the very beginning between change agent and researcher. Too often each works out a plan for his relationship with the client system and then challenges the other to interfere. The first step, however, should be a plan for their own relationship to each other. In working out such a plan they may very well come to a redefinition of their roles in which they agree to work co-operatively toward common goals instead of independently toward separate goals. Out of such co-operation we could expect the emergence of new insights into the nature of planned change—insights equally valuable to the agent interested in application and to the theorist interested in conceptualization.

THE DEVELOPMENT AND COMMUNICATION
OF SOCIAL INVENTIONS

Our work in studying this sample of change agents has been in many respects exciting. But it has been dismaying too. We have been excited, for instance, by our discovery of the real creativity which has gone into the business of giving help, but we have been dismayed to see the fruits of this creativity so often lost simply because they are not shared among the various kinds of professional helpers.

One of the marks of a skilled change agent is his readiness and ability to invent new procedures, techniques, and forms of behavior in order to help a particular client system solve a particular problem. But there are three steps which should be taken beyond the simple invention and use of a new technique. Because these steps are so seldom taken, we find a great waste of creative energy, a loss of inventions which must only be invented over again.

The first step which ought to be taken is an appraisal of the success or failure of the particular innovation in its particular context. This means much more than merely obtaining information to show whether or not the invention worked. It means trying to make a judgment as to why the invention failed or succeeded in the particular situation. Many brilliant techniques have been invented and then discarded after they were tried once, simply because it was not understood that slightly different conditions or minor adjustments would lead to success.

Once one knows what are the essential elements that have made the invention successful, one can take the next step. This is the description, for oneself and others, of the invention's basic formulas so that "models" of it can be constructed correctly in varying situations. It is tragic to see a useful and ingenious invention, such as the buzz group or the feedback session, for example, ruined by attempts to apply the same model with strict regularity to every situation. Instead, workers should seek variations of the technique which will make it suitable to the particular needs of each client system.

When the change agent understands the essential elements of his invention and hence can vary its use in practice, he is ready for the third step—telling his professional colleagues what he has done. He must communicate to them the basic structure of his invention and his experience in using it so that they can understand, appraise, and experiment with the results of his work.

If only 10 per cent of the brilliant social inventions of change agents received this type of nurturing and communication, the professional practice of giving help would achieve an entirely new quality.

THE SCIENTIFIC AND PROFESSIONAL

TRAINING OF CHANGE AGENTS

11

The main purpose of this final chapter is to review what we have already said and see how it applies to the problem of training professional change agents in all fields. This means that we must examine the question of specialized versus general training. At our present juncture in the advancement of education, specialized training for change agents has probably been most fully developed in the fields of psychiatry, social casework, and clinical psychology. Training for specialized work with groups, organizations, and communities is less developed, although there are a few centers where trainees may concentrate on these studies. Just what directions the further development of training for work with groups, organizations, and communities should take is a question of real importance for curriculum development both in our professional schools and in the behavioral science departments of our colleges and universities.

The very rapid growth of the field of industrial relations as a professional specialty dramatizes the fact that our larger social systems, whether organizations or communities, are becoming more and more aware of their problems in the area of social prog-

ress in human relations and are turning more and more often to
sources of outside professional help for assistance in solving them.
Everything leads us to believe that we can expect this trend to
continue: an increasingly wider range of client systems will seek
more and more professional help. This will be encouraged by the
development of specialized training programs in our universities,
where more and more change agents will be trained. Several of the
preceding chapters have pointed up also the need for "training"
potential client systems so that they can recognize their own requirement for help and know where to go to find it. Hence in this
chapter we shall look briefly at the possibilities for educating potential client systems as well as at the need for expanded educational facilities for change agents.

WHAT CHANGE AGENTS MUST LEARN

Before we turn to the problems of specialized training itself, we
must identify some of the general areas of training experience
which seem to be required for all types of professional change
agents. These areas can be discerned by examining the functions
of the change agent as we have already analyzed them.

Conceptual-diagnostic training

In Chapters 2 and 3 it was pointed out that every change agent
acquires some conceptual framework in terms of which he ana-
lyzes the meaning of the facts which are presented to him by the
particular client system with which he is working. He must be able
to view each case as a complex of recognizable phenomena which
can be understood in terms of previously established concepts.
These conceptual models may emphasize internal processes, structural conformations, or interaction between the system and its
environment, or they may combine all three aspects. But certainly
some systematic conceptual orientation is a necessity. At the
same time, this conceptual orientation is not very helpful unless it is coupled with certain specific skills of interpretation and
fact finding. Consequently, one whole area of training for change

agents should include education not only in change concepts but also in the skills of diagnosis—techniques for asking the right questions, for establishing valid patterns of observation or measurement, for using reliable methods to collect, process, and interpret data.

Orientation to theories and methods of change

As we have seen in Chapters 5 through 9, the formulation of a process of planned change requires more than a sound diagnostic orientation. Change passes through several phases, making a complex movement which can only be understood in terms of some theoretical model of the process of change. Translating diagnostic interpretations into change goals and plans, for instance, requires that the change agent know what the whole process of change is and that he think about it in terms which are generally applicable. He must possess a theoretical basis for understanding the progress of the relationship between the change agent and the client system. He must be oriented toward a theory of change. Much research has been done on such processes as learning, identification, empathy, and problem solving, and the results of these investigations furnish the foundation for developing a theoretical orientation. But again it is obviously important that this ability to formulate systematically the process of change should be coupled with technical skills in applying the theory. The agent must know how to collect information about the movement of the change effort if he is to guide the effort intelligently. He must know how to conduct himself toward the client system in each phase of movement.

Orientation to the ethical and evaluative functions of the change agent

At many points in this book we have noted that the change agent, simply by virtue of being a change agent, commits himself to the responsibility for making intelligent value judgments. He must pass judgment on unproductive or maladjusted problem-solving processes; he must determine standards of efficiency; he must propose ways to improve interpersonal relationships. Even in nondirective work the agent usually must help to plan a good relationship between himself and the client system; that is to say, he must propose a reasonable *modus operandi*. Moreover, he usually collaborates in establishing a specific change goal. All of these functions involve the change agent in ethical judgments. He cannot make consistent decisions about these and hundreds of other problems unless he relies upon a comprehensive social philosophy. In addition, there are the specifically moral problems he must face. Is this client worth helping? What is the client's motive in asking for help? What are my own qualifications and responsibilities? All of these questions and many others involve moral choice. Consequently, it is important that training for all change agents should include a general study of social values as well as a specific study of professional ethics and an analysis of personal motivations.

Knowledge of the sources of help

As systematic research throws more and more light on the nature of personality and social systems and their problems, it will probably become evident that a variety of specialized services may be required to help solve a particular type of problem. Consequently, change agents need to know about the different kinds of professional help which are available. They need to know where to turn when they require special advice or particular kinds of information. All this, in turn, means that the change agent must have a realistic understanding of his own resources, and he must be willing to turn to others when his own resources are inadequate. Professional training for helpers should therefore include at least some general consideration of all the helping professions so that agents may know what helping skills are available and how to take advantage of them.

Operational and relational skills

The change agent's cognitive skills, that is, the skills of conceptualization, evaluation, and self-appraisal, must be integrated with another body of detailed knowledge which we call "action skills." These are the skills of relating effectively to a client system and performing effectively as a professional helper—therapist, counselor, caseworker, trainer, consultant, or whatever. This means that the change agent's education must equip him with experience in the emotional mechanisms of a close working relationship (acceptance, dependency, and so forth) as well as with a good deal of supervised practice in the actual procedures of giving help. This practice should include also opportunities to develop the skills of collaborating with other change agents. Such collaboration may involve consulting specialists, working in interdisciplinary teams, or working on the staff of a training program or consulting organization.

THE PROBLEM OF TRAINING SPECIALISTS
AND GENERALISTS IN PLANNED CHANGE

The number and variety of conceptual orientations and methodological skills which are required to meet the wide range of helping problems seem to indicate that professional helpers cannot hope to succeed without a high degree of specialization. On the other hand, there is a danger that overspecialization will lead to fragmentation of the helping professions and a lack of correlation among them. Consequently, it is important for us to examine the areas and dimensions in which specialization should occur so that we can see where the divisions between the different parts of the curriculum should be made. The analyses which we have conducted so far in this book seem to suggest five main dimensions along which specialization develops, and these are what we must take into account in attempting to determine the organization of a training curriculum. First we will define each of these dimensions briefly, and then we can consider some of the problems of overspecialization and overgeneralization.

Specialization by type of client system

This is probably the most clearly developed criterion for specialization. For example, training programs in psychiatry, clinical psychology, social work, education, and industrial training tend to concentrate primarily upon the individual as the appropriate client system. Training programs in group work—work with families, committees, and so forth—naturally emphasize the skills of dealing with face-to-face groups. Comparable specialized programs of training are offered for work with communities and organizations, although these specializations, as we have already pointed out, are less developed and do not have such completely organized training curricula. Specialization by type of client system is forced by a number of factors. First of all, a good deal of our theoretical and empirical work in the behavioral sciences is based on one or another kind of system, and therefore our basic knowledge is organized in terms of these different systems. From the beginning, psychology has focused on the individual's internal processes and sociology has focused on larger social systems. The two fields have remained relatively distinct. Moreover, this type of specialization within the behavioral sciences is reinforced by the ever more specialized development of service programs within the general fields of social welfare and education.

Specialization in terms of diagnostic orientations and methods

This second dimension is somewhat fuzzier but still fairly well marked. It seems to contain two subdimensions. First, as we pointed out in Chapters 2 and 3, change agents at work with all types of client systems have acquired specialized diagnostic orientations which emphasize either internal problems of the client system or problems located in the relationship between the client system and the environment. These different orientations are quite distinct and determine, to a large extent, the individual change agent's whole outlook and choice of techniques. Beyond this, change agents at all levels differ greatly in the ways that they conduct their diagnostic investigations. Some rely heavily upon scientific and quantitative methods (testing, observation schedules, sample surveys, and the like) while others, at the opposite extreme, depend upon qualitative and intuitive methods by which they can become personally sensitive to the nature of the client system's problems. This kind of specialization depends, of course, upon the change agent's training.

Some professional schools and college and university departments in the behavioral sciences emphasize scientific methods of measurement and investigation, and others emphasize interactional sensitivities and operational skills.

Specialization by areas of change objectives

Specialization often occurs in terms of the various kinds of problems which demand professional help. That is to say, the "content" of the problem determines the kind of professional helper that will be needed. Some change agents specialize primarily in problems of health, others in economic problems, still others in problems of political action, emotional adjustment, speech defects, reading deficiencies, community deterioration, or intergroup conflict, and so forth. In other words, specialization is determined by the problem, not by the client system—though the two may go together in many cases. Change agents who specialize in this way assume that they cannot function effectively until they have acquired knowledge and resourcefulness which will equip them to deal with all problems of a particular kind wherever they occur. We can see this kind of specialization developed to a very high degree in the field of medicine.

Specialization by "level" of problem

Here specialization occurs primarily in terms of the kind and degree of help which is needed to solve problems at different "depths." Surface problems, which are easily accessible and changeable, require one kind of change agent, and "deep" problems, which offer difficult resistance, require another kind. We can illustrate this dimension of specialization by the gradations of roles within a single field—psychoanalyst, psychotherapist, counselor, mental-hygiene educator, social-skills trainer, and so forth. This effort to define specialization in terms of depth of problem has become one of the chief issues in interprofessional relations (for example, between psychiatry and clinical psychology) during recent years.

Specialization by type of change method

This dimension is correlated with several of those we have already considered, but it still must be looked at separately. When we compare the work of change agents who are dealing with the same problems, the same depth of problem, and the same kind of client system, we still find a good many differences in their choice of helping techniques. To a large extent these differences of choice seem to depend on the methodological specializations which the agents acquired from their training. Different agents faced with the same problem of emotional maladjustment in an individual, for instance, may decide that the patient needs nondirective counseling, or assignment to a therapy group, or psychoanalysis, or directive counseling, or a series of psychodramatic sessions, or training in general semantics. In the same way, when a certain problem arises in a community one change agent may prescribe a leadership-training program, another a course in community development for selected persons in the community, another a self-survey, another a program of immediate action on almost any front, and another the establishment of a community council. To a certain extent, these various ways of prescribing for the same problem are the result of different assumptions about the variable factors which affect the problem and about the nature of the change process. But more often these different prescriptions are simply the result of the different change methods which the agents have been taught during their professional training. A man who has been taught the techniques of organizing and directing a community self-survey, for instance, is not likely to abandon his special skill in favor of some other technique if he can see any way to use what he has been taught.

SOME PROBLEMS OF SPECIALIZATION

At this point we are faced with a number of questions. If specialization can proceed in terms of any of various dimensions, including the five we have discussed here, then we must decide which of these dimensions will allow specialization to occur with the least danger. Which of the dimensions can be cut, so to speak, at points which will divide naturally into fields of specialization yet still permit the change agent to give adequate service in a reasonable range of professional cases? Is it desirable or feasible to combine specialized training in one part of the dimension with generalized training in the rest of the dimension? Do the professional training curricula which are now offered seem to cut the dimension at appropriate points? Let us look briefly at some of these problems. The whole future of our change professions and the enormous role they will occupy in our society may depend upon our ability to find the answers to these questions about professional education.

The main difficulty of specializing in terms of a particular type of client system is the fact that so many cases, when they are analyzed, reveal an overlapping and interdependence of systems. The client's problem is caused not by purely internal factors but by a complex of factors stemming from several systems. For example, many problems of individual systems are found to be determined in part by the dynamic operations of group systems and even organizational systems of which the individual system is a part. Work with small groups reveals quite dramatically that group problems are very often caused by the malfunctioning of the individual systems which make up the group and also often by factors which arise in the organizational or community systems in which the group finds itself. This does not mean, of course, that we should expect all change agents to be able to work equally well with two or three levels of client systems. On the contrary, specialization according to types of systems is probably very important. But at the same time change agents need training in a much broader spectrum of diagnostic sensitivity than most of them get now. They must be able to identify the various types of factors which enter into the cause of any particular problem, wherever these factors appear, and they must be able to understand realistically and precisely what aspects of a given problem they themselves can deal with and what aspects demand supplementary help from other kinds of change agents. Only in this way can the individual change agent who accepts the responsibility for a given problem be sure that he can supply or obtain the total pattern of help which the problem requires. One of the most common and serious weaknesses of much current professional help lies just in this area: agents regard the system with which they are working as a closed unit and ignore the aspects of the client's problem which spring from subsystems or more inclusive systems. The result, of course, is that the change program gets off to a lopsided start and never completely agrees with the realities of the client's situation. In order to understand the full breadth of the client's problem the change agent must very often possess a broader access to diagnostic information than is afforded by his particular specialization.

A number of difficulties appear when one considers specialization in terms of diagnostic orientations. Orientations based on scientific methods of quantitative research often are too narrow to uncover all of the important variables which bear on a given problem. On the other hand, orientations based on unsystematic "intuition" may handicap the change agent by encouraging him to rely on invalid or incomplete information. But perhaps even more serious than these problems of being too focused or too selective in collecting diagnostic information is the problem of knowing how to interpret whatever data are discovered. If the diagnostic orientation is too eclectic, there may be no consistent frame of reference to guide the change agent in interpreting data. It is not enough for him to know about present symptoms and their correlates; he must also have a means for making inferences about what caused the problem in the first place. He can only get this from specialized training in a particular theoretical orientation. However, the implication seems to be that this theoretical orientation needs to be broad enough in scope to allow him to recognize and assemble facts from all the levels of significant phenomena (that is, the individual, the group, the organization, and the community). In other words, his training must be to a certain extent interdisciplinary. Furthermore, it follows that the agent must possess a reasonably wide repertoire of diagnostic skills which he himself can use intelligently, although there will always be situations in which he must rely on collaborating specialists to furnish supplementary means for collecting and processing information.

Specialization in terms of problem content also involves serious dangers. The change agent who is equipped only to deal with a given kind of problem, for instance, may not be able to recognize the other problems which are connected with it. The agent may see only the problem that he has been trained to see, never realizing that it is symptomatic of a more basic problem or that it is part of a larger complex of problems. Our case materials on work with such problems as food habits, reading difficulties, intergroup conflict, and citizen apathy give us many illustrations of instances when agents have had to shift their attention from the original problem to a more basic problem in order to make any headway at all. Again, this seems to indicate that the agent must possess a wider range of diagnostic sensitivities than he can get from training which focuses on the content of one particular kind of problem. He must have basic training in general problem-solving methods of giving help as well as expertness in a particular content area.

Our fourth kind of specialization was that which distinguishes between "levels" or "depth" of problems. This dimension, together with specialization according to types of client systems, is probably one of the most important. Obviously, from the point of view of training and using our professional manpower most intelligently, it is important not to train everyone to a level of professionalization which is required only for work on "deep" problems. Here the greatest problem seems to us that of developing better methods of differential diagnosis and better ways to keep track of change progress and resistance to it. In other words, we need to be able to locate the level of a given client's problem, and we need to know more about the client's capacity to change and the sources of his resistance to change. It is certainly true that many adult educators and mental hygienists are wasting time and energy in trying to help people whose problems demand a much deeper level of help; and it is equally true that many highly trained specialists are working on problems which in the end will be seen to have needed only the help of an educational consultant. Again, this points to the need for diagnostic sensitivity covering a much broader area than that in which a change agent is prepared to offer specialized help. Probably all change agents should be trained

to secure systematic information on whether or not change is occurring in each new relationship with a client system. This would
help the change agent to find out in a given case whether or not
the level of help being offered was appropriate to the particular
problem and, if it was not, to make a more appropriate referral
without excessive loss of energy on his part and without too much
discouragement or harm to the client system. Here again, of course,
the agent must be skilled in referring appropriately to the specializations of his fellow helpers.

Our fifth dimension of specialization was that which distinguished among the different types of change methods in which
change agents are trained. It is clear that for many problems a
combination of methods is needed. Hence the change agent must
have a fairly broad repertoire of helping skills. It is also clear that
all client systems are in a sense unique and consequently present a
variety of problems. The agent who wants to perform well, even in
a fairly restricted area, must be able to use his skills flexibly and
resourcefully. This means that training for change agents must
include supervised practice in the use of a variety of helping methods and experience in working on teams which use various approaches at various times.

One rather empirical way to decide how much specialization we
need in professional training for change agents would be to find
out how many different kinds of client systems there are and how
many different kinds of problems they experience. Then a specialization could be set up for each kind. But this is an unsound approach. The fact is that as we go along new problems appear—or
rather we become newly aware of them. As our knowledge of social
and personality processes increases, we see more and more clearly
the ways in which problems are differentiated, either because they
stem from different causes or because they appear in different systems. Furthermore, as we pointed out in Chapter 7, the change
process must often be initiated by the change agent; his specialized
sensitivity to certain problems permits him to see them before the
client does. Consequently, no purely quantitative census of help
needs would aid us significantly in deciding on the most suitable
areas for specialization. What is needed, on the contrary, is a

theoretical and philosophical analysis of our help needs, now and especially in the future, so that we can establish those training curricula for professional change agents which will be most effectively oriented to current and emerging problems of personality and social systems.

Should there not also be a certain number of generalists? This is a challenging question. Should some of our students be trained to a comprehensive view of change theory and change methods? Do we need people who can play integrative or co-ordinative roles not only in our universities but even on the job, where multiple problems may be faced by teams of many specialists working together?

With these questions in mind, let us turn to some of the possible designs for training curricula which seem to suggest themselves.

CURRICULA FOR TRAINING CHANGE AGENTS

In the suggestions which we shall make on this important business of education for change agents, we shall try to steer a middle course. We do not want to be restricted by our knowledge of what is currently taught in professional schools and behavioral-science departments. On the other hand, we want to be practical; we want to keep in mind the current practices of professional specialization and certification. We have thought in terms of five different kinds of training: graduate training in a professional school; graduate training in a behavioral-science department; specialized undergraduate training; in-service training; and certain related features of general education. We shall not try to make concrete differentiations among professional schools (such as psychiatry, social work, education, public health, industrial relations, public administration, and the like) or among behavioral science departments (such as psychology, sociology, anthropology, and political science). Furthermore, we shall continue to base our suggestions on the facets of thought which have turned up in our preceding analyses rather than upon more general thinking about professional and scientific training.

The curriculum in the professional school

In the light of our discussion of the types of training which are needed by a change agent, it seems to us that the professional school has a number of definable tasks or objectives, whether its particular field of concentration is casework, group work, community organization, health education, elementary education, industrial relations, or another specialization. We shall outline these tasks briefly in the following paragraphs.

First of all, it seems to us that the professional school is responsible for selecting and organizing appropriate bodies of knowledge from the behavioral sciences. This knowledge includes both theory and empirical substantive data. In other words, the professional school must transplant the results of academic work in the behavioral sciences into a professional context. The job requires an active and close collaboration between teachers who are oriented to the practical problems of their profession and behavioral scientists who are well versed in the theoretical and substantive content of their academic field. Naturally, this applies to schools which specialize in training agents to work with individuals as well as to schools which specialize in training agents to work in a larger social context. In any behavioral science knowledge is continually being expanded and reorganized, and consequently it is essential that the professional schools be staffed in part by behavioral scientists who help keep the curriculum revision process up-to-date. The curriculum in such a professional school will never be finally established. It will be reorganized constantly to keep it commensurate with advances of knowledge. This is a pressing need and becomes a more and more acute problem with the accelerated accumulation of new, validated information in the behavioral sciences.

The professional school is also responsible for offering training in scientific methods of collecting data, especially as these methods are used in the processes of diagnosis. In most areas of professional help the diagnostic methods used by change agents lag behind the techniques for investigation and interpretation that have been developed in the behavioral sciences. Part of this lag is necessary and appropriate—the professional change agent cannot be expected to do the same things as the researcher—but part is due to the lack of proper methodological training in the professional schools. The behavioral scientists, in many cases at least, do not contribute as much as they could to finding and teaching methods of information gathering which will be useful to the change agent as well as the research student.

A third important contribution which the behavioral scientists should be asked to make to the professional school is an orientation of students to the variety of specializations which exists within the behavioral-science disciplines. Change agents must know how these specializations can be used in working on various types of helping problems. They must know how each academic specialty contributes to a unified theory of change. Professional schools differ greatly in the degree to which they emphasize a conceptualization of the change process and the change relationship. Certainly all of them offer some framework for understanding the rationale of professional help. But very few of them, unfortunately, help their students to think seriously about a general theory of change or to understand the contributions of the various types of change agents whose work contributes to a general theory of change. Here again the major weakness of the professional-school curriculum seems to appear in the area of methodology. By methodology we mean specifically the skills of collecting evidence about the progress of change and the techniques for measuring the effects which certain helping methods have produced. Not only do schools neglect the methods of research which contribute specifically to the change agent's evaluative procedures, but when they do teach these methods they teach them outside the context of the helping relationship. In other words, students are not taught to regard evaluation as an integral part of the helping process but as something special and often rather futile. We suggest again that no change agent can control the dynamic process of change unless he knows what has happened and what is happening. The techniques which enable him to find out what has happened and is happening are therefore exceedingly important.

Another of the professional school's objectives is the teaching of professional standards and ethics as well as social values in general. This aspect of the change agent's education is rather heavily emphasized at most schools. Students leave the professional school with a fairly well-developed concept of the ethical basis for social action and an active sense of responsibility to the ideals of our society. What we should emphasize here is that this awareness of social values should be coupled with a self-awareness of the particular ethical responsibilities involved in the change agent's special role. As we have pointed out a number of times, the relationship between the change agent and the client system, like all relationships, is an ethical one, and it invariably involves both members in a series of moral choices. Consequently, we think that the professional training curriculum should include a certain amount of training in the explicit and implicit value judgments which are part of the change agent's job. Of course, it goes without saying that students should learn the normative standards of their own profession, whether these standards have been codified or not.

A fifth part of professional training is actual practice in exercising learned skills. In the case of the helping professions this means supervised field experience in giving help. Here again this is a part of professional training which has received a good deal of thoughtful emphasis in most professional schools. The schools recognize the importance of learning by doing. And they make sure that practice is carried out under skilled supervision and in a variety of operating situations. It seems to us that two particularly difficult problems arise in this connection. One is the problem of providing a real experience in the helping relationship over a long enough period of time to give the student a genuine insight into the continuity of association of change agent and client system. Only in this way can the student know what it is like to deal with a client in a real situation of change. Yet it is almost impossible to provide this kind of experience in many fields of change, and it is even more difficult in some to give the student experience with anything like an adequate variety of client systems. The second problem, which has received much attention in many schools, is that of finding a way to help the student integrate his theoretical knowledge and his operating experience. Many ways have been tried to bring the classroom and the field or laboratory together. But our analysis of what change agents have said about their work leads us to think that there is still a wide gap between practice and theory, between the skills of work and the skills of conceptualization. A surprising number of change agents cannot describe what they are doing in articulate, general terms that communicate effectively to their colleagues.

Finally, the professional school must offer follow-up support and in-service training. Our analysis of case materials has given us very little to go on in discussing this aspect of professional training. Yet there is a good analogy between professional training and the change process itself, and this would lead us to expect that students of planned change need at least a certain amount of continued support after they have left school and have undertaken active professional work. The change agent on his first job has a hard time bridging the gap from learning to practice. His school and professional society can help him and can continue to help him by supplying opportunities for in-service training throughout his career. In this way the change agent is encouraged to keep abreast of the new developments in his field of specialization, and his period of professional usefulness, even in our time of very rapid expansion in technical knowledge, is thus prolonged.

These brief comments on the training activities of professional schools have not been based on any careful comparative study of current training programs. The comments we have made, including the critical ones, have been derived by inference from our examination of our case materials and from what we know of the difficulties involved in any interdisciplinary effort of integration and theorizing. It seems to us that precisely this kind of interdisciplinary effort is very largely lacking now in the training of professional change agents.

Now let us turn to a similar summary of the curriculum problems which appear in the training of change agents in a behavioral science department.

The curriculum in the behavioral-science department

Perhaps the first question to be asked is why a behavioral-science department in a regular university should be training professional change agents at all. At the present stage of development in the behavioral sciences and in the helping professions, there are several different ways to answer this question.

First of all, an increasing number of those who receive advanced degrees in departments of psychology, sociology, and anthropology are being sought for operating positions in organizations, government agencies, and community programs. In many departments a larger number of doctoral candidates will wind up in these "active" jobs than will enter the traditional fields of academic research and teaching. As the resources of the social scientist have become better known and more respected, there has been a heightening of the prestige of basic scientific training, and this training alone is now sometimes considered enough to qualify a person as an expert in many operational contexts.

Besides being a source of satisfying an avowed need, the providing of professional training by departments of behavioral science has other advantages. The development of programs for training clinical psychologists in departments of psychology, for example, points to one of the most important of these advantages. The academic department seems to offer a better balance between basic training in scientific theory and training in the practical skills of application. Too often in professional schools, as we noticed earlier, professional training is divorced from contact with the personnel and resources of the academic departments. Many problems occur when scientific training and training in professional clinical skills are combined in the same academic department, but the advantages, at least in many cases, seem to outweigh the disadvantages.

Another advantage of training professional change agents in departments of behavioral science seems to us to be the important stimulation of basic research which results when students become interested in applying fundamental concepts to particular working situations. The scientist may be qualified to do many kinds of research, but there are also many research problems where the professional man's experience is especially valuable. The behavioral-science department is better equipped than most professional schools to stimulate an interest in research among its students. Probably this is because the direct and immediate contact of two kinds of training, professional and scientific, leads students to think more clearly and aggressively about problems of theory.

Still another beneficial effect of professional training in behavioral-science departments is that which is produced on the faculty itself. The scientists are given an opportunity to see the practical results of their theoretical work, and often they are called upon to give actual assistance on applied problems, either as consultants on evaluation research or as theoreticians who can help formulate integrative judgments. Perhaps it is not too much to say that this provides the scientists with a needed leaven of practicality.

In addition to these advantages of professional training in behavioral-science departments there are a number of disadvantages. Perhaps the biggest problem is that which occurs in shifting from the "intellectual" role of understanding phenomena to the "active" role of doing something about them. Most graduate training in behavioral science helps the student to learn the concepts and methods which he can use in amplifying and clarifying our knowledge about social phenomena. This kind of diagnostic sophistication is an important professional skill of the change agent. But it is important that it be coupled with a skill in active change efforts. The phenomena must not only be looked at; they must be dealt with. There is an increasing number of behavioral scientists who agree with Kurt Lewin that the scientist who begins to play this more active role finds himself coming to grips with new phenomena and new variables which force him to extend his basic scientific concepts. There are many others, of course, who find the "action orientation" distracting to their creative preoccupation with refining theoretical understandings.

Another problem which arises when professional change agents are trained in a behavioral-science department derives from the fact that most change problems call for the use of a conceptual framework that cuts across disciplinary boundaries. Actually, however, these disciplinary boundaries are breaking down very rapidly under the stress of the new trends toward integrative thinking throughout the social sciences.

A third major weakness of most academic departments as places for professional training is that they often do not offer very much in the way of facilities for supervised field work in actual operational environments. This is an aspect of training which has been much more fully developed in the professional schools. The training programs in clinical psychology have developed rapidly in this respect.

As a sidelight to our consideration of moral standards, it is interesting to note that the ethical code recently published by the American Psychological Association shows that there are a great many similarities between the ethical problems faced by the research worker and those faced by the professional helper. The professional helper, however, also faces a good many additional problems, and all of his problems are likely to be cast in a sharper, more urgent form than those of the research worker. The academic teacher and the research worker are not called upon to put their professional ethics into practice in virtually everything they do, but the change agent is.

What emerges from all this is the observation that the professional-school curriculum tends to be strong where the behavioral-science curriculum is weak, and the training of the behavioral scientist is strong in the areas where the professional schools are weak. Clearly, it is time for a much more active exploration of ways to share training resources among schools and departments. This sharing is most likely to be productive where both the school and the department are involved in trying to carry out programs of training which are related to the practical application of the social sciences. This would mean that the sharing could be equal in both directions. An example is the kind of relationship which might develop between, on the one hand, a psychology or sociology department that would give some training to social psychologists and, on the other, a school of social work which, with its curriculum for the training of group workers, would extend its facilities to students in behavioral-science departments. Here there would be an excellent opportunity to exchange courses of training in the theory of behavioral science with courses of supervised field training in the applications of behavioral science (that is, relating to small groups as client systems). The same type of exchange could occur between a sociology department which is attempting to increase the applied skills of sociologists who are being trained in community dynamics and a school of social work or a school of education which is trying to develop better training in behavioral science for students in community organization or adult education. These are only illustrations, of course, of the potential working relationships which exist on many campuses. What is most probable is that certain types of change agents will always get their training most effectively in behavioral-science departments, and others will be trained most effectively in professional schools. This division already exists to a considerable degree in training for work with organizations and communities, where change agents who specialize in diagnostic research methods typically are trained in science departments and change agents who specialize in teaching the skills of human relations typically are trained in professional schools.

Finally, we think—though it is just a hunch—that the area of a general theory of change into which we have attempted a preliminary foray in this book is one of the primary areas which offer a great opportunity for collaboration between behavioral-science departments and professional schools. Here teaching and research go hand in hand, and the contributions which can be made by both academicians and fieldworkers are very important.

Undergraduate and lower-level graduate training for change agents

In our discussion of the dimensions in which specialization has occurred we pointed out the possibility of training professional change agents to specialize in problems of different "depths" or "levels." Great progress has been made in the profession of nursing, for instance, by organizing training programs in this way.

The specializations of professional and practical nursing have led to a clarification of levels of responsibility. Comparable developments have occurred in the field of clinical psychology, where there has been a differentiation in training for psychotherapy, personnel counseling, and diagnostic testing. A recent analysis of developmental needs in the field of social welfare seems to suggest that there are a great many types of jobs which do not require a high level of graduate professional training but which do call for a certain degree of specialized training in the theory and technique of giving help. Would it not be desirable and appropriate for some of our professional schools and behavioral-science departments to collaborate in offering terminal undergraduate training? Our evidence seems to point in this direction. Specialized undergraduate professional schools such as George Williams College and Springfield College have already shown that effective undergraduate training in some fields of professional social service is completely feasible.

A comment on general education

In previous chapters we have commented on the frequency with which systems are unaware of the serious personal or social problems which develop within them, and we have pointed out how often systems do not know how to find help when they need it. Obviously, more people should be made aware of the kinds of problems which can, in general, occur in different systems, and they should learn about the various kinds of professional help that are available. This is something that our colleges and universities can help accomplish. We suggest that every college should offer as part of its program of general education at least a certain amount of instruction in the theory of planned social change. Every college-trained person should be oriented to the scope and function of professional help and should know something about the types of problems which require specialized attention.

Furthermore, we think that general education should also include the notion that all college training, and high-school training too, is directed in part toward the development of skilled citizens and parents. This means that students should be instructed in the nature of the citizen role, which certainly includes the ability to work with and influence other people through leadership and guidance. Unless we build some professionalization of citizenship and parenthood into our current educational programs we can expect our group and community systems to become ever more fragmented, demoralized, and ineffective. It takes special training to learn the roles of leadership and active membership in our complex urban society. It requires a special consciousness of modern problems and their causes to recognize and act upon the need for professional help.

Adult education for individuals and groups

Our various programs of adult education, which are expanding rapidly, offer an excellent opportunity to inform individuals and groups of the kinds of problems which can arise in modern life and the kinds of professional help which are available to meet them. Actually, many community adult-education programs are already giving people a chance to work through their problems— both individual and social—with skilled change agents. It is not hard to think of other ways in which adult-education programs might help. For instance, they might compile directories of local sources of professional help for individuals, groups, and organizations. Anything which spreads information of this kind to more and more people is a real benefit. The newspapers tell us every day of cases where help has arrived too late because no one knew how to ask for it.

Professional in-service training

In-service training institutes and workshops for professional change agents are another very important part of the total curriculum for effective social change. Most universities are now providing a fairly wide variety of "refresher" courses in their institutes, conferences, clinics, and summer workshops. Obviously, this kind of training is needed. The acceleration of basic research into individual and social dynamics produces an ever-changing array of theories and methods which the professional worker is hard

pressed to keep up with. Refresher courses help, and they also give
the change agent an excellent opportunity to share his professional
experiences with his colleagues. Many new and renewed insights
have developed from such programs.

We have been able to give here only a very sketchy outline of
some of the directions in which we think the development of training programs for professional change agents might proceed, and
we have been able to say even less about the education of potential
client systems. We have thought it inadvisable at this point to try
to spell out in detail the ingredients of a particular curriculum.
Instead we have attempted a summary of some of the implications
of our analysis of change, and we have tried to show how our belief in the eventual formulation of a consistent theory of change
affects the concepts of education which govern the training of our
professional change agents in every field. We have been convinced
by our examination of case materials that it would be very profit-
able for behavioral science in general if a few behavioral-science
departments would launch trial programs of general training for
change agents. Such programs might give us help precisely where
we need it most—in finding out how to apply the newest advances
of theory to the practical work of the professional change agent.
At the same time, such a program would have a significant effect
on the development of systematic theory and the progress of research into the processes of change and the helping relationship.
Furthermore, it seems to us imperative that the professional schools
make increasing use of the resources of basic social science; they
should involve themselves in a broader orientation to change and
theories of change in all types of systems. Such cross-fertilization
is already occurring, though slowly, within the sciences themselves.
Each year we see a few more behavioral scientists who are willing
to reach out across the barriers of the different disciplines in order
to gather together and unite all our knowledge of the way men
live. But the application of this knowledge to the actual problems
of men too often lags tragically far behind.

BIBLIOGRAPHY

The bibliography has been divided into five sections:

I. Change agents working with the individual as client system
II. Change agents working with the small group as client system
III. Change agents working with the organization as client system
IV. Change agents working with the community as client system
V. Additional references that proved helpful in analysis

Authors are listed in that section of the bibliography which represents their major emphasis. In some cases, however, the same author is included in more than one section because of the multiple focus of his work.

I. Work with the individual as client system

1. Bettelheim, Bruno, *Love is not enough*, Glencoe, Ill., Free Press, 1950.
2. Blocksma, D., R. Fox, R. Lippitt, and others, "An experimental study of three methods of improving the social acceptance and social participation of rejected children," Ann Arbor, Research Center for Group Dynamics, U. of Michigan. Research in progress, Grant M919, National Institute of Mental Health.
3. Bradford, Leland, and others, *Explorations in human relations training*, Washington, D. C., National Training Laboratories, 1953.
4. Brim, Orville, "The acceptance of new behavior in child-rearing," *Human Relations*, 1954, 7, 473-93.

5. Clifton, E., and F. Hollis, eds., *Child therapy: A casework symposium*, New York, Family Service Association of America, 1948.

6. Curle, Adam, and E. L. Trist, "Transitional communities and social reconnection," *Human Relations*, 1947, *1*, two parts in Nos. 1 and 2.

7. Fenichel, Otto, *The psychoanalytic theory of neurosis*, New York, Norton, 1945.

8. Fromm-Reichmann, Frieda, *Principles of intensive psychotherapy*, Chicago, U. of Chicago Press, 1950.

9. Hollis, Florence, *Women in marital conflict: A casework study*, New York, Family Service Association of America, 1949.

10. Jones, Maxwell, *The therapeutic community*, New York, Basic Books, 1953.

11. Lippitt, Gordon, "Feedback of interpersonal perceptions as a training procedure." Unpublished experiment conducted by National Training Laboratories, Washington, D. C.

12. Lippitt, Ronald, *Training in community relations*, New York, Harper, 1949.

13. Redl, Fritz, and David Wineman, *Children who hate*. Glencoe, Ill., Free Press, 1951.

14. Redl, Fritz, and David Wineman, *Controls from within*, Glencoe, Ill., Free Press, 1952.

15. Rogers, Carl R., *Client-centered therapy*, Boston, Houghton Mifflin, 1951.

16. Taft, Jessie, ed., *A functional approach to family casework*, Philadelphia, U. of Pennsylvania Press, 1941.

II. Work with the group and interpersonal system as client system

17. Allen, Frederick H., *Psychotherapy with children*, New York, Norton, 1942.

18. Bach, George R., *Intensive group psychotherapy*, New York, Ronald Press, 1954.

19. Barron, M., and G. Krulee, "Case study of a basic skill training group," *J. of Soc. Issues*, 1948, *2*, 10-31.

20. Bradford, L., and T. Mallinson, "Group formation and development," Washington, National Training Laboratories, 1951 (dittoed).

21. Corey, Stephen M., *Action research to improve school practices*, New York, Bureau of Publications, Columbia Teachers College, 1953.

22. Cunningham, Ruth, and others, *Understanding group behavior of boys and girls* (especially Chaps. 9, 10, 11), New York, Bureau of Publications, Columbia Teachers College, 1951.

23. Hogrefe, Russell W., "An agency works with street gangs," in Clyde E. Murray, Marx G. Bowens, and Russell Hogrefe, eds., *Group work in community life*, New York, Association Press, 1954.

24. Jenkins, D., and R. Lippitt, *Interpersonal perceptions of teachers, students, and parents*, Washington, D. C., National Education Assn., 1951.

25. Lau, James, "Attitude change as related to change in perception of the group norm." Unpublished Ph.D. dissertation, U. of Michigan, 1954.

26. Lewin, Kurt, "Forces behind food habits and methods of change," Washington, D. C., National Research Council, Bulletin CVIII, 1943.

27. Lippitt, R., and H. Coffey, "A training relationship with an agency staff." Unpublished case study.

28. Maier, Norman R. F., *Principles of human relations*, New York, Wiley, 1952.

29. Moreno, J. L., *Psychodrama*, *I*, New York, Beacon House, 1946. See especially pp. 315-83.

30. Powdermaker, Florence B., and Jerome D. Frank, *Group psychotherapy*, Cambridge, Mass., Harvard U. Press, 1953.

31. Taft, Jessie, ed., *A functional approach to family casework*, Philadelphia, U. of Pennsylvania Press, 1944.

32. Thelen, H., *The dynamics of groups at work* (Chap. 5), Chicago, U. of Chicago Press, 1954.

33. Watson, J., and R. Lippitt, *Learning across cultures*, Ann Arbor, Mich., Institute for Social Research, 1956.

III. Work with the organization or institution as client system

34. Bradford, L., and R. Lippitt, "Role-playing in supervisory training," *Personnel*, 1946, *22*, 13-14.

35. Coch, Lester, and John R. P. French, Jr., "Overcoming resistance to change," *Human Relations*, 1948, *1*, 512-32.

36. Jaques, Elliott, *The changing culture of a factory*, New York, Dryden, 1952.

37. Jones, Maxwell, *The therapeutic community*, New York, Basic Books, 1953.

38. Krulee, Gilbert K., "A study of organizational change." Unpublished Ph.D. dissertation, Massachusetts Institute of Technology, 1950 (study of the Scanlon Plan).

39. Lippitt, Ronald, "Three-level training in a hospital." Unpublished case study.

40. Lippitt, Ronald, "Three-level training in a government bureau." Unpublished case study.

41. Maier, Norman, R. F., *Principles of human relations,* New York, Wiley, 1952.

42. Mann, Floyd C., "Changing superior-subordinate relationships," *J. Soc. Issues,* 1951, 7, 56-63.

43. Mann, Floyd C., "Human relations skills in social research," *Human Relations,* 1951, *4,* 341-51.

44. Mann, Floyd C., *The survey feedback experiment,* Ann Arbor, Survey Research Center, U. of Michigan, 1953.

45. Morse, N., and E. Reimer, "The experimental change of a major organizational variable," *J. Abnorm. Soc. Psychol.,* 1956, *52,* 1.

46. Nylen, Donald, Wayne Dick, and others, "A program of group development study and human relations training," Seattle Public Schools, 1953 (mimeographed).

47. Richardson, F. L. W., Jr., and Charles R. Walker, *Human relations in an expanding company,* New Haven, Labor and Management Center, Yale U., 1948.

48. Scanlon, Joseph N., "Profit sharing under collective bargaining: Three case studies," *Industr. Lab. Rela. Rev.,* 1948, *2,* 58-75.

49. Sorenson, Roy, and Hedley Dimock, *Designing education in values: A case study of institutional change,* New York, Association Press, 1955.

50. Taylor, F. W., *The principles of scientific management,* New York, Harper, 1911.

IV. Work with the community as client system

51. Aberle, David F., "Introducing preventive psychiatry into a community," *Human Organization,* 1950, *9,* 5-9.

52. Alinsky, Saul D., *Reveille for radicals,* Chicago, U. of Chicago Press, 1946.

53. Biddle, William W., *The cultivation of community leaders,* New York, Harper, 1953.

54. Bowens, Marx G., "The neighborhood center for block organization: An experiment in self-help at the neighborhood level," in Clyde C. Murray, Marx G. Bowens, and Russell Hogrefe, eds., *Group work in community life,* New York, Association Press, 1954.

55. Brashear, Ellen L., Eleanor T. Kenney, A. D. Buchmueller, and Margaret C.-L. Gildea, "A community program of mental health education using group discussion methods," *Amer. J. Orthopsychiat.*, 1954, *24*, 554.

56. Buchmueller, A. D., Frances Porter, and Margaret C.-L. Gildea, "A group therapy project with parents of behavior problem children in public schools: A comparative study of behavior problems in two school districts," *Nerv. Child*, 1954, *10*, 415.

57. Buchmueller, A. D., and H. R. Domke, "The role of the public health department in preventive mental health services," *Children*, 1956, *3*, 225-31.

58. Cannell, Charles F., Fred G. Wale, and Stephen B. Withey, issue eds., "Community change: An action program in Puerto Rico," *J. Soc. Issues*, 1953, *9*, No. 2.

59. Clark, Kenneth, "Desegregation: An appraisal of the evidence," *J. Soc. Issues*, 1953, *9*, No. 4.

60. Curle, Adam, and E. L. Trist, "Transitional communities and social reconnection," *Human Relations*, 1947, *1*, two parts in Nos. 1 and 2.

61. DuBois, Rachel Davis, *Neighbors in Action: A manual for local leaders in inter-group relations*, New York, Harper, 1950.

62. Festinger, Leon, and Harold H. Kelley, *Changing attitudes through social contact*, Ann Arbor, Research Center for Group Dynamics, U. of Michigan, 1951.

63. Glidewell, J. C., I. N. Mensh, H. R. Domke, Margaret C.-L. Gildea, and A. D. Buchmueller, "Methods for community mental health research: I. Hypothesis formation," *Amer. J. Orthopsychiat.*, 1957, *27*, No. 1.

64. Lindemann, Erich, and Lydia G. Dawes, "The use of psychoanalytic constructs in preventive psychiatry," *The psychoanalytic study of the child*, New York, International Universities Press, 1951, 7, 429-48.

65. Loomis, C., and A. Beegle, *Rural sociology and anthropology*, New York, Prentice-Hall, 1956.

66. McClusky, Howard Y., "The community in council," *Adult Leadership*, 1956, *5*, 12-14.

67. McClusky, Howard Y., and W. G. Robinson, "The area conference for community self-help," Community Adult Education, U. of Michigan, 1956 (mimeographed).

68. McClusky, Howard Y., "The community: Partner in power," *Community News*, Illinois College, Jacksonville, Ill., 1955, *6*, 4-12.

69. Ogden, Jean, and Jess Ogden, *These things we tried*, Charlottesville, U. of Virginia, 1947.

70. Ogden, Jean, and Jess Ogden, *Small communities in action*, New York, Harper, 1946.

71. Poston, Richard W., *Small town renaissance*, New York, Harper, 1950.

72. Poston, Richard W., *Democracy is you*, New York, Harper, 1953.

73. Reid, J. T., *It happened in Taos*, Albuquerque, U. of New Mexico Press, 1946.

74. Sarchet, Bettie B., *Block groups and community change*, Human Dynamics Laboratory, U. of Chicago, 1955.

75. Selltiz, Claire, and Margaret H. Wormser, eds., "Community self-surveys: An approach to social change," *J. Soc. Issues*, 1949, *5*, No. 2.

76. Thelen, Herbert, *The dynamics of groups at work*, Chicago, U. of Chicago Press, 1954.

77. Thelen, Herbert, "Social process vs. community deterioration," *Group Psychother.*, 1951, *4*, 206-12.

78. Thelen, Herbert, and B. Sarchet, "Neighbors in action," Human Dynamics Laboratory, U. of Chicago, 1954.

79. Zander, Alvin (chairman), Report of the committee on field services, Community Adult Education, U. of Michigan, May 1949 (mimeographed).

V. Additional references that proved helpful in our analysis

80. Aptekar, Herbert, *The dynamics of casework and counseling*, Boston, Houghton Mifflin, 1955.

81. Bavelas, Alex, "Some problems of organizational change," *J. Soc. Issues*, 1948, *4*, 48-52.

82. Benne, K. D., and G. E. Swanson, eds., "Values and the social scientist," *J. Soc. Issues*, 1950, *6*, No. 4.

83. Bobbitt, Joseph M., and John A. Clausen, "Psychotherapy and its public health implications," in C. H. Mowrer, *et al.*, *Psychotherapy theory and research*, New York, Ronald Press, 1953.

84. Cartwright, D., "Basic and applied social psychology," *Phil. Sci.*, 1949, *16*, No. 3.

85. Cattell, Raymond, "Concepts and methods in the measurement of group syntality," *Psychol. Rev.*, 1948, *55*, 48-63.

86. Ezriel, Henry, "Experimentation within the psycho-analytic session," *Brit. J. Phil. Sci.*, 1956, *7*, 29-48.

87. Lewin, Kurt, "Frontiers in group dynamics," *Human Relations,* 1947, *1,* 5-41.

88. Likert, R., and R. Lippitt, "The utilization of social science," Chap. 13 in L. Festinger and D. Katz, eds., *Research methods in the behavioral sciences,* New York, Dryden, 1953.

89. Lippitt, R., "The strategy of socio-psychological research in group life," Chap. 2 in J. G. Miller, ed., *Experiments in social process,* New York, McGraw-Hill, 1950.

90. Long, Nicholas, "A study of the relationship between the growth of the whole child and an experimental attempt to change the social power of the rejected child." Unpublished Ph.D. dissertation, U. of Michigan, 1957.

91. Luszki, Margaret, *Interdisciplinary Team Research: Methods and Problems,* New York, New York U. Press, 1957.

92. McGregor, Douglas, "The staff function in human relations," *J. Soc. Issues,* 1948, *4,* 5-22.

93. Merton, R. K., "The role of applied social science in the formation of policy," *Phil. Sci.,* 1949, *16,* No. 3.

94. Merton, R. K., "Selected problems of field work in the planned community," *Amer. Sociol. Rev.,* 1947, *12,* 304-12.

95. Parsons, Talcott, "The problem of controlled institutional change," in *Essays in sociological theory,* rev. ed., Glencoe, Ill., Free Press, 1954.

96. Polansky, N., and J. Kounin, "Clients' reactions to initial interviews: A field study," *Human Relations,* 1956, *9,* 237-65.

97. Polansky, N., and others, "Problems of interpersonal relations in research on groups," *Human Relations,* 1949, *2,* 281-91.

98. Schanck, R. L., "A study of the community and its institutions conceived of as behavior of individuals," *Psychol. Monogr.,* 1932, *43,* No. 2.

99. Selznick, Philip, *TVA and the grass roots,* Berkeley, U. of California Press, 1949.

INDEX